A HISTORY OF THE OTTOMAN
EMPIRE TO 1730

A HISTORY OF
THE OTTOMAN EMPIRE
TO 1730

*Chapters from The Cambridge
History of Islam and The New
Cambridge Modern History*
by

V. J. PARRY

H. İNALCIK, A. N. KURAT AND J. S. BROMLEY

Edited with an introduction by
M. A. COOK

Cambridge University Press

CAMBRIDGE
LONDON · NEW YORK · MELBOURNE

Published by the Syndics of the Cambridge University Press
The Pitt Building, Trumpington Street, Cambridge CB2 IRP
Bentley House, 200 Euston Road, London NW1 2DB
32 East 57th Street, New York, NY 10022, USA
296 Beaconsfield Parade, Middle Park, Melbourne 3206, Australia

First published 1976

Printed in Great Britain
at the
University Printing House, Cambridge
(Euan Phillips, University Printer)

Library of Congress Cataloguing in Publication Data

Main entry under title:
A History of the Ottoman Empire to 1730.
  Bibliography: p.
  Includes index.

  CONTENTS: İnalcik, H. The rise of the Ottoman
Empire. – Parry, V. J. The reigns of Bāyezīd II and
Selīm I, 1481–1520. – Parry, V. J. The reign of
Sulaimān the Magnificent, 1520–66. [etc.]

  1. Turkey – History – 1288–1453. 2. Turkey –
History – 1453–1683. 3. Turkey – History – 1683–1829.
I. Parry, Vernon J. II. Cook, M. A. III. The Cambridge
history of Islam. 1. The central Islamic lands.
Selections. 1976. IV. The New Cambridge modern
history. V. 1–6. Selections. 1976.

DR486.H57 949.6 75–38188
ISBN 0 521 20891 2 hard covers
ISBN 0 521 09991 9 paperback

CONTENTS

MAPS

PUBLISHER'S PREFACE

This book is intended to make available within one pair of covers a number of valuable and enduring essays hitherto scattered in different volumes of the Cambridge Histories and not always readily available to students outside the confines of their libraries. The Syndics of the Cambridge University Press felt that there was a need for collections of this sort particularly where original work on relatively little studied themes was concerned. It was with this need in mind that the Syndics invited Mr Michael Cook to edit and see through the Press a selection of chapters on Ottoman history between the late thirteenth and early eighteenth century, first published in volumes of *The Cambridge History of Islam* (*CHI*) and *The New Cambridge Modern History* (*NCMH*).

The essays are reproduced substantially unchanged. Mr Cook has amended certain errors and added cross-references, provided an original introduction and a bibliographical note, suggested the use of relevant maps (from *CHI* and *NCMH Atlas*) and supervised the preparation of the index (by Mrs B. Britton). In reprinting these chapters no attempt has been made to reduce the conventions of transcription employed by the various authors to a uniform system. All significant variants are however entered and cross-referenced in the index. There is in fact only one point of difference which is likely to perplex the non-specialist reader: the Turkish form of the name Muḥammad appears in some chapters as Mehemmed and in others as Meḥmed (or Mehmed).

It is sad to report the deaths of two of the authors whose work is represented here, Mr V. J. Parry and Professor A. N. Kurat. In a sense this volume is a memorial to Mr Parry, four of whose contributions are included, and who published relatively little during his lifetime. The Cambridge University Press gratefully acknowledges the permission given by Mrs Parry and Professors İnalcik and Bromley to include contributions in this collection. It is hoped that this book will provide a concise and convenient introduction to the internal development of the Ottoman empire during its heyday and fill a lacuna in the secondary literature on this subject.

INTRODUCTION

IN terms of the history of Europe, the Ottoman presence is at once intimate and alien. The intimacy is a direct result of Ottoman military power. But the alienness is in a way more curious. At a very basic level the history of the Ottoman Empire was made up from the same ingredients as that of Europe: in each case a Christian Roman empire had fallen prey to a barbarian conquest. And yet the outcome of the demise of the eastern empire at the hands of the Turks was very different indeed from that of the demise of the western empire at the hands of the Germans.

In the first place, the degree of continuity in the Roman imperial tradition was vastly less. The Goths initially preserved the Roman empire they conquered, the Franks eventually restored it; not so the Turks. It was true of course that the Turks in effect reconstituted the original territories of the eastern empire to a degree unknown since Justinian. And with the territory they inherited also the name: in one widespread usage the Ottomans were identified as *Rum*—that is, etymologically, as Romans.[1] It is thus not altogether surprising to encounter a fifteenth-century Byzantine scholar who acclaims Mehmed II as the legitimate Roman emperor (p. 41), and even a toying with the notion of Ottoman descent from one of the Byzantine imperial families. Yet this sense of an Ottoman inheritance of the Byzantine tradition was still-born: the Ottomans in the event inherited from the Byzantines little more than the site for their empire.[2] When the Ottomans went in search of an imperial precedent for the extent of their empire, they picked not the Roman Justinian but the Macedonian Alexander; just as when they went in search of an imperial precedent for justice, they picked not the Roman Marcus Aurelius but the Persian Anushirvan. There was in fifteenth-century Europe a 'Holy Roman Empire of the German nation'; but there was no 'Holy Roman Empire of the Turkish nation' in the contemporary Middle East.

In the second place, the degree of continuity in the history of the barbarian conquerors was much less than in Europe: the Turkic tribesmen whose conquest of Byzantine Anatolia was eventually to issue in the

[1] This usage appears, for example, in Ottoman documents with reference to the heartlands of the empire, and in Arabic chronicles, especially those of Syria and Arabia; it was even picked up by the Portuguese in the Indian Ocean. It goes back to the sultanate of *Rum* established in the aftermath of the Turkic conquest of Anatolia in the eleventh century.
[2] For the Byzantine heritage of the Ottomans, see S. Vryonis, *The Decline of Medieval Hellenism in Asia Minor* (Berkeley and Los Angeles, 1971), chapter 7.

1

Ottoman Empire passed on only the vestiges of a political tradition from their barbarian past. And this seems much more paradoxical. The Turcicization of Anatolia in the aftermath of the invasion was quite as impressive as the Germanization of Europe; and if the Ottomans were identified in one usage as 'Romans', in another equally well-established one they were 'Turks',[1] an identification reinforced by the fact that their primary literary language was Turkish throughout. And yet 'Turks' in standard Ottoman usage came to refer not to the Ottoman proprietors of the state, but to the Anatolian tribesmen who had to be kept out of it. Not only was there no Ottoman Holy Roman Empire; there was no Turkish nation to have one.

It is worth emphasizing this point by taking it a little further afield. The Mongol invaders of the Islamic world in the thirteenth century, in contrast to the Turkic invaders of the eleventh, did to some extent leave a barbarian political tradition behind them. Most strikingly, they established in certain areas the notions of the exclusive right to rule of members of a royal lineage, the Chingizids, and of the supremacy of an ethnic Mongol law, the Yasa. This tradition was accessible to the Ottomans in two ways. In the first place, it was rapidly Turcicized: a Mongol tradition short of Mongols was appropriated by Turks short of tradition. In the second place, the tradition was politically well within the Ottoman field of vision: to take the most striking, though not the most important example, the Crimea was ruled by Chingizid monarchs in accordance with a Mongol law. It is not therefore surprising that the Ottomans came under the influence of the Mongol heritage. In particular, there appears in the fifteenth century an Ottoman calque on Chingizid descent in the form of a fabricated genealogy for the ruling dynasty going back to the Turkic tribes of Central Asia.[2] Yet in the event very little came of this Mongol fallout at the level of political values. The Central Asian genealogy of the Ottoman sultans lived on, but it did so more as antiquarianism than as legitimism; just as the memory of the Mongol Yasa lived on not as a sanction for Ottoman administrative law but merely as a foil to demonstrate its superiority.[3] The Turkish conquest of the eastern Roman empire thus issued in no real tradition of barbarian kingship and barbarian law of the kind so prominent in the history of post-Roman Europe.[4]

The cause of this muting of both the imperial and the barbarian traditions whose collision was to issue in the Ottoman Empire is not of course far to

[1] The Ottomans were 'Turks' to most outsiders (the Balkan and European Christians, the North African Muslims), and terms suggestive of a Turkish ethnicity can be found in Ottoman sources.

[2] See P. Wittek, *The Rise of the Ottoman Empire* (London, 1938), chapter 1.

[3] Contrast the statements of Tursun Beg and Huseyn Hezarfenn cited in U. Heyd, *Studies in Old Ottoman Criminal Law*, ed. V. L. Ménage (Oxford, 1973), pp. 169–70.

[4] Contrast equally the marked sense of their barbarian ethnicity and heritage retained by the Manchu conquerors of China, whose tradition was even more of a calque on the Mongol tradition than was that of the Turks.

seek. Both the eastern and the western Roman empires had converted to Christianity before falling victim to barbarian conquest. But whereas the sharpest break in the subsequent religious history of Europe was a Reformation which took place *within* Christianity long after the barbarians had settled down, in the eastern empire Christianity was displaced by a rival faith, and one which the barbarians themselves brought with them. The Turkic invasion of Anatolia in the eleventh century and the Ottoman conquest of Constantinople in the fifteenth brought to completion the assault of Islam on the eastern Roman empire initiated by the Arabs in the seventh. Now Islam was a religion of a very different stamp from Christianity. Doctrinally it represented a far more intransigent form of their shared Judaic monotheism; and politically it spread primarily as a result of the efforts not of missionaries but of conquerors. The result was a faith a good deal less disposed to accommodate and perpetuate the cultures it encountered than was Christianity. Hence the drastic discontinuity in the Byzantine imperial tradition brought about by the linking of barbarian invasion with Islam. The Turks could not simply settle down as the eastern Slavs of the Byzantine world, a military menace but eventually a cultural province in the manner of the Bulgars.[1] But it is equally this domineering character of Islam that explains the striking etiolation, alongside the tradition of the conquered empire, of the tradition of the conquering barbarians themselves.

The corollary of this was that the constitutive role of religion in the Ottoman polity was out of all proportion to its role in Europe. In Europe it was the Romans and the Germans who provided the substantive components of the 'Holy Roman Empire of the German nation'; the holiness was adjectival. In the Ottoman case, by contrast, it was religion which provided the key term in one of the commonest designations of the empire, 'the lands of Islam'. If Byzantium provided little more than a site and the Turks little more than a language, it was Islam which gave the venture its meaning.

Initially the embodiment of this meaning in concrete reality was an uncomplicated one. The empire began as a *ghazi* state, an organization of warriors engaged in the sacred struggle with the infidel; and Islam provided direct and emphatic scriptural sanction for this military enterprise, as Christianity did not do even for so godly an institution as the New Model Army.[2] But the Ottoman polity evolved by virtue of its very success in this Islamic task from an organisation of *ghazis* into a slave army backed by a fiscal bureaucracy; and as the balance shifted from the conquest of infidels to the administration of subjects, the relationship of the

[1] Cf. the eventual division of the Byzantine heritage: the Ottomans took the territory, but it was the Slavs who got the imperial tradition.

[2] Or to take an even closer parallel, there was no Ottoman equivalent to the devious casuistries and painful public debates that arose from the Spanish conquest of infidels in the New World, for all that Sulaiman the Magnificent had as tender a religious conscience as Philip II.

Ottoman state to its Islamic legitimation lost its initial clarity.[1] At first sight this is surprising. By the mid-sixteenth century the Ottomans had reconstituted the political unity of the Islamic world more effectively than anyone since the ninth century: the Ottoman Empire was in a very concrete sense *the* Islamic state of its day. But this concrete sense was not in fact a deeply normative one; and it is striking how the Ottomans, in referring to their political reunification of the Middle East, tend to cite as precedent not the early rulers of Islam whose heirs they might have claimed to be, but rather Alexander the Great, who for all his role as a cosmopolitan symbol of political adventure left no heirs outside Hellenistic history and the tribal chiefs of the Pamirs.

The core of the problem lay in the fact that the Islamic tradition, for reasons arising from the history of its formation, was unsuited to the legitimation of the settled, bureaucratic government of a territorial state. It could aptly legitimate a *ghazi* state, but the Ottoman state soon passed beyond this; it could aptly legitimate the mobilization of tribesmen to conquer a settled state, but that role was arrogated in the Ottoman context by their greatest Muslim enemies, the Safavids. The problems of religious conscience which Philip II experienced in respect of the relations of his state to the infidels he conquered, Sulaiman the Magnificent experienced in respect of the faithful he ruled.

The tension between the Ottoman polity and its Islamic political values is particularly apparent in three areas. The first is the claim of the Ottoman sultans to be caliphs.[2] The ruler of the early Islamic polity was neither a king nor an emperor, neither a Theodoric nor a Charlemagne, but a caliph: the occupant, that is, of an intrinsically religious office. With the demise of caliphal power from the ninth century on, effective rule passed into the hands of potentates who lacked this religious legitimation—to employ a term which became common usage, they were merely sultans. But when the Mongols in the thirteenth century brought to an end even the nominal existence of the caliphate, there was a natural tendency for the sultans of the Islamic world to seek to elevate their status by debasing the caliphal title; it thus became normal for any Islamic ruler of any significance to make some gesture in the direction of caliphal status, and the Ottomans were no exception to the general scramble. But the trouble was that the caliphate was more than a mere honorific to grace the titulature of existing rulers. In particular, one of its more inconvenient requirements was descent from Quraysh, the Arab tribe into which the Muslim Prophet had been born. In this situation there were only two coherent courses for

[1] Compare the venture of Ahmad Grañ, a *ghazi* who in the sixteenth century initiated an abortive Islamic conquest of Christian Ethiopia. Here as in the early Ottoman context we encounter the title 'Commander of the Faithful' as the highest dignity that could be won in Holy War; but Ahmad, unlike the Ottomans, had the moral good luck that his conquest issued in no enduring state organization.

[2] See H. A. R. Gibb, 'Luṭfī Paşa on the Ottoman Caliphate', in *Oriens* (1962); also the comments of H. İnalcık in *The Cambridge History of Islam*, I, 320–3.

4

the Ottomans to take. They could have adopted a Qurashi genealogy in the manner of the contemporary rulers of the Yemen or Morocco; or they could have rejected the genealogical criterion altogether in the manner of the contemporary heretics of Oman. But having adopted a Turkic tribal descent, they could hardly rewrite their genealogy; and having adopted orthodox Islam with its clear emphasis on Qurashi descent, they could hardly rewrite the criterion. There was one man, Lutfi Pasha, who in a pamphlet written in 1554 was unwise enough to confront this intractable issue. It is characteristic that he should have been a well-intentioned amateur—a retired Grand Vizier rather than the Grand Mufti—and unsurprising that the result should have been embarrassed and unpersuasive.[1] It was as if the legitimacy of the rule of Philip II had been open to question on the ground that he was not descended from the House of David; and conversely, it was this embarrassment which the Ottomans would have been spared had their religious culture permitted them to be the heirs of Byzantium in the manner of the Tsars, or barbarian kings in the manner of the Chingizids.

The second area of tension was the relative status of the Holy Law of Islam, the *Shari'a*, and the administrative law of the state, the *Kanun*.[2] Just as the Islamic polity was to be headed by an intrinsically religious ruler, so also it was to be ruled in accordance with an intrinsically religious law. But just as the Ottoman rulers were in fact sultans, for all their pretensions to the caliphate, so also their administrative code was in fact a law of their own making, for all their deference to the *Shari'a*. Given this fundamental tension between *Kanun* and *Shari'a*, the Ottomans could either avoid the issue and save face, or face up to it and choose. As might be expected, they did their best to take the first course. Hence denials of the incompatibility of the two laws, attempts to subsume the *Kanun* under the marginal religious recognition of the category of custom, and so forth.[3] But we also find less evasive responses to the tension. Given their religious values, the Ottomans could hardly choose the *Kanun* to the exclusion of the *Shari'a*: that response came only in the twentieth century, by which time the *Kanun* in question was no longer Ottoman but Swiss. But they could and did on occasion choose the *Shari'a* to the exclusion of *Kanun*. Thus in the field of criminal law, the insistence of one sixteenth-century writer that the way to suppress crime is actually to apply the *Shari'a* finds concrete embodiment in the insistence of a sultanic decree of 1696 that no penalties be inflicted other than those prescribed by God and the Prophet;

[1] Particularly striking is the *risqué* use which Lutfi Pasha makes of Shiism: on the one hand he invokes as orthodox the Shiite tradition that one who dies without knowing the *imam* (i.e. caliph) of the age in effect dies a pagan; and on the other he attempts to dismiss the orthodox requirement of Qurashi descent as Shiite heresy.

[2] See H. İnalcik, 'Suleiman the Lawgiver and Ottoman Law', in *Archivum Ottomanicum* (1969), and Heyd, *Studies in Old Ottoman Criminal Law*, pp. 167–207.

[3] In criminal law the standard move is to play up the discretionary power vested in the ruler under the *Shari'a*; in fiscal law there is a similar attempt to append the *Kanun* to a marginal category of the Holy Law.

while in the field of fiscal law, we have the bizarre spectacle of the Ottoman conquerors of Crete setting about the recreation of the system of taxation they believed to have been that of the earliest Islamic conquests. In each case, religious fundamentalism is associated with an explicit condemnation of the traditional rulings of the *Kanun*. It was as if canon law, or even the law of Moses, had been the only accredited law of medieval Europe; and similarly, it was this embarrassment which the Ottomans would have avoided had their religious culture permitted them to dignify their *Kanun* as Roman Law, somewhat in the manner of the aspiring despots of contemporary Europe, or as Turkic tribal law, in the manner of the Yasa of the Chingizids.

The third area of tension was the position of the Islamic scholars, the *'ulema*, within the state.[1] On the one hand the Islamic tradition demanded of its scholars a moral purity untainted by involvement in the corrupting milieu of political power; but on the other, the Ottoman state was unusual in Islamic history in the extent to which it integrated its religious scholars into the apparatus of the state through a system of colleges and career opportunities created and regulated by the state itself. The resulting tension between an ethic of purity and the complicities of office appears most clearly in the case of the Grand Mufti. A sort of institutionalized religious conscience of the empire, the contradictory requirements of his role could be brought into some kind of balance only by playing it with an element of almost ritual intransigence: if the intransigence ceased to be merely ritual, the Mufti stood to lose his job, while if the ritual ceased to be intransigent, he stood to lose his integrity.

In sum, the legitimatory force of Islam in the Ottoman polity was a distinctly ambivalent one. Islam provided a clear terminal value for the Ottoman polity in the shape of the Holy War against the infidel, and in consequence it provided also a fairly persuasive instrumental status for the concrete machinery of the state as a means to victory in this struggle. But it was a legitimacy that was very much one of achievement rather than ascription: Islam conferred little intrinsic legitimacy on the structure of the state. Powerfully focused on the battlefields of Europe in the good times, the meaning of the Ottoman polity tended to evaporate in the internal disarray of the bad times which followed.[2]

This analysis of what the Islamic character of the Ottoman state meant for its political values can be restated in terms bearing more closely on the realities of political power.[3] To put it negatively, the striking thing about

[1] See R. Repp, 'Some Observations on the Development of the Ottoman Learned Hierarchy', in N. R. Keddie (ed.), *Scholars, Saints, and Sufis* (Berkeley, 1972).

[2] Contrast the abundance of profane meaning in the internal bickerings of European countries in the same period, with their estates, ancient constitutions, common and Roman lawyers etc.

[3] For an illuminating presentation of the Ottoman (and Islamic) pattern in a rich comparative perspective, see P. Anderson, *Lineages of the Absolutist State* (London, 1974).

the Ottoman Empire is the relative absence of those accredited structures which in post-feudal Europe so densely populate the social and political space between the state and its subjects. Two closely related aspects of this contrast are particularly noteworthy. The first is the absence of 'nations' in the Ottoman context. Absorption into the Ottoman Empire was very much more likely than absorption into a European state to strip a subject people of its traditional political structures. The Hungarians under Habsburg rule remained a nation throughout: the residue of their medieval polity was entrenched in institutions of unquestionable legitimacy and elaborately articulated in terms of history and law; and if the Czechs failed to do the same, it was their intransigence in a religious conflict which led to the political catastrophe. But in Ottoman Anatolia, by contrast, the survival of the pre-Ottoman polities was literally nominal.[1] The second aspect of the contrast is the lack of an Ottoman aristocracy. Where Europe made a fundamental social distinction between noble and commoner, the Ottomans made a fundamental political distinction between members and non-members of the state apparatus. There was of course present in the state a subordinate category of rural feof-holders, the *Sipahis*; and they would clearly have provided the natural locus for the evolution from aristocracy of service to aristocracy of blood had the category itself existed. But the *Sipahis* were no more an Ottoman gentry than Abaza Mehmed Pasha, the most outstanding representative of provincial hostility to the Janissaries, was an Ottoman archduke (pp. 142–3). The obverse of all this was of course that feature of the Ottoman polity of which the Janissaries are the prime example, the role of slaves in constituting the military and administrative backbone of the state. This system was not in any intrinsic way Islamic; but it was characteristically Muslim both by association—it is virtually unknown in non-Muslim societies[2]—and by genesis—it had developed in the ninth century precisely in response to the failure of Islamic society to domesticate the category of aristocracy.

This combination of the absence of nations and aristocracy on the one hand with the prominence of slaves on the other meant that the Ottoman state was in a sense the only serious attempt at an absolute monarchy in Europe. Everywhere in Christian Europe the state accepted aristocracy

[1] There were of course at all times client states of the Ottoman Empire; the most interesting case is perhaps the Crimea, inasmuch as it retained from its Mongol heritages a real dynastic and aristocratic legitimism. But in general the status of these states is well expressed in Sulaiman's observations on Hungary (p. 92).

[2] There is one noteworthy parallel in European history: the Teutonic Order in Prussia presents significant structural analogies to both the great Islamic slave states, the Ottoman Empire and the Mamluk regime of late medieval Egypt. As in both, we have a military and administrative apparatus renewed in each generation by the recruitment of outsiders. As in the Mamluk case, the Knights chose their ruler from among themselves. As in the Ottoman case, there was an enduring tension between this state of outsiders and the local and more or less hereditary feof-holders. But if the structures are similar the cultural background is quite different.

as a fact of life. It was in the relationship between the two that the changes were rung: compare Poland, where the organized power of the aristocracy virtually absorbed that of the state, with Prussia, where the organized power of the state virtually absorbed that of the aristocracy. Only one European country, and that the most marginal, presents a closer parallel with the Ottoman system: if the Poland of Henry of Anjou was a country where the aristocracy nearly ate the state, the Russia of Ivan the Terrible was the one European country where the state nearly ate the aristocracy. The curious experiment through which this attempt was made—the creation of a ruling institution at once delinquent and quasi-monastic—is a venture that can in some ways be compared with the Ottoman slave state.[1] And yet even in Russia aristocracy proved to be a fact of life: Ivan himself abolished his new order, and its long-term effect was not to destroy the category of aristocracy but simply to replace one aristocracy by another.

This static picture has significant dynamic implications. In the first place, the combination of a society with few socially entrenched bulwarks against the state and of a political elite with little real linkage to local society made for a markedly unstable relationship between the two: if central control of the military and administrative machine were allowed to slip, the apparatus collapsed onto the society it ruled in a fashion which combined minimum central control with maximum local irresponsibility. In the second place, the instrumental status of the internal structures of the empire rendered the will to exercise this control more than usually contingent: the Ottoman state was not built to cultivate its own garden, and if was failing to engross the gardens of others, it was more than likely to let its own go to seed. The alternations between order and disorder in Ottoman history illustrate both these points. First, the great succession crises of the fifteenth and sixteenth centuries show how readily chaos could break out even at the best of times—just as the careers of the great 'strong men' of the seventeenth century show how chaos could be brought to heel even at the worst of times. Secondly, the contrast between the occasionally disrupted order of the earlier period and the occasionally interrupted disorder of the later period points to a basic long-term change: after the late sixteenth century, the maintenance of central power no longer ensured dramatic rewards in terms of imperial expansion (p. 96)—whereas it was not until the end of the eighteenth century that it became clear that the absence of central control meant dramatic penalties in terms of imperial contraction. The despotism which was the terror of the infidel

[1] But note that whereas in the case of the Teutonic Order the analogy lies in the structure of the institution and not in its relationship to the cultural background, in the Russian case it is rather the other way round. Russia in this period is in some ways suggestive of an Islamic society *manqué*. Politically, Muscovite Russia had taken shape as an autocracy against which the society possessed few legitimate defences; culturally, the Russians stood heirs to a Byzantine tradition arbitrarily shorn of its Hellenism; nationally, they were a people unusual even at the time in the extent to which they had vested their identity in their religion. It is hard to avoid a sense that what an obscurantist Christianity did for the Russians, Islam could have done better.

and the chaos which was the terror of the servants of God were thus but two sides of the same coin.

There is however one very striking achievement of the Ottoman state even in disarray: the longevity of the imperial framework is a phenomenon more European than Islamic. There was no radical discontinuity in the history of the Ottoman state between the early fifteenth century, when it was temporarily put out of action by Timur, and the early nineteenth century, when it blew up its own Janissaries in the hope of avoiding such a fate at the hands of its modern enemies.[1] At the centre, the Ottoman order withstood both external assault and internal subversion (the dynasty did not succumb to the ambitions of mayors of the palace, as did the 'Abbasids, nor did it suffer displacement by its own slave soldiers, as did the Ayyubids). Equally it displayed a comparable durability in the provinces. The pattern of Ottoman provincial history in the seventeenth and eighteenth centuries was one of unstable adventures in the gathering and dissipation of local power, but it is strikingly lacking in examples of successful secession: if the state had lost the will or the way to impose centralized order on its provinces, it still retained a spoiling power in virtue of which it could prevent the consolidation of emergent patterns of localized order.[2] The Ottoman Empire of the nineteenth century may have been the 'Sick Man of Europe'; but it was a sickness that few other Islamic states would have survived to endure. And in so far as an explanation of this longevity can be sought in the terms of the analysis set out above, it has to be found in the otherwise much etiolated heritages of Byzantium and the steppes. On the one hand the Ottoman Empire was in an obvious way the first Islamic state with a plausible imperial site; and on the other, it was in a more elusive way the leading beneficiary of that reinforcement of the dynastic and institutional structures of profane power was the gift to Islamic history of the Turks and Mongols.[3]

[1] For an Ottoman sultan who seems to have entertained the notion of doing something of the kind two hundred years earlier, see p. 138.

[2] For a clear presentation of this point in one provincial context, see S. Shamir, 'As'ad Pasha al-'Azm and Ottoman rule in Damascus (1743–58)', in *Bulletin of the School of Oriental and African Studies* (1963). Egypt is to some extent an exception.

[3] Cf. the suggestive comments of B. Lewis, 'The Mongols, the Turks and the Muslim Polity', in *Transactions of the Royal Historical Society* (1968), reprinted in his *Islam in History* (London, 1973).

I

THE RISE OF THE OTTOMAN EMPIRE

IN the second half of the seventh/thirteenth century, as the Seljuk
state fell apart, a number of principalities (*beyliks*) of a new kind
came into being in the western marches of Anatolia. They were in
territory conquered as a result of holy wars (sing., *ghazā*) waged against
Byzantium, and hence are known as *ghāzī* states. The Ottoman principality was one of these. It was destined within a century to unite Anatolia and the Balkans under its sovereignty, and to develop into an
Islamic empire. Let us now examine as a whole the formation of these
ghāzī principalities. The emergence of the Ottoman state can be understood only in the context of the general history of the marches.

THE EMERGENCE OF TURCOMAN BORDER PRINCIPALITIES IN WESTERN ANATOLIA

When the state of the Anatolian Seljuks developed into a fully formed
Islamic sultanate, three areas came to be designated as marches *par
excellence,* and attracted settlements of Muslim *ghāzīs*. In the south,
facing Cilicia (Chukurova) the 'realm of the Lord of the Coasts' was
centred round 'Alā'iyya and Antalya and directed against Lesser Armenia
and the kingdom of Cyprus. In the north, on the borders of the Byzantine
empire of Trebizond and along the shores of the Black Sea, the Muslim
marches consisted of two parts, the eastern, centred round Simere,
Samsun and Bafra, and the western centred round Kastamonu and
Sinop. Finally, the western marches, whose principal cities were Kastamonu, Karahiṣār-i Devle (Afyonkarahisar), Kütahya and Denizli lay
along the Byzantine frontier from the area of Kastamonu to the gulf
of Makri in the south.

It appears that in each of these three areas of the marches the Seljuk
state was represented by a governor-general known as commander
(*emīr*) of the marches. These powerful *emīrs* who represented the central
authority, generally kept their positions in their families as a hereditary
dignity. The post of commander of the western marches on the Byzantine frontier came to be the most important of all. This position was
given in 659/1261 to Nuṣrat al-Dīn Ḥasan and Tāj al-Dīn Ḥusayn, the
sons of the powerful Seljuk *vezīr* Fakhr al-Dīn 'Alī. We know that this

emirate took in the whole area between Kütahya, Beyshehir and Akshehir. Its capital was the impregnable fortress of Karaḥiṣār. The area of the marches formed the basis of the power of Fakhr al-Dīn ʿAlī. The main strength of the marches lay in the Turcoman tribes, governed by their own hereditary leaders, or beys. It should be noted, however, that these tribes were loose social units which could dissolve and reform around leading *ghāzīs* in the marches. They were then usually named after their new leaders, e.g. Aydınlı, Sarukhanlı and ʿOsmanlı, i.e. Ottoman. These beys of the marches were linked to the *emīr* of the marches largely by bonds of personal loyalty. They exercised independent authority over their own groups. The marches were a frontier area where nomads driven there forcibly by the Seljuk state, as well as refugees from Mongol conquests and oppression, came together in search of a new life. This mountain region which lay between the plateau of central Anatolia and the coastal plains provided abundant summer pastures, and a large proportion of its population was made up of semi-nomadic Turcomans. At the same time highly developed urban forms of Seljuk civilization had also taken root in such border towns as Denizli, Kütahya, Karaḥiṣār, Eskishehir and Kastamonu. These urban centres were destined to influence profoundly the future development of the border principalities. Seljuk chroniclers, who stood for the interests of the Mongol-Seljuk central authority, tended to describe the population of the marches as robber rebels ready to mutiny at a moment's notice.

The Turcomans of the western marches were seen to play an important part in determining the political development of Anatolia at the time of the struggle between Kılıj Arslan IV, who was supported by the Mongols, and Kay-Kāvūs II (643–59/1246–61) who tried to base himself on the western provinces and marches. Kay-Kāvūs was finally forced to seek refuge in Byzantium in 659/1261. The Mongol and Seljuk troops led by Muʿīn al-Dīn Pervāne came to the frontier and pacified the Turcomans. Nevertheless, we know that a fairly numerous group of semi-nomadic Turcomans joined Kay-Kāvūs in Byzantine territory, and were later settled in the Dobruja. At roughly the same time one Menteshe Bey, a coastal bey who was probably a vassal of Kay-Kāvūs, left the southern coastal marches and led a *ghazā* raid against Byzantine possessions in Caria. As the result of these sea raids, Menteshe Bey succeeded in establishing himself first of all in the Carian seaports (659/1261 to 667/1269). It appears that he then co-operated with a numerous group of Turcoman nomads, migrating between summer pastures in the mountains of Denizli and winter pastures on the coast. After organizing these Turcomans, Menteshe Bey extended his authority over the whole of Caria. Then in 677/1278 he advanced in the direction of the valley of the Büyük Menderes, and captured the cities of Priene, Miletus and Magedon. In 681/1282 he advanced further to capture Tralles (Aydın) and Nyssa. Menteshe Bey's conquests were continued by his son-in-law Sasa Bey. Turkish conquests in western Anatolia had by that time assumed the nature of a general advance.

We have already referred to the importance of the area of Denizli and Kütahya in the western marches. Here the most advanced position was occupied by the semi-nomadic Germiyan Turks, who were subject to the 'Alīshīr family in the region of Kütahya-Sandıklı. Karīm al-Dīn 'Alīshīr, who belonged to an old-established family of *emīrs,* had been a supporter of Kay-Kāvūs II, and when the latter fled to Byzantium he was executed by the Mongols. The descendants of 'Alīshīr and the Germiyan Turks were then under the sway of the dynasty of Fakhr al-Dīn 'Alī. In 676/1277 when great disorders broke out throughout Anatolia, they fought bravely on the side of Fakhr al-Dīn 'Alī and of the Seljuk Sultan Kay-Khusraw III and captured the rebel Jimri. Fakhr al-Dīn then suppressed the rebellion of the chief *emīr* of the marches in the area of Denizli. He also pacified the Turcomans who had mutinied round Karahişār and Sandıklı. Fakhr al-Dīn's two sons were killed in the battle against the rebel Jimri. The 'Alīshīr dynasty which supported Fakhr al-Dīn then became a force to be reckoned with in the marches.

When, however, the Mongols appointed Sultan Mas'ūd II to the Seljuk throne, the successors of 'Alīshīr turned against Fakhr al-Dīn and the central government. It appears that important adherents of the old régime who had sought refuge in the marches incited the Turcomans to rebel. Not only those who had been threatened by the change of sultan but also people dissatisfied with the taxation and land policies of the Mongols fled to the marches. In the summer of 685/1286 the Germiyan Turks raided the province of Gargorum lying between the marches and Konya. Mongol and Seljuk forces had to wage an intense struggle against them until 688/1289. The house of 'Alīshīr joined forces with two other border dynasties, the Karamanlıs and the Eshrefoghlus. The struggle ended with the house of 'Alīshīr winning the position in the marches formerly held by the house of Fakhr al-Dīn. An inscription in Ankara by Ya'qūb Bey I, the son of 'Alīshīr, shows that he held sway over the city while also recognizing the authority of the Seljuk sultan. Under Ya'qūb Bey (d. after 720/1320), who can be considered as the real founder of the Germiyan principality, the descendants of 'Alīshīr turned their forces and their energy against Byzantine territory where they could act independently. They captured Kula and closed in on Alashehir (Philadelphia). The commanders (sing., *su-bashı*) whom Ya'qūb Bey sent to the valleys of the Menderes and of the Gediz founded their own principality: Meḥmed Bey, the son of Aydın, the principality of the house of Aydın, Sarukhan Bey, the principality of the house of Sarukhan, and in the north, in Mysia, Qalam Bey and his son Karası Bey, the principality of Karası. Thus new conquests were made in Byzantine territory outside the province of the marches, and principalities of a new type were founded. The Ottoman principality was one of these. True, these principalities were, legally speaking, considered to be part of the marches and to come under the *emirs* of the marches, the Seljuk sultans and the Mongol Īl-Khāns in Tabrīz. In reality, however, the *ghāzī* beys felt themselves independent in the Byzantine territories which they had conquered. The formation of independent states by forces in the marches and, later, the emergence of one such state, which turned back from its area of new conquest to win dominion over the old Seljuk part of Anatolia were among the most important developments of the history of the Near East in the seventh/thirteenth and eighth/fourteenth centuries.

THE EMERGENCE OF THE OTTOMAN FRONTIER PRINCIPALITY

The marches from the Byzantine frontier along the River Sakarya to Kastamonu were subject to the *emir* of Kastamonu. About 690/1291 Kastamonu was ruled by Muẓaffar al-Dīn Yavlak Arslan, a descendant of the famous Seljuk *Emir* Ḥusām al-Dīn Choban. Yavlak Arslan held the title of captain-general of the marches. A contemporary source, Pachymeres, attributes the emergence of 'Osmān Ghāzī to a struggle with the dynasty of 'Amurios', *emirs* of Kastamonu. When the sons of Kay-Kāvus II returned to Anatolia from the Crimea, one of them, Mas'ūd, obtained the Seljuk throne from the Mongol, Arghūn Khān. At his orders his brother Rukn al-Dīn Kılıj Arslan settled in the marches, probably near Akshehir. When after the death of Arghūn Khān and the election of Gaykhātū to the khanate (23 Rajab 690/22 July 1291) a struggle for the throne broke out among the Mongols of Persia, a state of anarchy developed in Anatolia. The frontier Turcomans rebelled.

Kılıj Arslan rebelled against his brother Mas'ūd. When Gaykhātū arrived in Anatolia in Dhu'l-Qa'da 690/November 1291, Kılıj Arslan went to the march of Kastamonu and gathered the Turcomans round him. He killed the *emīr* of the marches, Muẓaffar al-Dīn Yavlak Arslan, who had been a supporter of Mas'ūd. Sultan Mas'ūd who was sent to the area by Gaykhātū, was at first defeated but was later victorious thanks to the Mongol forces at his disposal (Dhu'l-Ḥijja 690/December 1291). Kılıj Arslan escaped, but was later killed when caught in a raid by Yavlak Arslan's son, 'Alī. 'Alī, who after the events of 690/1291 renounced his allegiance to the Seljuks and their Mongol overlords, attacked Byzantine territory, and conquered the land stretching as far as the River Sakarya. He even raided the far bank of the river. Later, however, he established peaceful relations with the Byzantines. 'Osmān Ghāzī's area lay to the south of him, on the far bank of the middle stretch of the River Sakarya around Sögüd. Pachymeres states clearly that when 'Alī broke off the struggle 'Osmān took over the leadership of the raids and started waging violent *ghaẓā* warfare on Byzantine territory. The *ghāẓīs* started gathering under his banner. Pachymeres says that they came from Paphlagonia, in other words from the territory subject to the *emīr* of Kastamonu.

By 700/1301 'Osmān had advanced far enough to press in close on the old Byzantine capital of Nicaea (Iznik). Old Ottoman traditions on his origin and on his activities before that date, show that he had come under the pressure of the Germiyan dynasty and was thus forced to work in the most forward part of the marches. It was this circumstance which made for his future success and for that of the principality which he founded. According to the same traditions, 'Osmān's early activity did not amount to a general and ceaseless struggle against the Byzantines. At first he tried to get on with the more powerful of the Byzantine lords (*tekfurs*) in his area. He appeared in the light of a bey of a semi-nomadic group of Turcomans in conflict with the *tekfurs* who controlled their summer and winter pastures.[1] Old sources, which are legendary in character, attribute 'Osmān's decision to come forward as a *ghāzī* to the influence of Shaykh Ede Bali. In fact, however, the factors which

---

[1] On 'Osmān's tribal origin and his membership of the Kayi tribe of the Oghuz Turks, see M. F. Köprülü, 'Osmanlı imparatorluğunun etnik menşei meseleleri', in *Belleten*, 28, 219–303, who defends against P. Wittek the view that 'Osmān was the leader of a small clan of the Kayı. According to Köprülü, this tribal nucleus played a negligible part in the formation of a state which did not have a tribal character even at its inception; on this point Köprülü is in agreement with Wittek and Giese.

impelled 'Osmān to become a leader of *ghāzīs* were the same factors as motivated the whole activity in the marches of western Anatolia, in other words the pressure of population and the need for expansion resulting from the movement of immigration from central Anatolia, the decay of the Byzantine frontier-defence system, and religious and social discontent in the Byzantine frontier areas, as well as the desire of Anatolian Turks to escape from Mongol oppression and to start a new life in new territory.

'Osmān had become master of an area stretching from Eskishehir to the plains of Iznik and Brusa (Bursa), and had organized a fairly powerful principality. When he started threatening Iznik, anxiety was for the first time felt in the Byzantine capital on his score. It was then that the Byzantine empire began counting him among the most important beys of the marches alongside the houses of 'Alīshīr, Aydın and Menteshe. In 701/1301 the Byzantine emperor despatched against 'Osmān a force of 2,000 men under the command of the *Hetaereiarch* Muzalon charged with the task of relieving Iznik. When 'Osmān ambushed this force and destroyed it at Baphaeon, the local population was panic-stricken and started to leave, seeking shelter in the castle of Nicomedia (Izmit). In another direction 'Osmān's forward raiders advanced as far as the approaches of Bursa. In Ottoman tradition this victory is known as the victory won near Yalakova over the forces of the emperor during the siege of Iznik. It was at this time that 'Osmān is said to have been recognized by the Seljuk sultan as a bey, in other words as a person wielding political authority. After 701/1301 'Osmān's fame is reported to have spread to distant Muslim countries, and his territory was filled with wave upon wave of immigrant Turkish households.

The importance attached by the Byzantine empire to the Ottoman threat is shown by the fact that, in order to stop 'Osmān, the emperor tried to conclude an alliance with Ghāzān Khān, and, after the latter's death, with Öljeitü Khān and to bring the Mongol army into play. Nevertheless, around the end of the century the conquests in western Anatolia of the house of Germiyan and its commanders, and of Sasa, the son-in-law of Menteshe, seemed to pose the greater threat. In 677/1278 and 695/1296 the empire tried to reconquer lost territory here by sending two armies, but both attempts proved unsuccessful. The expedition of mercenary Alan and Catalan troops were also fruitless (701/1302 and 703/1304). Ephesus (Seljuk) fell immediately after the withdrawal of the

Catalans. Meḥmed Bey, son of Aydın, captured Birgi (Pyrgion) in 708/1308, made it his capital and, by extending his power as far as Smyrna (Izmir), became the most powerful prince in western Anatolia. Sarukhan Bey captured Manisa (Magnesia) in 713/1313, made it the centre of his principality and became an independent ruler. Further to the north, in Mysia, Karası Bey captured Balıkesir (Palaeocastron) and, having resettled it, made it his capital. This principality expanded, probably after 728/1328, to the shores of the sea of Marmora, of the Hellespont and of the gulf of Adrammytion (Edremid). To the east lay 'Oṣmān's territory. He too made extensive new conquests after 1301, occupied the environs of Iznik and Bursa, and blockaded these powerful fortresses by means of towers which were built nearby. He thus tried to starve them out.

When the Mongol governor Timurtash Noyon, who had forcibly tried to exact obedience from the princes of the marches, had to seek refuge with the Mamluks in 728/1328, after having been proclaimed a rebel, the authority of the Īl-Khāns in the Anatolian marches became weaker than ever before. The tax-register for the year 1349 still shows Karaman, the principality of Ḥamīd, Denizli, Aydın, Germiyan, the Ottoman principality, Gerdebolu, Kastamonu, Eghridir and Sinop as lying within the borders of the Mongol state, grouped under the general name of marches, but these princes of the marches had long ago become independent rulers, paying only nominal tribute, and minting coins in their own names.

THE CULTURE OF THE MARCHES

The principalities of the marches had a distinct way of life, which could be described as a frontier culture, and this distinguished them clearly from the hinterland. This culture was dominated by the Islamic conception of Holy War or *ghazā*. By God's command the *ghazā* had to be fought against the infidels' dominions, *dār al-ḥarb* (the abode of war), ceaselessly and relentlessly until they submitted. According to the *Sharī'a* the property of the infidels, captured in these raids, could be legally kept as booty, their country could be destroyed, and the population taken into captivity or killed. The actions of the *ghāzīs* were regulated by the *Sharī'a* to which they paid heed. Ceaseless warfare led to the formation of groups commanded by *ghāzī* leaders specially blessed by shaykhs. The *ghāzī* groups were often named after their leaders.

Successful leaders naturally attracted the greatest number of *ghāzīs*. In the Seljuk marches which were dominated by Turcoman nomads, these leaders were also often chiefs of tribal clans. But, as we have seen, many of them had been commanders under the Seljuk sultans. Usually these *ghāzī* beys paid no taxes to the central government, or they sent only nominal taxes as a token of loyalty.

Life in the marches was dangerous, and required great personal initiative. At the other side of the border there was a similar Christian frontier organization, moved by the same spirit, the Byzantine *akritai*. Ethnically, frontier society was very mixed. It included highly mobile nomads, refugees from central authority, heterodox elements and adventurers. In contrast with the highly developed conservative civilization of the hinterland, with its theology, palace literature, and the *Sharī'a,* the marches had a mystical and eclectic popular culture, which had not yet frozen into a final form. They sheltered heterodox sects, bred a mystical and an epic literature and obeyed customary or tribal law. Their ethos was chivalrous and romantic.

References to the life of 'Osmān Ghāzī in old Ottoman traditions strongly reflect this way of life. It should not be forgotten, however, that there are considerable distortions of reality in these legends. According to Oruj, the Ottomans were

Ghāzīs and champions striving in the way of truth and the path of Allāh, gathering the fruits of *ghazā* and expending them in the way of Allāh, choosing truth, striving for religion, lacking pride in the world, following the way of the *Sharī'a,* taking revenge on polytheists, friends of strangers, blazing forth the way of Islam from the East to the West.[1]

In 1354 they told Gregory Palamas that the constant expansion westwards of Muslim power was a predestined event reflecting the will of God.[2] They considered themselves as the sword of God, and this view was widespread not only among themselves but also among the Byzantines. Later on, Luther was to view the Ottomans in the same light. In old Ottoman traditions people described as *alplar* (heroes), *alp-erenler,* and *akhiler* were among the closest companions of 'Osmān. 'Osmān became a *ghāzī*, it was said, as a result of the preaching of Shaykh Ede Bali, who was probably a member of the *akhī* confraternity and who, in accordance with the *akhī* custom tied a sword to 'Osmān's waist. As

[1] Oruj, *Tavārikh-i Āl-i 'Osmān,* ed. F. Babinger (Hanover, 1925), 3.
[2] G. Arnakis, 'Gregory Palamas among the Turks', in *Speculum,* XXVI, 110.

for the *alplar,* they followed the heroic tradition of Central Asian Turks. In the marches, the *alplar* cloaked themselves in the Islamic *ghazā* tradition and became known as *alp-erenler.* According to a contemporary source there were seven conditions for becoming an *alp-eren*: courage, strength of arm, endeavour, a good horse, a special dress, a bow and arrows, a good sword, a lance and an appropriate companion. Köprülü believes that the traditions and customs of Central Asian Turks survived strongly among the semi-nomadic Turcomans of the Anatolian marches. Wittek, on the other hand, thinks that it was rather the Islamic traditions relating to the Byzantine frontier districts, developed under the caliphate, that were dominant.[1] It is really a question of degree to determine the strength of each of the two traditions in forming the common way of life in the marches.

Between 730/1330 and 746/1345 the most brilliant *ghazā* exploits in the marches were achieved by Umur Bey of the house of Aydın. Umur Bey extended the *ghazā* to naval engagements. To counter his raids in the Aegean, Christian states agreed on a crusade against him and signed a preliminary agreement on 14 Dhu'l-Ḥijja 732/6 September 1332. They formed a fleet of twenty galleys. In 734/1334 many Turkish ships were sunk in the Aegean, the fleet of Yakhshi Bey, lord of Karası, being destroyed in the gulf of Edremid. On 19 Jumādā II 745/28 October 1344, the castle in the port of Izmir was raided and captured by the Christian forces. Umur was killed in an attempt to recapture it (Ṣafar 749/May 1348). The new bey of Aydın, Khiḍr, seeing the fate of his brother, gave up the policy of *ghazā,* preferring the advantages deriving from trade. Acting through the papacy he made peace with the Christian states concerned and granted them full privileges, allowing them to trade freely in his dominions (20 Jumādā I 749/17 August 1348). He stated in this document that he had put an end to his war with the Christians, that he would protect them in the future, would not alter customs-dues and would allow consuls of the Knights of Rhodes, of Venice, and of Cyprus to establish themselves on his land, and would permit their ships to make use of his ports.

Writing *c.* 730/1330 al-'Umarī describes the beys of Karası, Sarukhan, Menteshe and Aydın as maritime *ghāzīs,* but he distinguishes Umur Bey as one waging ceaseless Holy War (*jihād*).[2] When these principalities were

---

[1] P. Wittek, *The rise of the Ottoman Empire* (London, 1938), 17-19.
[2] Al-'Umarī, *Masālik al-abṣār,* ed. Fr. Taeschner (Leipzig, 1929), 30-47.

fought to a standstill by the Christian League in the Aegean, they lost their function as bases for the *ghazā*, and, like the Knights of Rhodes, they came to prefer the advantages of trade. Once this choice was made, the classical way of life and the institutions of Islamic society of the hinterland began to predominate. The leadership of the *ghazā* then passed to the Ottomans, who occupied the front line of the marches and crossed into the Balkans, where they established themselves.

The *ghāzī* beys of the marches demonstrated the original spirit of unity of the marches through common action in some of their raids and by helping each other. Cantacuzenus says that a bey embarking on a *ghazā* expedition would willingly accept in his troop *ghāzīs* coming from neighbouring principalities.[1] Nevertheless, there were also frequent dynastic wars in these principalities. In accordance with old Turkish tradition, a bey divided his country among his sons. He then ruled from the centre over his semi-dependent sons. There were frequent internal struggles between brothers. In the Ottoman dominions, which were faced with greater dangers and greater efforts to destroy them, unity was better preserved.

In western Anatolia after the *ghāzī* beys had settled in the rich plains, and conquered international commercial ports, their countries developed commercially and culturally, and assumed the character of little sultanates which had adopted the higher forms of Islamic civilization. This is demonstrated by the accounts of al-'Umarī and Ibn Baṭṭūṭa in 730/1330 and 733/1333. Ibn Baṭṭūṭa admires the beautiful markets, palaces and mosques in these cities. He says that Denizli with its seven mosques and beautiful markets is 'one of the most attractive and immense cities'. Balıkesir, the chief city of Karası, is 'a fine and populous city with pleasant bazaars' and, finally, Bursa is 'a great important city with fine bazaars and wide streets'.[2] In western Anatolia, Ayasolug (Altoluogo, Ephesus) and Balat (Miletus) were two important centres of the Levant trade. In the middle of the eighth/fourteenth century there were Venetian consuls in both cities, and wealthy Christian merchants had settled there. In Ayasolug, the city built on the hill by the Turks was the main commercial centre. Merchants from all over the world came there. Italians bought the products of Anatolia: cotton, rice, wheat, saffron, wax, wool, hemp,

---

[1] P. Lemerle, *L'émirat d'Aydın, Byzance et l'Occident. Recherches sur la geste d'Umur Pacha* (Paris, 1957), 212–13.

[2] H. A. R. Gibb (tr.), *The travels of Ibn Baṭṭūṭa*, II (Cambridge, 1961), 425, 449–50.

raisins, alum, and valonia as well as slaves. Valuable cotton textiles woven in Denizli and precious silks woven in Balıkesir could also be bought by Western merchants, who sold in exchange valuable woollen cloth, which was used in the Īl-Khān's palace under the name *saqirlāt*. Other imports were tin and lead. In order to facilitate this expanding trade the Turcoman beys minted in Balat, Ayasolug and Manisa silver coins known as *gigliati*, with Latin inscriptions, modelled on Neapolitan coins.

Ibn Baṭṭūṭa mentions the pages dressed in silks whom he saw at Birgi in the palace of the Aydın prince. He stresses the importance and prestige of the Muslim jurists in the courts of the beys. The first *vezīrs* were undoubtedly chosen from among the jurists invited from the great urban centres of the interior. This was also the case with the first Ottoman *vezīrs* and with the jurists who organized the Ottoman state. Orkhān Bey opened a *medrese* in Iznik in 731/1331, and converted to a *medrese* the monastery inside the castle of Bursa. The complex of buildings, including a mosque, an alms-house, bath and a caravanserai, which Orkhān Bey built in Bursa remains to this day at the centre of the city's life.

The most salient characteristic of the culture which developed in these Turcoman principalities, was the survival of essentially Turkish cultural traditions within the context of Islamic culture. Most significantly, the Turkish language had a predominant position as a language both of the state and of literature. We know that, at the order of these Turcoman princes, classical Persian and Arabic works were translated into Turkish. Creative literary activity began in the second half of the eighth/fourteenth century with writers such as Sheykhoghlu Muṣṭafā and Aḥmedī. In these principalities, deeds of endowment (sing., *waqfiyya*) were drawn up not only in Arabic and Persian but also in Turkish. As for the works of architecture which came into being under the beys in western Anatolia, the two most important ones are the Great Mosque in Birgi built in 712/1312 and the mosque of Orkhān, built in Bursa in 741/1340. In the second half of the century there were such other great works of architecture as the Great Mosque in Manisa, the mosque of 'Īsā Bey in Ayasolug (777/1375), the *medrese* of Aḥmed Ghāzī in Pechin (777/1375) and the Green Mosque in Iznik (781/1379). These demonstrate a refined artistic taste. In decoration these buildings are simpler than the monuments of Seljuk architecture, while their plans also show novel features.

EXPANSION IN THE BALKANS AND ANATOLIA UNDER
ORKHĀN AND MURĀD

By capturing in quick succession Byzantine fortresses such as Bursa, Iznik and Izmid, which had long been blockaded, Orkhān Ghāzī, the son and successor of 'Osmān, became pre-eminent among the beys of the marches. Bursa fell on 2 Jumādā I 726/6 April 1326. In 729/1329 the effort made by the Emperor Andronicus III to relieve Iznik was defeated, and the town surrendered on 21 Jumādā I 731/2 March 1331. Andronicus having failed to relieve Izmid, that city too fell in 738/1337.

By annexing the principality of Karası by 746/1345, the Ottomans became masters of the area between the gulf of Edremid and Kapı-daghı (Cyzicus), and found themselves facing Europe. The Karası *ghāzīs* entered the service of Orkhān, and encouraged his energetic son, Süleymān, appointed by his father bey of the important march of Karası, to extend his conquests into the Balkans (Rumeli, whence the English term Rumelia). Umur Bey, who was at that time engaged in the Aegean Sea with the Crusaders, had an ally in John Cantacuzenus, to whom he recommended Orkhān. In 747/1346 Orkhān married Theodora, daughter of Cantacuzenus, became his faithful ally, and won the opportunity of intervening in Byzantine affairs as well as in operations in Thrace. At this time the command of the marches was given, in accordance with the old Turco-Mongol tradition, to Orkhān's eldest son, Süleymān, who then moved to Adrianople (Edirne) in Thrace in order to help Cantacuzenus. On his way he occupied the castle of Tzympe (Jinbi) on the isthmus of Gallipoli (Gelibolu) and refused to evacuate this bridge-head in spite of all the efforts and pressing requests of Cantacuzenus. By concluding an agreement with the Genoese in 755/1354 Orkhān obtained valuable allies for his operations in the area of the Hellespont. Süleymān strengthened his position by moving a stream of *ghāzīs* over the Straits and capturing the castle of Hexamilion (Eksamil) which dominated the isthmus of Gallipoli. The great fortress of Gallipoli was thus isolated from Thrace. The embattled front facing Gallipoli was immediately constituted under the command of Ya'qūb Eje and Ghāzī Fāżil who thus formed a new march. Another was formed on the left flank, under the command of Ḥājjī Ilbegi and Evrenuz (Evrenos) in order to extend the conquests to the north. Süleymān himself operated in the middle sector. In the night of 7 Ṣafar 755/2 March 1354, a violent earthquake brought down the walls of Gallipoli and of other fortresses around it. These were immediately occupied and re-fortified by the *ghāzīs*. This event, which allowed the Ottomans to establish a permanent foothold in Europe and opened limitless possibilities before the *ghāzīs,* caused great concern and excitement among the Byzantines and in the Western Christian world. The Venetian ambassador (*bailo*) wrote in Shaʿbān 755/August 1354 that Constantinople was ready to accept the protection of a powerful Christian state. Cantacuzenus, who was deemed responsible for this turn of events, had to renounce the throne. In Europe people began to say that a crusade had to be organized, this time not against the Aydın dynasty in Izmir but against the Ottomans. Gallipoli became a base for the *ghāzīs*.

When Süleymān died unexpectedly in an accident in 758/1357 his brother Murād accompanied by his tutor was sent to the command of the marches. In 760/1359 he launched a great offensive against Edirne, which surrendered in 762/1361. Rumours spread in Italy that Constantinople was about to fall. Under papal leadership a stimulus was given to exchanges between the king of Hungary, the Byzantine emperor and the Italian states with a view to organizing a crusade. By a bull dated 25 December 1366 the pope proclaimed a crusade to expel the Turks from the Balkans. The only ruler to respond was the duke of Savoy, Amadeus VI, who led his fleet to Gallipoli and recaptured it from the Ottomans (767/1366). The following year he handed over the castle to the Byzantines. This, however, did not check the Ottoman advance.

Murād I (763-91/1362-89) had now succeeded Orkhān, and threatened both the Byzantine empire and the Serbian. When the journey of the Byzantine Emperor John V Palaeologus to Italy to meet the pope and mobilize aid failed to produce results, and when the last joint operation of the Serbian princes in Macedonia was defeated on the Maritza (battle of Chirmen 15 Rabīʿ I 773/26 September 1371), the emperor and the rulers of the Balkans acknowledged Ottoman suzerainty, one after the other. As early as 773/1372 or 774/1373 John V realized that no hope was left, and agreed to accept the suzerainty of Murād I, taking part in his Anatolian expeditions as an Ottoman vassal. Later, his son Andronicus IV obtained the protection of the Ottomans, thanks to which he succeeded to the Byzantine throne (778/1376). Then he returned Gallipoli to the Ottomans (781/1379).

In brief, Murād had succeeded by 782/1380 in creating in Anatolia and Rumelia an embryo empire made up of vassal principalities. Relations with these were at first so regulated that in exchange for aid or formal alliances the Ottomans subjected local princes to a number of obligations which eventually turned them into Ottoman vassals. When this process was complete, the Ottomans forced these princes and beys to send their sons to the Ottoman court as hostages, to pay tribute, and to participate in Ottoman expeditions with forces commanded by these princes in person or by their sons. At the same time these vassal states remained under the constant pressure of the beys of the marches, lest they should escape from Ottoman dominion. The moment that they renounced their subject status, their territories were considered *dār al-ḥarb,* i.e. a field of battle which attracted the terrifying onslaughts of the *akınjı* raiders (see below, pp. 31 ff). Under Murād I, Ottoman occupation of roads and centres of population in the Balkans followed three main directions: in the centre, the valley of the Maritza, which the Ottomans followed, reaching the foothills of the Balkan range as early as 767/1366 and then going on to conquer Sofia *c.* 787/1385 and Nish in 788/1386; on the right the valley of the Tunja, and on the left, the southern march, commanded by Evrenuz, where Serez (Serrae) was occupied on 21 Rajab 785/19 September 1383, an event which was followed by the beginning of the siege of Salonica. This second largest city in the Byzantine dominions surrendered in Ramaḍān 789/September 1387. Divisions and rivalries in the Balkans and attempts by Balkan states to ally themselves to the Ottomans and win their protection, facilitated these advances. Thus in 766–7/1365–6 the Bulgarian King Shishman, threatened from the north by an invasion of Hungarians and of the prince of Wallachia, and from the Black Sea by the fleet of Amadeus of Savoy's Crusaders, had sought safety in becoming an ally of the Ottomans. It appears that he accepted Turkish help, as Cantacuzenus had earlier done. Between 767/1366 and 771/1370 there are references in chronicles to Bulgarian-Turkish co-operation and to Turkish units fighting alongside the Bulgarians on the Danube. Let us add that Prince Wladislaw of Wallachia also sought Ottoman help in 775/1373 when he turned his back on the Hungarians.

The reign of Murād I also saw the expansion and consolidation of Ottoman power in Anatolia. In 755/1354 the Ottomans had captured Ankara, which was at that time an important economic and political centre. This marked the start of Ottoman expansion into the former Seljuk-Mongol area—the old Islamic hinterland. It embroiled the Ottomans with the *emīr* of Sivas, and with his neighbours and powerful allies, the house of Karaman. The princes of Karaman were the most powerful of the Turcoman frontier-beys in the south. After a long struggle, they had established themselves firmly in the old Seljuk capital of Konya, whence they considered themselves as heirs to the Seljuks— sovereigns of the sultanate of Rūm and suzerains of the other beys of the marches. The Ottomans, greatly strengthened by the success of their *ghazā* in the Balkans, came up against the house of Karaman with precisely the same claim. Resistance to Ottoman overlordship was crushed in 789/1387, when Murād I marched on Konya and won a pitched battle there.

But while Murād was in Anatolia, there was a revolt in the Balkans by the Serbians, whom the ruler of Bosnia joined. The Bulgarians sided with them. Thereupon an expedition was undertaken against Shishman the Bulgarian king in the first place. In 790/1387 he was eliminated from the fray, and Bulgaria was occupied. The following spring Murād marched down to the plain of Kosova against the Serbs. The victory which the Ottomans won (19 Jumādā II 791/15 June 1389) showed that they were destined to stay in the Balkans as the ruling power. Murād was mortally wounded on the battlefield and was immediately succeeded by his son Bāyezīd, called *Yıldırım,* 'the Thunderbolt'. To avoid a civil war Bāyezīd's brother was executed.

BĀYEZĪD I AND THE CLASH WITH TĪMŪR

As soon as news was received of the death of Murād, the beys of Anatolia revolted once again. Thereupon Bāyezīd immediately crossed into Anatolia with prestige of the great victory won at Kosova. Within a year he occupied and annexed to the empire what remained of the *ghazī* principalities of western Anatolia, i.e. the principalities of Aydın, Sarukhan and Menteshe and the remnants of those of Ḥamīd and Germiyan. He then marched on the prince of Karaman, and forced him to sue for peace (793/1391). He crushed the bey of Kastamonu, and added his territories to the empire. However, in the area of Amasya, further to the east, he was faced with a dangerous rival in the person of the sultan of Sivas, Qāḍī Burhān al-Dīn. In the meantime the Wallachians, acting under Hungarian protection, established themselves on the south bank of the Danube in Silistre (Silistria) and in the Dobruja, while the Byzantines reoccupied Salonica. Once again Bāyezīd crossed over to the Balkans (795/1393) and annexed the Dobruja; Tirnova, Shishman's capital, was occupied on 7 Ramaḍān 795/17 July 1393. He summoned all the vassal princes of Rumelia to attend on him. His object was to underline his rights as suzerain and to punish the Palaeologi who were gravitating towards Venice. However, the princes succeeded in evading the summons. Bāyezīd then reoccupied Salonica (19 Jumādā II 796/21 April 1394) and sent his *akınjı* raiders into the Morea. Having done this, he appeared before the walls of Constantinople and blockaded the city in the hope of forcing it to surrender through the exercise of unrelenting pressure. He then made an expedition into Hungary in order to intimidate the Hungarians and subdue the Wallachians. The army, which he commanded in person, devastated southern Hungary and then entered Wallachia, where he had a fierce battle with a Wallachian army at Argeshe. On his way back, Bāyezīd crossed the Danube at Nicopolis, and had Shishman arrested and executed. This marked the extinction of the Bulgarian kingdom. These operations led to the formation of a crusading army made up of groups of knights from all over western Europe under the command of King Sigismund of Hungary. The Crusaders came as far as Nicopolis, while the Venetian navy stood guard over the Hellespont. Bāyezīd was at that time near Constantinople. He immediately marched off, and encountered the Crusaders outside Nicopolis, which they were besieging. The Crusaders were completely routed (21 Dhu'l-Ḥijja 798/25 September 1396). This victory won the sultan great fame as a *ghāzī* throughout the Muslim world. Returning to Anatolia, with this victory behind him, Bāyezīd occupied Konya the following year and destroyed the state of Karaman (beginning of 800/autumn of 1397). The following year he also put an end to the state of Qāḍī Burhān al-Dīn around Sivas, and, entering the territory of the Mamluks in the upper valley of the Euphrates, occupied several cities including Malaṭya and Elbistan. Thus Bāyezīd was at one and the same time waging war on the most powerful Muslim sultan, the Mamluk ruler, and encroaching on Tīmūr's sphere of influence in eastern Anatolia as far as Erzinjan. His pressure on Constantinople was such that the Emperor Manuel II went himself to Europe (802/1399) in order to plead for a crusade. The sultan of the *ghāzīs* in this way eliminated the petty states of Anatolia and Rumelia and, having founded an empire within a brief spell of time, put it in the forefront of a world-wide struggle for power. Envoys were exchanged between Tīmūr and the king of France. Tīmūr went into action, crushed Bāyezīd's imperial army, which was not yet well integrated, and captured the sultan himself in a battle of Ankara on 27 Dhu'l-Ḥijja 804/28 July 1402.

Bāyezīd, encouraged by his victories and by the forces at his disposal,

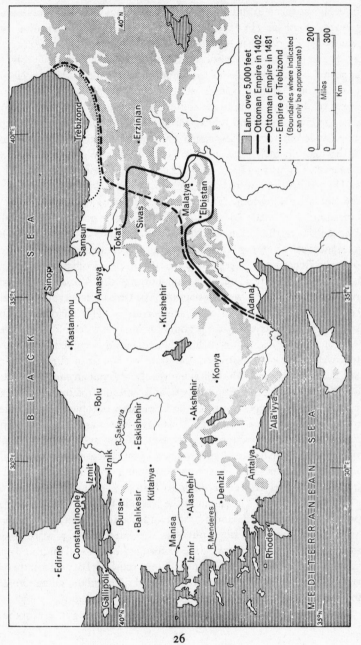

Map I. Anatolia in the fifteenth century.

had tried to transform the empire made up of vassal principalities, which existed under Murād I, into a true empire coming under a centralized administration. He acted with force and determination. He tried to eliminate Hungarian influence from the Balkans. By establishing a fortified naval base at Gallipoli he won control over the Hellespont and challenged Venice at sea. He sought to conquer Constantinople and make it the capital of his empire, joining Anatolia and Rumelia. While challenging the entire Christian world, he sought from the caliph in Egypt the official title of *sulṭān al-Rūm*, as the legitimate heir to the Seljuk possessions in Anatolia. Meanwhile, however, Tīmūr had raised his banner in the East, espousing the cause of the descendants of Chingiz Khān, and seeking recognition of his right to rule over Anatolia and with it over Bāyezīd, whom he considered as simply a bey of the marches. After crushing Bāyezīd at Ankara, Tīmūr revived the Anatolian principalities and placed them under his protection against any further Ottoman encroachments.

The nucleus of the Ottoman dominions was divided among three brothers, Süleymān in Edirne, Meḥmed in Amasya, and 'Īsā in Bursa. These recognized Tīmūr as their suzerain. Ottoman possessions in Anatolia having now been reduced to the area which they had occupied under Murād I, the centre of gravity of the state moved to Rumelia, Edirne becoming from this date the main Ottoman capital. Even before Tīmūr died in 807/1405, a civil war started among the brothers for possession of the two Ottoman capitals, Edirne and Bursa, and for undivided rule over the empire. This period is known as the interregnum. Finally Meḥmed I triumphed over his rivals and re-established the unity of the Ottoman state in 816/1413. With this end in view Meḥmed adopted a policy of conciliating the beys, princes and local lords, who had reappeared in Anatolia and Rumelia and, above all, of getting on peacefully with the Byzantines. This policy forced him into important concessions. The states in question regained some of their former possessions and won a greater freedom of action in the face of the Ottoman sultan. After the experience of Tīmūr's onslaught, the Ottomans made a point of advancing their policy of conquest and of *ghazā* with greater care, avoiding as far as possible giving rise to crusades in the west and to a fresh intervention in Anatolia, this time by Tīmūr's son, Shāh-Rukh. It was only in the reign of Meḥmed II the Conqueror that the Ottomans launched an offensive policy both in the east and in the west in order to revive the empire of Bāyezīd.

To understand why the Ottomans succeeded in re-establishing the unity of their state, one must remember above all that Bāyezīd had abandoned the traditions of the marches and had introduced the highly developed classical Turkish-Islamic system of central government into the administration of the state. Provincial land and population surveys, fiscal methods developed in the Īl-Khān state in Persia, a central treasury and a bureaucracy which sought from the capital to regulate affairs of the state throughout the provinces, were introduced or strengthened in his reign. The system of control through the sultan's own slaves (sing., *ghulām, kapı-kulu*), which was above all instrumental in establishing the absolute authority of the sultan in the provinces, came to dominate the administration in the time of Bāyezīd I.[1] Military and administrative commanders were chosen largely from among the *ich-oghlans* (slaves educated at the sultan's court), and even the majority of *timar* fiefs in the provinces were granted to the sultan's slaves brought up within the *ghulām* system. The military units made up of the sultan's slaves came to number 7,000 men. These elements helped in the re-establishment of a centrally administered empire, for, as long as there were rival sultans, neither the holders of *timar* fiefs nor members of the *kapı-kulu* slave class could be certain of their positions. The rights and influence which they had acquired could only be guaranteed by a stable centralized administration. It is they who supported first Meḥmed I and then Murād II against his rival, *Düzme* Muṣṭafā. They defended the absolute central authority of a single sultan against the divisive tendencies of the marches.

Furthermore, although weakened in Anatolia after Tīmūr's incursion, the Ottomans maintained their former strength in Rumelia. They were then able to come back to Anatolia from the Balkans and re-establish their supremacy.

THE OTTOMAN RECOVERY

The reign of Murād II (824–55/1421–51) was a time of preparation for the extension of the empire under Meḥmed II the Conqueror. When Murād ascended the throne in Bursa, Edirne and the whole of Rumelia gave allegiance to his uncle Muṣṭafā, known as *Düzme*, 'the Impostor'. Muṣṭafā was also supported by the Byzantines, who hoped to regain Gallipoli. In Anatolia the princes of the Germiyan and Karaman dynasties

---

[1] Thus *kapı-kulus* were recruited originally from the Sultan's share of prisoners-of-war, and subsequently from a periodical levy (*devshirme*) of Christian boys. Most of the youths entered the Janissary corps.

supported Murād's younger brother, also called Muṣṭafā, who was a governor in Ḥamīd. Like his father, Murād spent the first two years of his reign in dangerous struggles to establish himself on his throne and ensure the unity of his state. The beys of Anatolia did not recognize him. The prince of Karaman occupied Ḥamīd, while the bey of Kastamonu made himself master of the area round Tosya and Qal'ejik. Things had returned once again to the state of affairs which had prevailed in 804/1402. However, Murād II succeeded finally in crushing *Düzme* Muṣṭafā. He besieged the Byzantines in Constantinople as a punishment for the support which they had given to Muṣṭafā (Rajab 825/June 1422). But the beys of Anatolia attacked him and established his younger brother Muṣṭafā as sultan in Iznik. Thereupon Murād, who had been besieging Constantinople for fifty days with guns, crossed into Anatolia. He had Muṣṭafā arrested and executed. He forced the princes of Karaman and Kastamonu into submission, obliging them to return their newly won lands. He annexed the *ghāzī* principalities of western Anatolia, those of Izmir-Aydın, of Menteshe and the Teke branch of the Ḥamīd dynasty. Nevertheless, he followed a policy of conciliation towards the principalities of Jandar and Karaman in so far as they were part of the old Seljuk area of Anatolia which came under the protection of Shāh-Rukh. When the Byzantines who had regained Salonica in 805/1402, ceded the town to Venice in 826/1423 the Ottomans started a war against Venice. This war dragged on for a long time, from 826/1423 to 833/1430, because of the weakness of the Ottoman navy, and passed through some dangerous phases. In the meantime Hungary attempted to establish its supremacy over Wallachia and Serbia. This led to clashes which were ended by the truce signed for three years in 831/1428. The princes of Wallachia, Serbia and Bosnia reaffirmed their allegiance to the sultan. Finally Salonica was occupied in 833/1430.

Although Murād was described as a peace-loving sultan, his court was nevertheless under the influence of people who wished to return to the forceful policy of conquest pursued by Bāyezīd. Their counsels were particularly strong between 837/1434 and 846/1442. In 837/1434 struggle was renewed with Hungary for supremacy in Serbia and Wallachia. Benefiting from the death of King Sigismund in 841/1437 the sultan himself led an army into Hungary (1438). In 843/1439 he occupied and annexed Serbia. The following year the Ottomans made the first attempt to gain from the Hungarians the fortress of Belgrade, which was the gate leading to central Europe. Murād's withdrawal from

Belgrade was a turning point. In 845/1441 and 846/1442 there were large-scale Ottoman raids in Transylvania (Erdel). These were, however, totally crushed by the attacks led by John Hunyadi. These Ottoman defeats raised the hopes of Crusaders in the Christian world. The Hungarians launched a counter-offensive. In another surprise attack Hunyadi captured Nish and Sofia, and pressing on the last Balkan passes, threatened Edirne. Murād II succeeded with difficulty in halting the invading army at the battle of Izladi (Zlatića), on 1 Shaʿbān 847/24 November 1443, and thereupon returned suddenly to a pacific and conciliatory policy. He signed a peace with the Hungarians and with the despot of Serbia, George Branković, promising to return Serbia to him and to refrain from crossing the Danube (24 Ṣafar 848/12 June 1444). He then made peace with the prince of Karaman, who had once again gone over to the attack (summer 848/1444). By this agreement Ḥamīd was ceded to Karaman. Thinking that he had thus made peace on all sides, he voluntarily renounced the throne in favour of his son, Meḥmed II (summer 848/1444). The king of Hungary, the Byzantine emperor and the pope saw in this a golden opportunity, and pushed on with their preparations for a crusade. A Hungarian-Wallachian army crossed the Danube. At the same time the Venetian navy held the Hellespont. However, the despot of Serbia, who had been reinstated by the Ottomans, did not join the allies. The army of the crusaders reached the neighbourhood of Varna. Panic broke out in Edirne. In answer to pressing requests and petitions, Murād II came back to command the Ottoman army. Its victory at the pitched battle of Varna (28 Rajab 848/10 November 1444) is one of the vital battles in the history not only of the Balkans and of Byzantium, but also of Europe as a whole. Although Hunyadi later entered the Balkans for a third time, planning to co-operate with the Albanian, Iskender Bey (Scanderbeg), he was again defeated at Kosova (18–21 Shaʿbān 852/17–20 October 1448). This proved to be the last effort to free the Balkans and relieve Constantinople.

Among factors which paved the way to the conquest of Constantinople, certain internal developments in the Ottoman state hold an important place. In the first phase of the reign of Meḥmed II, who in 848/1444 was only twelve years old, the sultan was surrounded by a circle of commanders thirsting for war and conquest. This group tried to break the absolute power of the grand *vezīr* Chandarlı Khalīl, who came from the *'ulemā'*, and to supplant him. Chandarlı succeeded, however, in retaining the support of the Janissaries, and engineered the return to the throne of Murād II (Ṣafar 850/May 1446). Chandarlı refrained from threatening subject-states, fearing lest this should lead the Ottomans into adventures similar to those of 848/1444. When Murād II died on 1 Muḥarram 855/3 February 1451, Meḥmed II, who was then nineteen years of age, ascended the Ottoman throne for a second time. Power then passed to his governors Shihāb al-Dīn Shāhīn Pasha and Zaganuz Pasha, both of them advocates of further conquests, who had already tried to persuade Meḥmed II to attempt the conquest of Constantinople in 848/1444. The young sultan and his entourage needed a great victory in order to reaffirm their power and their influence against the grand *veẓīr*. Preparations were immediately put in hand for the siege of Constantinople.

FACTORS IN THE OTTOMAN CONQUESTS

The Ghāzīs *and the* Akınjıs

The Holy War or *ghaẓā* was the foundation stone of the Ottoman state. The tradition of the *ghāzīs* of the marches, which lay at its origin, dominated all its history, and constituted the fundamental principle of its policies and its organization. The concept of the *ghaẓā* stimulated great initiatives and endeavours, and, later, attempts at renewal; it inspired both individuals and society. The Ottomans took in all seriousness the duty of protecting and extending Islam, and even tried to justify their claim to sovereignty over the whole Islamic world, by the argument that they alone were carrying out that duty.

For *ghāzīs* in the marches, it was a religious duty to ravage the countries of the infidels who resisted Islam, and to force them into subjection. The only way of avoiding the onslaughts of the *ghāzīs* was to become subjects of the Islamic state. Non-Muslims could then enjoy the status of *dhimmīs,* living under its protection. Most Christian sources confuse these two stages in the Ottoman conquests. The Ottomans, however, were careful to abide by these rules, and this helped in the expansion of their empire. Faced with the terrifying onslaught of the *ghāzīs,* the population living outside the confines of the empire, in the 'abode of war', often renounced the ineffective protection of Christian states, and sought refuge in subjection to the Ottoman empire. Peasants in open country in particular lost nothing by this change. The institutions and traditions of the marches which existed at the time of 'Osmān Ghāzī lived on in Ottoman history, moving, however, to new frontiers. Later

31

ghāzīs became known as *akınjıs* (raiders) and the old term *uj* (march) gave place to *serḥadd* (frontier), but the concepts remained unchanged. An investigation into them can give us a clearer picture of the old marches.

From the point of view of organization the *sanjaks* (provinces) of the marches differed considerably from those of the interior. This was particularly true in the eighth/fourteenth and ninth/fifteenth centuries. In Üsküp, for example, the free *sipahi* cavalry was loyal to the person of the bey of the march. These beys of the marches were often descendants of the original frontier leaders and they formed dynasties such as the houses of Evrenuz, Mikhal, Turakhan and Malkoch, which inherited their *sanjaks* and ruled them more or less independently. We have already mentioned that they could at times receive tribute from foreign states. They disposed of vast properties in freehold or in *waqf*. Each of these main leaders, who enjoyed great power and renown in the marches, became a subject of legends, and epic poems were written about their exploits. The troops of these great beys of the marches in the Balkans were known by the names of their leaders as late as the tenth/sixteenth century. The *akınjıs* of the right flank were known as *Mikhallıs*, those of the left flank as *Turakhanlıs*. Seven thousand of the latter were active in the Morea in 966/1559. Under Murād II (824–55/1421–51) the Ottoman sultan began to appoint his personal slaves to commands in the marches, a custom which had existed under the Seljuks.

As for the *ghāzīs* themselves, known now under their new name of *akınjı*, these in the eighth/fourteenth century consisted largely of volunteers (sing., *gönüllü*) who had come from Anatolia, drawn by the prospect of warfare and of booty or by the hope of gaining a fief for themselves. These *akınjıs* were, unlike the old *ghāzīs*, a kind of auxiliary militia. We know also that nomad *yürüks*, and Christian *voynuks* and *martolos* (Greek: *armatolos*, armed irregulars) were enrolled as *akınjıs* for service in the frontier areas, and that they were used for intelligence and other purposes in enemy territory. The *akınjıs* normally set off on an expedition with two horses. The weapons of the *akınjıs*, who constituted a kind of light cavalry, were a sword, a shield, a scimitar, a lance and a mace. The *akınjıs* were formed in units of tens, hundreds and thousands. Their officers were known as *tovija* and were rewarded with fiefs (sing., *timar*). They were commanded by a *sanjak beyi* known as the bey of the *akınjıs*. In the tenth/sixteenth century the duties of the *akınjıs* on an expedition were to penetrate into enemy territory ahead of the main army and destroy the enemy's preparations, to carry out raids, to destroy the enemy's sources and routes of supply, to open roads for the Ottoman army, to check bridges and roads which the army had to cross, and to capture prisoners for intelligence purposes. From the end of this century raids became more difficult and, therefore, less frequent in central Europe. From then on Crimean auxiliaries came only when an expedition was in progress and carried out the duties of *akınjıs*. The organization of the *akınjıs* was thus considerably weakened. In 1034/1625 there were only two or three thousand left.

During the early stage of Ottoman history when the Ottoman state could still be considered a frontier principality, the marches played an important part in home politics. Ottoman beys of the marches or members of the ruling house might well have established independent principalities in the Balkans, following the example of the other frontier principalities. However, faced as they were with particularly strong enemies in the Balkans, the Ottoman beys of the marches needed the help which only the central government could provide. What is more, the Ottoman sultans were always personally active on the field of the *ghazā*. Thanks to the *beylerbeyi* organization and the force of the sultan's own retainers or slaves (*kapı-kulus*) the Ottoman sovereigns had the practical means of exerting their authority. Bāyezīd both as a great *ghāzī* himself and thanks to his *kapı-kulu* forces, was fully master of the marches. After his death, when his sons and grandsons struggled for power, the marches once again came to the fore. Contenders who could gain the support of the hereditary beys of the *akınjıs* in the marches could become masters of all Ottoman possessions in the Balkans. They could then ascend the throne in Edirne which had become the main royal residence since 805/1402. Mūsā Chelebi, who had been closely associated with the *akınjıs* in his father's lifetime, utilized their help to defeat his brother Süleymān in the Balkans, and this allowed him to gain the throne (22 Shawwāl 813/17 February 1411). His first action was to appoint to the dignity of *beylerbeyi* the famous bey of the *akınjıs* Mikhal-oghlu. Since the time of Orkhan the function of *beylerbeyi* had been given to the sultan's slaves and this allowed the central government to maintain its authority over the *sipahi* cavalry and the marches in the Balkans. There was always jealousy, open or hidden, between the *beylerbeyis,* who stood for the interests of the central authority, and the beys of the marches. The appointment of Mikhaloghlu meant that the bey of the *akınjıs* was in control of all the military forces in the Balkans. From their side the *akınjıs,* and their officers, the *tovijas,* viewed with jealousy the *sipahis* who had rich *timars* in the interior. Mikhaloghlu and the chief judge (*qāḍī 'asker*) Shaykh Badr al-Dīn, who was known for his extreme views, granted fiefs in the interior to many *akınjıs* from the Dobruja. Nonetheless, Mūsā continued the tradition of appointing his own slaves to key positions to counteract the influence of the beys of the marches. At the death of Meḥmed I (824/1421), his brother, *Düzme* Muṣṭafā became master of the Balkans and of Edirne, largely through the support of the house of Evrenuz. To outweigh this, Murād released Mikhaloghlu, who had been imprisoned in Tokat after the fall of Mūsā, and with his help succeeded in winning over the beys of the marches and eliminating his rival. Under Murād II the refusal of Turakhan, a powerful bey of the marches, to obey the *beylerbeyi* of Rumeli was one of the factors which led to Murād's abdication. In 1444 a pretender to the throne named Orkhan went from Istanbul to the Dobruja, where he tried to organize a rebellion of the forces in the marches. Meḥmed the Conqueror, as a great *ghāzī* himself, was able to dominate the marches, and attach them to the central government.

Expansion in Byzantine and Balkan territories

When the Ottomans appeared as a dynamic unifying force amidst the anarchy of the Balkans, Byzantine territories and the Balkans were prey not only to political but also to deep social and religious divisions. Civil wars and the absence of a central authority had allowed local lords in the provinces to strengthen their hold over the land and to subject the peasantry to a more or less arbitrary régime. The Byzantine administration struggled hopelessly to free from the grasp of these lords the estates which it wished to see returned to central control. This struggle over land between the central government and local lords was undoubtedly one of the main problems of Balkan history. Serfs tied to the land had to pay the lord a tax on produce as well as render free service in compulsory *corvées*. These services included the provision of firewood and hay, and free labour with oxen two or three days a week. When Ottoman administration was established, there was almost a social revolution through the application of the following principles: first, all agricultural land passed to the overriding ownership of the state, in other words the state established close control over the land. Land which thus passed to the state became known as *mirī* land. Secondly, all local feudal rights which limited the state's control over the land and the peasants were abolished. Local manorial rights were eliminated. The rights of local lords and, in some cases, of monasteries to exact forced labour from the peasants, and all similar privileges were suppressed. The Ottoman administration was always and everywhere opposed to the *corvée* system. The obligation to transport firewood and hay, and to work manorial estates, was replaced by a tax, known as plough dues (*chift resmi*) amounting to 22 aspers. The commutation of feudal service, which could easily be abused, into an easily payable fixed monetary tax was a major social reform. In addition, it was in principle forbidden to compel the peasants to any service. In brief, the Ottoman régime represented a strong and impartial central administration which extended to the peasants effective protection against feudal lords.

It is true that at the same time the Ottoman invasion deprived the Balkan peoples of their national cultural institutions and of the ruling class which embodied them. The Ottomans incorporated in the *timar* fief-system the local Balkan aristocracy which adhered to them. They left it part of its old lands, which these local nobles continued to hold in the changed capacity of holders of *timars*. In this way they entered the ruling group and came under the close control of the new empire, becoming in time ottomanized. Some of the more important noblemen tried, however, to preserve their position during the Ottoman conquest by relying for help on the Western Catholic world, and eventually fled to the West. Even before the conquest of Constantinople, the Ottomans appeared as protectors of the Church, and considered the Greek Orthodox ecclesiastical organization as part of their administrative system. Greek Orthodox archbishops were granted *timars*. The struggle between Greek Orthodox and Catholics in the Balkans was founded on deep-rooted social causes. It is an historical commonplace that the popular masses, fanatically attached to Greek Orthodoxy in Byzantine territories, preferred the Ottomans to Latin Catholics, and disowned their own ruling class and aristocracy which tried to unite with the Catholics. The ruler of Bosnia complained in 1463 to the pope that the peasants seemed to favour the Ottomans, who treated them well and promised them freedom. In any case, we know that the Balkan peasantry did not support the local feudal lords against the Ottomans, with whom, on the contrary, they sometimes co-operated.

Attempts to describe the conquests made by Anatolian Turks in western Anatolia and the Balkans as a large-scale movement of population have been borne out by recent research in the Ottoman archives. This movement of population not only modified the ethnic composition of the territories in which it occurred, but almost inevitably stimulated further conquests.

Population registers for the provinces (*sanjaks*) of Aydın and of Thrace in the middle of the ninth/fifteenth century show that the overwhelming majority (eighty to ninety per cent) of the population of these areas was already by that time made up of Muslim Turks. It appears therefore that Byzantine sources do not exaggerate when they say that the Turks came to settle in masses. After moving into the Balkans, the Ottomans encouraged immigration into the newly conquered territories where they transferred nomads *en masse*. This old system of transfer of population, known as *sürgün* or 'exile', had already been used on a large scale by the Seljuks. Nomad Turks who were known in the Balkans by the name of *yürük* (yörük), were especially numerous in the districts which lay in the path of the conquering armies and in the marches. *Waqf* deeds and registers of the ninth/fifteenth century show also that there was a wide movement of colonization of western Anatolian peasantry settling in Thrace and the eastern Balkans and founding hundreds of new villages. The newly arrived Muslim Turks did not usually mix with Christian peasants, but settled in their own villages. Villages which kept their old names and where the population was mixed were usually old Byzantine villages converted to Islam. Muslims were also settled in cities which had put up resistance to the Ottomans. These soon became Muslim cities. For example the frontier town of Üsküp (Skopje) which was captured in 793/1391 had by 859/1455 twenty-two Muslim quarters as against only eight Christian ones. But the cities which surrendered remained in most cases Christian. This widespread wave of Turkish emigration to western Anatolia and the Balkans coincided with the conquests of the eighth/fourteenth century. A fresh wave was set off by the conquests of Tīmūr. It appears that emigration slowed down in the second half of the fifteenth century, since we do not see similar concentrations of new settlers in Serbia, Albania and the Morea.

As new conquests were added, the area of the marches moved forward. During the reign of Bāyezīd I (791–806/1389–1403) the march of the Dobruja and Deliorman, centred on Silistria, faced Wallachia (Eflak) and Moldavia (Boghdan); the march of Vidin faced Serbia and Hungary; the march of Üsküp faced Bosnia, Serbia and Albania; and, finally the march of Tırkhala (Trikkala) faced Epirus and the Morea. After the conquest of Serbia and Bosnia, Semendere and Saray-Bosna (Sarajevo) became the centres of the marches facing Hungary. After the conquest of Hungary the marches moved again, this time to the *sanjaks* bordering on Habsburg territory. In Albania, Avlonya (Valona) was the centre of the march facing Italy. The islands of the Aegean, the Morea and the old maritime *ghāzī* principalities of western Anatolia were the marches of the sailor *ghāzīs* of the Mediterranean. These pushed their operations as far as the western Mediterranean, and turned Algeria and Tunisia into a fresh march as a base for expeditions against the Spanish monarchy, which had driven the Muslims from Spain, and against Spanish possessions in Italy. Such is the brief history of the role of the marches in the expansion of the Ottoman empire.

Expansion in Muslim Anatolia

The concepts of the *ghazā* and the marches were applied by the Ottomans not only to conquests of infidel territory, but also to expansion within the confines of the Islamic world. When they annexed the Turcoman principalities of Anatolia, by peaceful means, by threats, or, when necessary, by war, they granted to the former beys, as a general rule, rich *timars* in the Balkans. This often enabled the Ottomans to annex the beys' territories without a struggle. In any case, religion forbade a Muslim, and particularly a *ghāzī*, to use arms on another Muslim (Qur'ān, 4. 90). The reputation of the Ottomans as *ghāzīs* was vulnerable to criticism in the case of wars waged against other Muslims. The Ottomans therefore tried to pass off as licit acts annexations achieved through pressure and threats. The Ottomans argued, for example, that they had acquired through canonically licit ways the lands of the houses of Ḥamīd and Germiyan which were a bone of contention between them and the house of Karaman. The latter refused of course to countenance the acquisition by the Ottomans of centres like Ankara and the land of Ḥamīd, formerly a part of the sultanate of Konya. The struggle between the houses of Karaman and of 'Osmān revolved, in the main, round this territory.

As a general rule, whenever they wanted to wage war on Karaman or any other Muslim state, the Ottomans did not neglect to provide themselves with a legal ruling (*fetvā*; Arabic, *fatwā*) from the *'ulemā'* demonstrating that their actions were in accordance with the *Sharī'a* and therefore licit. It was thus argued that it was canonically mandatory to wage war against those who attacked them in the rear while they were engaged in a *ghazā* against the infidels. The house of Karaman and others were thus proclaimed rebels against religion. This view recurs constantly in Ottoman sources. In 848/1444 Murād II obtained from the independent *'ulamā'* of Egypt a *fatwā* proclaiming to the Muslim world and particularly to Tīmūr's successor, Shāh-Rukh, the legality of the expedition against Karaman which he was about to launch. The Ottomans insisted in particular that the house of Karaman collaborated with the Christians, a fact which is confirmed by Western sources.

The second direction of Ottoman expansion in Anatolia followed the Persian silk road. Not content with the capture of Ankara they used that city as well as the city of Bolu as a base for operations aimed ostensibly at protecting the weak *emīrs* of the region of Tokat and Amasya, lying to the east of them, against the pressure of Qāḍī Burhān al-Dīn in Sivas. When Murād I crossed over to the Balkans for an expedition against Serbia in 790/1388, Burhān al-Dīn's commanders argued that a golden opportunity had presented itself for an offensive against the Ottomans. However, the Qāḍī rejected their advice saying that it was tantamount to weakening Islam and strengthening the infidels. Nevertheless, when Murād I was killed on the battlefield of Kosova, as soon as news of it reached Anatolia, Qāḍī Burhān al-Dīn had Mürüvvet Bey capture Kirshehir, while Karaman regained Beyshehir, and the house of Germiyan the territory which it had lost to the Ottomans.

For political reasons the Ottoman sultans attached the greatest importance to safeguarding and strengthening the reputation which they enjoyed as *ghāzīs* in the Muslim world. When they won victories in the *ghazā* in the Balkans they used to send accounts of them (sing., *fetḥ-nāme*) as well as slaves and booty to eastern Muslim potentates. Knights captured by *Yıldırım* Bāyezīd I at his victory over the Crusaders at Nicopolis in 798/1396, and sent to Cairo, Baghdād and Tabrīz were paraded through the streets, and occasioned great demonstrations in favour of the Ottomans. This widespread fame as *ghāzīs* was the source of extensive political advantages to the Ottomans. For example, Tīmūr's entourage long resisted launching an attack on the sultan of the *ghāzīs*. When Tīmūr defeated the Ottoman sultan in 804/1402, he himself felt the need of waging a token *ghazā* by capturing Izmir from the Crusaders. In a letter written some time before 1420 Meḥmed I emphasizes his title as *ghāzī* in order to parry the threats of Shāh-Rukh, and says that he is about to set off on a *ghazā* against the infidels. In a letter sent to Shāh-Rukh justifying his expedition against Karaman, Murād II argues that the latter had impeded the *ghazā* by attacking him from the rear.

Map 2. Ottoman expansion in Europe to 1606.

In the *feth-nāme* which he sent to the sultan of Egypt after his great victory in Constantinople, Meḥmed the Conqueror concedes to him the duty of 'reviving the obligation of the Pilgrimage', reserving for himself that of being the only king to 'fit out the people waging the holy wars of *ghazā* and *jihād*'.[1] The *ghazā* became so important as a source of political influence and power in the Muslim world that other Muslim kings also tried to gain the title of *ghāzi*, e.g. Tīmūr and Uzun Ḥasan. But none of them could compare in stature with the Ottoman sultans who fought for Islam in ceaseless wars in Europe, the Mediterranean and the Indian Ocean. This is why as the Christian threat grew for the Muslim countries of Asia, the influence and the power of the Ottomans

---

[1] Ferīdūn, *Munsha'āt al-salāṭīn* (Istanbul, 1274), I, 236.

increased proportionately in the Muslim world. The Ottomans did not fail to make the most of this. In Asia as in Europe, the *ghazā* was the main factor in Ottoman expansion.

SULTAN MEḤMED THE CONQUEROR

Imperial expansion

Two independent sources report that Meḥmed II made the following points at the meeting which decided to proceed with the conquest of Constantinople: 'The *ghazā* is our basic duty, as it was in the case of our fathers. Constantinople, situated as it is in the middle of our dominions, protects the enemies of our state and incites them against us. The conquest of this city is, therefore, essential to the future and the safety of the Ottoman state'.[1] These words reaffirmed the policy of conquest pursued by Bāyezīd. They drew attention to cases when the Byzantine empire had given refuge to claimants to the Ottoman throne, thus causing frequent civil wars. They also showed that it was the Byzantine empire which had been the main instigator of crusades. It was also within the bounds of possibility that Constantinople could be surrendered to Western Catholics, as Salonica had been. This would have meant that the Ottoman empire would never be fully integrated. In brief, the conquest of Constantinople was a matter of vital concern to the Ottomans.

The siege of Constantinople lasted for fifty-four days (25 Rabīʿ I–20 Jumādā I 857/6 April–29 May 1453). In the Turkish camp Chandarlı continued to draw attention to the great danger of provoking the Western Christian world, and to advocate a compromise. Zaganuz Pasha argued against this that the Ottomans' adversaries could never unite, and that even if an army were sent from the West, Ottoman forces would prove superior, but that, more probably, the city could be captured before the arrival of assistance from Italy. Success depended on speed. The Venetian navy had already left port. News had come of preparations by the Hungarians. When, therefore, his surrender terms had been rejected by the Byzantine Emperor Constantine XI Palaeologus, Meḥmed II ordered his army on 20 Jumādā I/29 May to deliver a general assault and pillage the city. In any case the sultan could not prevent the pillaging of a city captured against resistance, and we know that he later

[1] H. Inalcık, *Fatih devri üzerinde tedkikler ve vesikalar* (Ankara, 1954), 126.

allowed the return of those Greeks who, after the conquest, paid ransom or who had left the city before the siege. They were granted immunity from taxation for a certain time. The day after the conquest Chandarlı was dismissed and imprisoned. His rival, Zaganuz, was appointed grand *vezīr* in his place.

The conquest of Constantinople turned Meḥmed II overnight into the most celebrated sultan in the Muslim world. He began to see himself in the light of an heir to a world-wide empire. He believed in the absolute character of his power, and wished Istanbul to become the centre of the world in all respects. He devoted thirty years of his reign to the realization of these aims. It was Meḥmed the Conqueror who established the distinctive character and nature of the Ottoman empire.

The ideal of universal empire entertained by Meḥmed the Conqueror was derived from various sources. As far back as the reign of Murād II, a chronicler claimed that as ʿOsmān Ghāzī had come from the tribe of Kayı, he had been chosen sovereign by the Turkish beys of the marches. He then adds: 'According to the tradition of the Oghuz bequeathed by Gün Khān, as long as the clan of Kayı remains in existence, none other deserves the khanate and sovereignty.' Whatever the historical value of this claim, the Ottoman dynasty made this view its own in order to give a legal title to its dominion over other Turkish princes and, particularly, in order to rebut the claims to overlordship advanced by Tīmūr and his descendants. This is also why the *damgha* or seal of the Kayı clan was used on Ottoman coinage.

At the same time the Ottomans believed strongly in the teaching of Islam on the sources of sovereignty. We have emphasized earlier the great lengths to which Meḥmed the Conqueror himself went to rest his authority on his title of *ghāzī*. But, with the conquest of Constantinople, Meḥmed the Conqueror became heir to a third tradition: in 870/1466 G. Trapezuntios addressed the Conqueror in the following manner: 'No one doubts that you are the Emperor of the Romans. Whoever is legally master of the capital of the Empire is the Emperor and Constantinople is the capital of the Roman Empire.'[1] According to Giacomo de' Languschi, a contemporary of the Conqueror, 'In his [the Conqueror's] view, there should be only one Empire, only one faith and only one sovereign in the whole world. No place was more deserving than Istanbul for the creation of this unity in the world. The Conqueror believed that thanks to this city he could extend his rule over the whole

[1] F. Babinger, *Mehmed II. der Eroberer und seine Zeit* (Munich, 1953), 266.

Christian world.'[1] No doubt Meḥmed II used this tradition as a political weapon and as a point of departure for his conquests. He saw in all three titles, the titles of Khan, *Ghāzī* and Caesar, gates leading to dominion over the whole world. It was for this reason that Meḥmed the Conqueror saw to it that the Greek Orthodox patriarch, the Armenian patriarch and the Jewish chief rabbi all resided in his capital, Istanbul, and ordered the making of a *mappa mundi*. The Conqueror created in his person the prototype of Ottoman sultans combining Turkish, Islamic and Byzantine traditions.

His conquests make it clear that his first aim was to revive the Byzantine empire under his rule. As Kemāl Pasha-zāde says, he sought to leave no one 'among the Byzantine Greeks who could be named king (*tekfur*)'.[2] He thus eliminated the Byzantine empire of Trebizond, the two despots of the Palaeologus dynasty in the Morea, and the Gattilusi family which was related to the Palaeologi. Secondly, he placed the whole Balkan peninsula south of the Danube under his direct rule, removing all local dynasties. Finally, he occupied the ports in southern Crimea (880/1475) and the city of Otranto in southern Italy (885/1480) which used to belong to the Byzantine empire.

The attempt at establishing undivided rule over the Balkans brought Meḥmed the Conqueror into conflict with Hungary across the Danube, and with Venice in Albania, Greece and the Aegean Sea. The papacy tried to lead the whole of Europe on a crusade in support of these two states.

The Conqueror and Venice both tried to avoid war, until it became inevitable in 867/1463. The Conqueror knew that his navy was weak, while Venice had obtained favourable terms for trade under an agreement which it made with the sultan in 858/1454. Freedom of trade was granted to the republic and customs duty at entry and exit was fixed at only two per cent *ad valorem*. Permission was granted to the Venetians to keep a permanent *bailo* in Istanbul to look after their interests. A similar privilege to trade freely was given to the Genoese in the Archipelago and in the Crimea on condition of payment of tribute, i.e. of accepting Ottoman suzerainty. Meḥmed the Conqueror realized the prime importance of trade with the West for his country and for his treasury. In 867/1463, when he broke with the Venetians, he encouraged the Florentines to take charge of trade with Europe.

[1] F. Babinger, 'Mehmed II der Eroberer und Italien', in *Byzantion*, XXI (1951), 140.
[2] Kemāl Pasha-zāde (facsimile edn., TTK, Ankara, 1954), 186, 613.

Between 858/1454 and 867/1463 Meḥmed fought for mastery in the Balkans. In the north, the Serbian principality, revived in 848/1444, formed a gap through which Hungarian influence penetrated to the heart of the Balkans. In the south, the Morea could at any time fall into the hands of the Venetians. Meḥmed led two expeditions into Serbia in 858/1454 and 859/1455, and succeeded in making Serbia more firmly a part of the Ottoman empire. He failed, however, to defeat the Hungarians at Belgrade (860/1456). When Branković, the despot of Serbia, died in 862/1458, Serbia became once again an apple of discord between the Hungarians and the Ottomans. There was a Hungarian party and an Ottoman party in the country. After two further expeditions, in 862/1458 and in 863/1459, the independent existence of the principality was terminated and Serbia was annexed to the Ottoman empire. The Ottomans incorporated the local military class into their own army organization and maintained certain local laws. In the Morea a violent struggle developed between two Palaeologi princes, Demetrius having sought the protection of the Ottomans, while Thomas requested that of Venice. After two expeditions, in 862/1458 and 864/1460, Meḥmed succeeded in occupying the Morea. Nevertheless, the Venetians kept a foothold in the fortresses of Nauplia, Modon and Coron, which were built in inaccessible coastal fastnesses, and could be supplied by sea. When, in 867/1463, local Greeks surrendered the castle of Argos to the Ottomans, the Venetians launched a general offensive. They held the isthmus of Corinth and occupied the peninsula. The Ottomans then declared war on the Venetians. The war lasted from 867/1463 to 884/1479, and brought Meḥmed many problems.

In 867/1463 the Ottoman occupation of Bosnia led to renewed hostilities with Hungary. The Hungarians established themselves in Gajče in northern Bosnia, and acted in alliance with Venice. The allies gave encouragement to Iskender Bey (Scanderbeg), whose rebellion in northern Albania had started in 847/1443. Envoys were exchanged between Venice and Uzun Ḥasan, ruler of the Ak-Koyunlu dynasty, with a view to an alliance. Pope Pius II summoned the crusading armies to Ancona, where he went in person the following year. The allies drew up plans for the partition of the Ottoman empire. The Venetian navy cruised outside the mouth of the Dardanelles. Meḥmed had recourse to extraordinary measures to parry the danger. To cover Istanbul and his naval base at Gallipoli, he built two powerful fortresses facing each other across the Dardanelles, in the winter of

868/1463–4. In Istanbul he had a new shipyard built, and strengthened his navy. He despatched Maḥmūd Pasha at the head of a powerful army into the Morea, which was reoccupied. He himself led two expeditions into Albania in 870/1466 and 871/1467.

The greatest crisis of the war arose in Anatolia on account of the Karaman dynasty. A struggle for succession between members of the dynasty brought Mehmed into collision with Uzun Ḥasan. In 873/1468 Mehmed finally annexed the territory of Karaman. Nevertheless, members of the Karaman dynasty continued the struggle at the head of warlike tribes in the Taurus Mountains. In 876/1471 Uzun Ḥasan used his position of ruler of Persia to interfere in central Anatolia, thus following in the footsteps of Tīmūr. He extended his protection to the beys of Anatolia, some of whom had been forced by the Conqueror to leave their lands, and had sought refuge in Persia. In 877/1472 Venice, Cyprus, the Knights of Rhodes and Uzun Ḥasan formed an alliance. Uzun Ḥasan promised to send a force of 30,000 men to the shores of the Mediterranean where they were to be joined by Venetians armed with firearms. In 877/1472 Uzun Ḥasan raided the city of Tokat, which was pillaged and destroyed. The joint army of Karaman and of the Ak-Koyunlu penetrated as far as Akshehir in western Anatolia. Faced with danger on all sides, Mehmed retaliated by mobilizing his entire army, estimated at 70,000 to 100,000 men, against Uzun Ḥasan. The following year Uzun Ḥasan's forces were completely routed at Bashkent in eastern Anatolia. This victory resolved the greatest crisis which Mehmed the Conqueror had to face. Uzun Ḥasan made peace, promising to refrain from further incursions into Ottoman territory. In the meantime Gedik Aḥmed Pasha suppressed the resistance of the Taurus tribes and, occupying the coast of the Mediterranean, completed the conquest of Karaman in 879/1474. Between 870/1466 and 875/1470 the Ottomans came up against the Mamluks, who had aided the Karaman dynasty and the Dulgadır (Dhu'l-Qadr) Turcomans further to the east. The struggle for suzerainty over the Dulgadır principality brought these two most powerful states of Islam to the brink of war.

Having thus resolved the problems of Anatolia and extended his rule over the whole country as far as the Euphrates, Mehmed turned his attention to the war with Venice. He besieged the castle of Scutari in 879/1474 and 883/1478. Ottoman *akınjı* raiders crossed the Isonzo and appeared in sight of Venice. The republic sued for peace. The peace treaty surrendered Scutari, Croia, and the islands of Lemnos and Euboea (Negroponte) to the Ottomans, and provided for the payment of an annual tribute of 10,000 gold pieces. Freedom to trade was, however, restored to Venice.

Meḥmed, having thus forced the strongest naval power in the Mediterranean to make peace, set two further goals to the Ottoman navy: the conquest of Rhodes, considered the gate to the Mediterranean, and the occupation of Italy, which seemed ripe for conquest. In 885/1480 while Mesīḥ Pasha made a landing in Rhodes, Gedik Aḥmed Pasha landed before Otranto. The Knights of St John defeated Mesīḥ Pasha's forces, but Gedik Aḥmed Pasha succeeded in his task, and captured Otranto on 4 Jumādā II 885/11 August 1480. He left a garrison in the city, which thus became an Ottoman bridgehead in Italy. He then returned to Albania, in order to bring together a strong army for further conquests the following year. The pope made preparations to flee to France.

After he had become the undisputed master of the Straits, Meḥmed II succeeded in extending his mastery over the Black Sea. In 858/1454 he forced the Genoese colonies there to pay tribute, and then occupied them one by one. He also exacted tribute from Moldavia (22 Shawwāl 859/5 October 1455). Most important of all, he secured the co-operation of the tribal aristocracy of the Crimea, whom he protected against the Genoese and the Golden Horde. The khanate of the Crimea thus became an Ottoman vassal state in 880/1475.

When Meḥmed the Conqueror died in 886/1481 at the age of forty-nine, the expeditions in Egypt, Italy and the Mediterranean were left unfinished. He had fought the *ghazā* war without a break, to a degree that even a contemporary historian found excessive; as he claimed, he had become, within a space of thirty years, the master of two seas and two continents, and had laid the foundations of Ottoman rule in Anatolia and the Balkans, which were to remain unshaken for four centuries. He also gave their final form to the institutions of the empire and determined the course of its future political development.

The development of a centralized absolutist administration

In order to become an absolute sultan, holding in his hands the authority of the state in its entirety, and ruling the whole empire from his capital, Meḥmed eliminated, or at least transformed, the elements which could have resisted him. At his accession to the throne he suppressed with a heavy hand a revolt of the Janissaries. Many Janissaries were expelled from the corps, and new units were formed from the palace huntsmen. These new formations were known as *Sekban,* and the commander (*agha*) of the Janissaries came to be chosen from among them. The pay of the Janissaries was increased, their weapons were improved and their strength raised from 5,000 to 10,000. Thus reorganized, the Janissaries became the nucleus of the Ottoman army. Thanks to this force, which was always ready for service, and which was immediately subordinate to the sultan, who chose their commanders personally, the sultan could overpower any opponent in the imperial territory or in the marches. The beys of the marches were thus reduced to the level of ordinary beys of *sanjaks.* Janissaries were used to garrison newly conquered castles. They were not subordinate to the local governor or to any local authority, and took their orders direct from the capital. No other force was allowed in the castles which they garrisoned. The Janissaries were also responsible for preventing oppression of non-Muslims by Muslims in the cities outside the castle walls, and for compelling obedience to the orders of the sultan. In brief, the Janissaries represented in the provinces the central authority of the sultan.

Mehmed viewed his own personal authority in a much wider light than his predecessors had done. He did not frequent the meetings of the Council of State (*Dīvān*), and arranged for affairs to be seen through a Chamber of Petitions, through which important matters were submitted to his decision. Murād II had allowed the grand *vezīr* Chandarlı Khalīl, who belonged to an established family of *vezīrs* and of '*ulemā*', to decide affairs of state. It was only after the conquest of Constantinople that Mehmed dared dismiss his aristocratic minister. Thereafter he chose all his ministers, with the exception of Karamanı Mehmed, from among his personal slaves. The grand *vezīr* became the obedient instrument of the sultan's commands. Mehmed did not hesitate to order the execution of his most famous *vezīr,* Mahmūd Pasha. On the other hand, the authority of the grand *vezīr* as his master's steward in all things, was widened. The sultan's old tutor, Mollā Gūrānī, was forced to resign from the office of *qāḍī 'asker* when he made appointments without consulting the grand *vezīr.* Since the time of the autonomous principalities, the *qāḍī 'askers* had always been counted among the sultan's most influential assistants and advisers. As we have seen, *vezīrs* were usually chosen from among them. However, in the reign of Mehmed, Mollā Gūrānī, when offered the position of *vezīr,* refused the offer on the grounds that this dignity

46

now went to slaves brought up in court. The grand *vezīr* Maḥmūd Pasha also held the post of *beylerbeyi* of Rumelia, which afforded him the control of the greatest force of *timar*-holding *sipahis* in the empire.

Under the Conqueror, not only the grand vezirate, but also a host of other functions went to the sultan's personal slaves. Governors, *timar*-holders, taxation officers and executive officers charged with applying the sultan's regulations and decrees were mostly chosen from among slaves. Under the *Sharī'a* and state (*'urfī*) law, the issue of judicial decisions and the control of the administration were the exclusive privilege of *qāḍīs*. The administration of justice was thus left in the hands of the *'ulemā'*. The execution of justice, on the other hand, fell to the charge of state officials, in other words, to the sultan's slaves representing their master's executive authority. There were, however, cases of members of the class of *Sharī'a* officials being transferred to the class of *beys* and of *qāḍīs* being appointed as *beylerbeyis*.

As the absolute steward of the sultan, the grand *vezīr* supervized the work and confirmed the decisions of the *defterdār,* who was in charge of the financial side of the administration, and of the *qāḍī 'asker* and *qāḍīs,* who were responsible for the administration of justice. These officials were, however, autonomous in their separate departments and directly answerable to the sultan. The grand *vezīr* was not entitled to issue orders directly to the commander of the Janissaries. This prevented him from concentrating in his hands the whole range of state authority. The sultan reserved for himself the last word in these three main areas of state affairs. A fourth area represented the chancery work of the central government and the province of state law. Representatives of these four branches of central government were *ex officio* members of the *Dīvān.* According to the Regulation (*Qānūn*) of Meḥmed the Conqueror, the right to draw up orders and decisions in the sultan's name belonged to the grand *vezīr* in general matters, to the *defterdār* in financial matters, and to the *qāḍī 'askers* in matters concerning litigation. Four days a week these officials attended the Council of Petitions and submitted matters to the sultan's decision. Meḥmed inherited this system from his predecessors, but he modified it and added to it, and codified the result in his *Qānūn-nāme,* which established the final form of the institutions of the state. The promulgation of a *qānūn-nāme,* or 'book of laws', which is foreign to Muslim traditions, derives from Turkish state traditions. Muslim Turkish sovereigns never surrendered their absolute authority to promulgate rules for the regulation of their policies and of their administration. In this manner the province of state law kept on expanding by the side of the *Sharī'a*. Until the beginning of the tenth/sixteenth century the Ottomans held that in his capacity of *pādishāh*, the sultan had the absolute right to promulgate state law without the intervention of *Sharī'a* jurists. Meḥmed the Conqueror made use of this right to issue many laws and regulations as the sultan's orders.

The Conqueror's contemporaries report that Meḥmed behaved with great severity in all matters affecting the implementation of laws and regulations and of affairs of state in general. He did not except his own children from the operation of the law. His prestige was such that no one dared object to his actions, in spite of the existence of discontent, and he reacted forcibly to attempts at interference by the *'ulemā'*.

In the Ottoman empire there was no law or rule regulating succession to the throne. To be exact, in accordance with old Turkish tradition, as the ruler derived his authority from God, God should decide who was to be ruler. No legal heir to the throne could therefore be appointed. An attempt by Meḥmed I to nominate a successor proved fruitless. All the sultan's sons were held to have an equal right to the throne. The death of a sultan was inevitably followed by strife among his sons. A striking instance of the danger which this represented for the empire was provided by the struggles among the sons and grandsons of Bāyezīd I. Pretenders who sought refuge with foreign princes were a source of constant danger. An Ottoman prince had fought against Meḥmed on the walls of Constantinople. When Meḥmed succeeded to the throne he had his infant brother strangled. Later, in his *Qānūn-nāme*, Meḥmed the Conqueror stipulated that it was appropriate for a sultan to execute his brothers on his accession to the throne 'for the order of the world' i.e. for the sake of peace in his dominions. An action necessary 'for the order of the world' was in any case canonically licit. He wanted to make no concessions from the principle of the indivisiblity of the state and of sovereignty. These principles were to be tested in the struggles between Jem and Bāyezīd II, and later among the sons of Bāyezīd II and Süleymān I, but the principle of the unity of the Ottoman realm was never sacrificed. However, the same Ottoman opinion which accepted fratricide as necessary for the preservation of order in the ninth/fifteenth century refused to countenance it towards the end of the tenth/sixteenth century. Then, with the help of certain special circumstances, the custom of seniority, viz., that the eldest surviving member of the dynasty was to succeed to the throne, established itself.

Finances, land reform and trade

Meḥmed II's financial and land policies also brought many reforms in their train. In order to be able to extend his empire, he strained to make the fullest possible use of the country's resources. This, however, led to extreme social and political tensions after his death. The Conqueror's measures can be summarized as follows:

Monetary policy. New coins were minted and the old withdrawn from circulation and bought by the mint at five-sixths of their face-value. This measure, which was subsequently used by every sultan on accession, was repeated by Meḥmed II on four occasions, causing great discontent in the country. It meant in effect that the state levied a tax of one-sixth on silver coinage circulating in the empire. To enforce this measure the sultan sent to the provinces executive officials known as 'silver seekers', who searched the houses of merchants and caravanserais, and had the right to confiscate any hidden coins which they found. Meḥmed's policy of changing the standard of silver led to complaints by both local and foreign merchants.

Monopolies. Meḥmed farmed out to private individuals provincial monopolies in essential goods such as salt, soap and candle-wax. The state treasury derived immense benefits from these monopolies, and the sultan's legislation provided for severe penalties for their infringement. A contemporary chronicler protests against these as unprecedented innovations (*bidʿat*) in the Ottoman realm.

Confiscation of waqfs *and private property.* A large part of the land held by *waqfs* and private individuals was confiscated by the state and became 'royal land' after 880/1475. This measure led to grave discontent throughout the empire. Much of this land, however, originally belonged to the state and was later transferred by various means to pious foundations or private individuals. Meḥmed ordered the investigation of titles to these lands, and laid down rules for the transfer of land to the state, as in the case of land that went with ruined buildings originally bequeathed as pious foundations. According to a chronicler 20,000 villages or estates held in this way were transferred to the state and then assigned in *timars* to *sipahi* cavalry. This reform was designed to increase the number of *sipahis* for the frequent expeditions. However, numerous people were harmed, and opposition centred round the sultan's son Bāyezīd, governor of Amasya, who was on bad terms with his father. The abolition of many pious foundations harmed mainly the '*ulemā*' and certain old-established Turkish Muslim families. Rich, influential families tried to convert the land which they controlled into *waqf* in the hope that their descendants might derive a sure income from it as trustees. Only a sultan as powerful as the Conqueror was capable of carrying through this reform, but at his death a violent reaction broke out.

The large-scale military and political operations on which the Ottoman empire embarked in the ninth/fifteenth century, were made possible by the development of commercial and economic life in the empire, and by the increase in state revenue which followed. The Ottoman empire tried to put an end to the political dominion and to the privileged economic position of the Franks (Europeans) in the Levant. It abolished the complete immunity from customs dues which the Venetians and Genoese had wrested from the Byzantine empire in its decline. Up to the time of Meḥmed II, customs dues were as low as two per cent. After 865/1460 he raised the tariff to four per cent for *dhimmīs,* and to five per cent to foreigners from non-Muslim lands (*dār al-ḥarb*) who were allowed to trade under treaties of capitulation (sing., *amān-nāme*). This policy was noisily greeted as a catastrophe by the Frankish merchants who were used to exploiting the Levant trade.[1] In fact, the political order established by the Ottomans produced conditions of safety, provided a link between remote areas and brought about an economic integration of the region as a whole. Istanbul, which developed rapidly in Meḥmed's reign, and cities such as Bursa, Edirne and Gallipoli, which had earlier become centres of international trade, profited from this commercial revival. In trade between provinces, Muslim merchants, as well as non-Muslim Ottoman subjects, such as Greeks, Armenians and Jews, took the place of Italians. Customs-registers show a preponderance of these newcomers. A well-established cotton industry in western Anatolia, the mohair industry in Ankara and Tosya, the silk industry in Istanbul and Bursa were exporters to European markets.

Bursa in the ninth/fifteenth century was also the international entrepôt for Astarābādī (*Staravi*) silks produced in Persia and greatly prized in Europe. It was the goal of annual silk caravans. Bursa was the last stage on the road to the West travelled by Muslim caravans, and was also the entrepôt for Arabian and Indian goods sent through Damascus. Although spices were expensive in Bursa, they were despatched from that city to Wallachia, Moldavia and Lemburg. The

[1] H. Inalcık, 'Bursa and the commerce of the Levant', *JESHO,* III/2 (1960), 131–47.

Florentines considered it more profitable to exchange spices against cloth in Bursa than to buy them with gold in Egypt and Syria. Towards the end of Meḥmed's reign, Maḥmūd Gāwān, the famous *wazīr* of the Bahmanids in India, sent his own agents with merchandise to Bursa, and these Indians then went on to the Balkans. Bursa was also the gateway for the export of European woollens to Eastern countries. Silk merchants took them from Bursa on their return journey to Persia.

Valuable merchandise such as spices, dyes and Indian cloth generally followed the old trade-routes, crossing Anatolia diagonally from Damascus through Adana and Konya. A second way was the sea-route from Egyptian and Syrian ports via Antalya to Bursa. This short and cheap route was used mainly for heavy goods. Logs, planks and iron ore were exported from Anatolia to Egypt by sea from the ports of Antalya and 'Alā'iyya. We know that around 885/1480 Turkish merchants from Bursa, engaged in this trade, formed a company with a capital of half a million aspers. As in Anatolia under the Seljuks, so too in the Ottoman empire in the ninth/fifteenth century, Turkish Muslims were still pre-eminent in trade and industry and formed an influential class *vis-à-vis* the administration. It was only after the tenth/sixteenth century, when western European trade grew in importance, that *dhimmīs,* such as Armenians, Greeks and Jews, came to dominate trade in the Ottoman empire.

The reconstruction of Istanbul

Among Meḥmed II's main concerns was to make Istanbul one of the world's political and economic centres, to turn it into a populous city, to develop it and adorn it with new buildings. Before the Ottoman conquest, Constantinople had been like a head without a body, and in the last days of the Byzantine empire, it was a poor and largely depopulated city of ruins. After the conquest, Meḥmed tried to repopulate the city, from which its old inhabitants had fled. Until the end of his reign Meḥmed continued to resettle the city through the system of forcible settlement (*sürgün*) and other measures. Greeks, Italians and Jews were brought for settlement to the city from Phocea in western Anatolia, from Argos and elsewhere in the Morea, from the islands of Thasos, Samothrace, Mytilene and Euboea, from Amasra, Trebizond and Kaffa in the Black Sea. Meḥmed encouraged Jews to come from as far away as Germany and Italy. Considerable numbers of Muslim Turks and Christians were forcibly brought from Konya, Aksaray, Bursa and Ereghli in

Anatolia. Prisoners of war were settled in new villages round the city. The Conqueror saw to the repair of roads and bridges leading into Istanbul. In the winter of 859/1455 he ordered the building of the famous covered market known as Büyük Bedesten, 'the Grand Bazaar'. The same year he issued instructions for the repair of aqueducts to ensure adequate water supplies for his capital. He often inspected in person the construction work which he had set afoot. He had his first palace (Eski Saray, 'the Old Palace') built in the centre of the city. Later he found it inconvenient and had another palace built on Seraglio Point, which became known as Yeni Saray, or 'the New Palace'; later the name was changed to Topkapı Sarayı or 'Palace of the Cannon Gate'. This second palace was completed in 868/1464.

As in the case of the development of other Ottoman cities, the institution of *waqfs* (pious foundations) played the primary role in the reconstruction of Istanbul. It was this institution which secured the performance of a variety of public services: the construction and maintenance of public buildings, mosques, premises for trade, lodgings for travellers, fountains, baths, bridges, schools and hospitals. No claim could be further from the truth than the allegation that the Ottoman state had no conception of public service and that it bent all its energies to the exploitation of its subjects. It was considered a religious duty to see to their prosperity.

The Ottoman empire was the most successful Muslim state in developing *waqfs* for this purpose.[1] *Waqfs* were under close official control. Private persons had formerly been allowed to set them up on the strength of a single deed (*waqfiyya*) drawn up by a *qāḍī*. This was later changed and it was made obligatory for *waqfiyyas* to be approved and registered by the central government. At his accession to the throne, each sultan had the *waqfiyyas* checked and then either confirmed them by a diploma (*berāt*) or cancelled them. Pious foundations set up by Christians were subject to the same control. Meḥmed abolished the trusts connected with some monasteries of Trebizond, but confirmed those relating to Mount Athos. In 934/1528 *waqfs* in Anatolia were charged with the upkeep of 45 almshouses for the poor and for travellers, 342 Friday mosques, 1,095 smaller mosques, 110 *medreses*, 626 dervish convents, 154 schools for

---

[1] In 934/1528 the expenses of pious foundations held in trust and freehold amounted to sixteen per cent of the state revenue: see Ö. L. Barkan, 'H 933-934 Malî Yılına ait bir Bütçe Örneği' in *Iktisat Fakültesi Mecmuası*, (Journal of the Faculty of Economics, Istanbul University), IV, 259.

children, 75 caravanserais, 238 bath-houses and other establishments. In the eighth/fourteenth and ninth/fifteenth centuries, *waqfs* helped numerous Ottoman cities, and not least Istanbul, to become distinctively Muslim Turkish.

2

THE REIGNS OF BĀYEZĪD II AND SELĪM I, 1481–1520

SULTAN MEHEMMED II (1451–81) had striven throughout his reign to realise one dominant aim: the consolidation of the Ottoman State. In 1453 he had conquered Constantinople which, impoverished and greatly depopulated during the last years of Greek rule, was to become once more, under his guidance, the proud capital of an empire. The sultan repaired the ancient walls and peopled the empty spaces of the city with groups of Muslims, Christians and Jews taken from all parts of his realm. Public buildings were erected, like the great mosque which he founded, with its baths and hospital, its accommodation for travellers, and its colleges where students were trained in the law of Islam. Constantinople was transformed into Istanbul, an imperial city which, reflecting in itself the rich and complex character of the Ottoman State, bound together the provinces of Anatolia and the Balkan lands as Adrianople, the former capital of the empire, could not do.

Consolidation was also the objective behind the ceaseless campaigns of the sultan. In 1459 the last remnants of independent Serbia were converted into the Ottoman frontier province of Semendria, the strong bridgehead of Belgrade, besieged in vain by Mehemmed in 1456, being left however to the Hungarians. Bosnia was overrun in 1463–4. The Bosnian aristocracy largely embraced Islam and played henceforth a great role in the defence of the frontier and in the attacks launched against Hungary and Austria. In Greece, the principality of Athens, held by a Florentine family, the Acciaiuoli, and the Greek Despotate of the Morea, ruled by the Palaeologi, were subjugated in 1458–60; while in the Aegean Sea the islands of Thasos and Samothrace, Imbros and Lemnos were taken over in 1455–6, and Lesbos in 1462. During a long war with Venice (1463–79) Negroponte fell to the sultan in 1470; but it was not until the Albanians, the allies of Venice, had weakened in their resistance after the death of their leader, Scanderbeg, in 1468, that the Ottomans secured a firm hold on the Adriatic littoral through the capture of Croia and Scutari in 1478–9.

The Black Sea became an Ottoman lake. Genoese Galata, a suburb of Constantinople, had been forced to submit to Mehemmed in 1453, Genoa being thus severed from her maritime empire in those waters. In 1461 Ottoman control was established over the southern shore of the sea, where Amastris, a centre of Genoese interests, together with the Turkish emirate of Kastamuni, including its port of Sinope, and also the Greek 'empire' of Trebizond yielded to the sultan. The northern shore was secured in 1475 when the Ottoman fleet seized the old Genoese emporium of Kaffa in the Crimea. Even the khan of the Krim Tatars now became a vassal of the Ottomans. In Anatolia most of Karaman, a Turkish principality which had long been a dangerous foe in the rear of the Ottoman State, was taken over in the years after the death of its ruler, Ibrāhīm Beg, in 1464. Princes of the old ruling house continued to resist in the mountainous regions of the land, thus necessitating further Ottoman campaigns, as in 1470 and 1474; but, although the tradition of independence remained alive for more than a generation after these events, Karaman was henceforth an integral part of the sultan's dominions.

In spite of these achievements the work of consolidation was not complete when Mehemmed died in 1481. In Europe the Ottoman hold on the Christian principalities of Wallachia and Moldavia was not yet assured. Wallachia, ravaged by the Ottomans in 1462, had given less trouble than Moldavia which, led by its able ruler, the *voivode* Stephen (1457–1504), had defeated the Ottoman frontier warriors of the Danube provinces on the River Racova in 1475. Although this reverse had been avenged in 1476 when Mehemmed had routed the Moldavians at Valea Albă, the Ottomans had still to win control over the estuaries of the Danube and the Dniester, in order to establish safe land communication with the Crimea. On the north-western frontiers of the empire, the Hungarians retained Belgrade and parts of Bosnia; while the Venetian fleet had at its disposal a number of strong bases on the Adriatic and in the Morea.

To the east, tension had grown in the later years of Mehemmed's reign with two neighbouring Muslim Powers—with Mamluk Egypt over the buffer state of Albistan, ruled by the house of Zu'l-Kadr and regarded by the Mamluks as their protectorate, and with Persia because the state lately founded there by Uzun Hasan was a serious threat to Ottoman Anatolia. Originally the chief of the Turcoman tribes known as the Ak Koyunlü, who had dominated the region around Diyarbekir, Uzun Hasan (1423?–78) had started on a career of conquest which, in the years after 1453, had made him master of western Persia, Azerbaijan, and Kurdistan. As the ally of Venice during her war with Mehemmed, he had invaded Anatolia, only to be repulsed at the battle of Terjan in 1473. None the less, the Ottoman frontier towards the Ak Koyunlü State remained ill-defined in 1481, and so, too, the frontier towards Mamluk Syria.

Mehemmed had raised to the status of a law the old Ottoman custom that a sultan, on ascending the throne, should eliminate all possible rivals by having his brothers and their male children put to death; but he had left the problem of the succession itself undecided. When he died on 3 May 1481 two sons survived him, Bāyezīd and Jem, each of whom, in accordance with the Ottoman procedure that princes, from an early age, should learn how to govern, had charge of a province in Anatolia. Bāyezīd, the elder son, was at Amasia, and Jem at Konia, the old capital of Karaman. A conflict between them was unavoidable. It would be resolved in favour of the prince fortunate enought to win the allegiance of the janissaries and the great officials of state. The high dignitaries were divided amongst themselves but several of them, including the beglerbeg, that is the governor-general, of Anatolia and, according to some of the sources, the agha in command of the janissaries, were married to sisters or daughters of Bāyezīd and were therefore staunch advocates of his claim. It is true that no less a figure than the grand vizier was the head of Jem's party, but this man, Mehemmed Pasha, was a most unpopular personality.

Sultan Mehemmed had died at Maltepe, not far from Scutari opposite Istanbul, at the commencement of a new campaign. The grand vizier concealed the sultan's death and sent messengers to Amasia and Konia, hoping that Jem would arrive before Bāyezīd. To prevent the janissaries still encamped at Maltepe from crossing to the capital, he returned to Istanbul and ordered the landing-places on the shores of the Bosphorus to be closed and all available shipping to be seized. His efforts were in vain, for the secret filtered out and the janissaries, rising in revolt, secured ships on the Anatolian shore, crossed the strait from Scutari, and slew him. At the same time the messengers bound for Konia were caught and held on the command of the beglerbeg of Anatolia. In order to ensure the accession of Bāyezīd, his partisans raised to the throne one of his sons, Korkūd, until Bāyezīd himself should arrive from Amasia. Thus, when Bāyezīd reached Istanbul on 20 May 1481, he was at once proclaimed sultan.

Jem, driven to armed resistance, gathered in Karaman and among the Turcoman tribes of the Taurus mountains, the Varsak and the Torghud, a powerful force which enabled him to take the old capital of his forefathers, Brusa, where he assumed the title of sultan. His troops, however, were no match for the janissaries. Defeated at Yenishehir in the neighbourhood of Brusa (20 June 1481), he sought refuge in Egypt with the Mamluk Sultan Kā'it Bāy (1468–95). Just at this time Kāsim Beg, of the dispossessed house of Karaman and hitherto an exile in Tabriz at the court of Uzun Hasan's son Ya'kūb Beg (1478–90), had invaded his ancestral lands but had been driven into Cilicia. He and Jem joined forces in the spring of 1482 and made a vain assault on Konia in June. Jem, despairing of success, fled to Rhodes where he found asylum with the Knights of St John (26 July 1482).

The knights, knowing how eager Bāyezīd was to gain possession of so dangerous a claimant to the Ottoman throne, sent Jem to France in September 1482. They undertook to keep the prince in safe confinement when Bāyezīd promised to refrain from all hostilities against Rhodes and, after further discussion in December 1482, to pay them a yearly pension of 45,000 Venetian ducats. To secure control of Jem, the Christian

Powers and even the Mamluk sultan began a long series of negotiations and intrigues, in the course of which the knights agreed, in 1486, to place him under the control of Pope Innocent VIII, who, once he had the prince in his care (1489), came to an understanding with Bāyezīd in November 1490 and received thereafter the pension formerly paid to the Knights of Rhodes. In 1494 emissaries from Pope Alexander VI alarmed Bāyezīd with the news that Charles VIII of France, then on the point of invading Italy, might well make use of Jem in a crusade against the Ottomans; but the sultan's fear was soon dispelled, for although the pope was indeed forced to hand over Jem to Charles VIII in January 1495, the prince died in February of the same year.

Almost fourteen years of Bāyezīd's reign had passed under the constant danger that a coalition of Christian Powers, using Jem as their instrument, might invade the Ottoman empire. Neither in the west nor in the east could the sultan commit his forces to a definite line of action. There were, indeed, various armed enterprises, but these were either raids due to the initiative of governors in the frontier provinces or campaigns strictly limited in scope. As long as Jem was alive, the Ottoman military machine was never irretrievably engaged in a great war.

In Europe along the frontier marked by the rivers Sava and Danube, from Bosnia to the Black Sea, Muslim and Christian border lords waged against one another a ceaseless guerilla warfare which the central authorities on both sides were impotent to hold in check. The Ottoman begs of Bosnia and Semendria must have regarded the death of Sultan Mehemmed as a specially favourable opportunity, for in 1481 their raids into Hungary became so menacing that, in reprisal, the Hungarian governor of Temesvár, Pál Kinizsi, laid waste the province of Semendria in November of that year. In the spring of 1483 the sultan repaired and strengthened the frontier defences along the river Morava. At the same time, he established full Ottoman control over the Herzegovina. Of all the Bosnian lands, only a small area in the north, guarded by the Hungarian-held fortress of Jajce, remained outside the Ottoman dominions. Neither Bāyezīd nor the Hungarian king, Matthias Corvinus (1458–90), was eager for a serious conflict, and hostilities ended in 1483 with a truce for five years, later extended until 1491.

The death of Matthias and the ensuing dissension amongst the Hungarians over the choice of a new king induced the Ottomans to attack once more when the truce came to an end. Hostilities took the form of massive raids directed not only against Hungary, but also against Croatia and the Austrian lands—Styria, Carniola, and Carinthia. The great incursions of 1492 brought swift and terrible ruin to the Christians. None the less, one raiding column, as it returned laden with plunder and captives, was trapped by the men of Carinthia near Villach, where a desperate battle was fought in which 10,000 Muslim warriors and 7000

Christians are said to have been slain; while other raids into Hungary were repulsed at Szörény and at the pass of the Red Tower in Transylvania. The incursions were renewed in 1493 with increased ferocity, Croatia and lower Styria being ravaged once more and the Croat nobility almost annihilated at Adbina on 9 September. There were further attacks on Styria and Temesvár in 1494, to which the Hungarians retaliated by devastating the region around Semendria in November. Peace was restored in 1495 when the sultan, worried by recent developments in Italy, concluded a truce with Hungary for three years.

While Jem was a captive in Christian hands, Bāyezīd himself made a notable campaign against Stephen, prince of Moldavia (p. 55). On 15 July 1484 he took the fortress of Kilia on the Danube estuary; and on 9 August, after the khan of the Krim Tatars, Menglī Girāi, had brought a large force of horsemen to his aid, he seized Akkerman at the mouth of the Dniester. Stephen now turned to Poland for assistance, recognising Casimir IV as his overlord at Kolomea on 15 September 1485; but, although in November of the same year, near Katlabug in southern Bessarabia, he succeeded, with the help of a Polish contingent, in repelling the Ottoman frontier warriors of the Danube led by Malkoch-oghlü Bali Beg, he could not recover Kilia and Akkerman. Poland, harassed by the Tatars of the Volga, was unable to give him effective aid. In 1487, therefore, he sent tribute once more to the sultan. Poland herself made peace with Bāyezīd in 1489 in the form of a truce which was prolonged in 1492 and again in 1494, on this latter occasion for a further period of three years.

In the east, the unsettled conditions along the Taurus frontier led to a war with Egypt which claimed an ill-defined protectorate over Cilicia and the neighbouring principality of Albistan. The latent hostility between the Ottomans and the Mamluks was brought to a head by the intrigues and alliances, now with Egypt and now with the Ottomans, of the local dynasties which ruled in this 'no-man's land'. To the west in Cilicia, in the region around Adana and Tarsus, the Ramazān-oghlü were vassals of the Mamluk sultan. The Mamluks even laid claim to the lands beyond the Taurus because in 1464, on the eve of the Ottoman conquest (p. 55), Ishāk, a prince of the old ruling house of Karaman, had belatedly placed himself under the protection of Egypt. To the east of Cilicia the buffer state of Albistan dominated the route down the Euphrates. Because of its great strategic importance, the Mamluks had long striven to maintain a firm hold over this principality, but with no enduring success. Throughout Cilicia and Albistan, powerful Turcoman tribes, the Varsak and the Torghud, ever eager for warfare and plunder, added to the instability of the Taurus frontier.

Friction between the Mamluks and the Ottomans had arisen in 1465 when, on the death of Arslān Beg, prince of Albistan, two of his brothers,

Budak and Shahsuwār, had fought against each other for the throne. At first Budak had been successful with the help of the Mamluk sultan Khushkadam (1461–7), who had also encouraged the princes of Karaman in their conflict with the Ottomans. In 1467, however, Shahsuwār had appealed for aid to Mehemmed II, who was himself married to a princess of Albistan, and, having received from him investiture as ruler of the land, had driven out Budak Beg. For some years Shahsuwār defied the efforts of Kā'it Bāy, sultan of Egypt, to evict him, but in the end he was captured and then executed at Cairo in 1472. Budak Beg now returned to Mar'ash, the chief town of the principality, to rule there as a vassal of the Mamluks. In order to have a free hand in dealing with Albistan, Kā'it Bāy had refrained from aiding the Karaman-oghlü in their resistance to the Ottomans and had assured Mehemmed that, far from wishing to exert full control over Albistan, he had acted only because of a personal grievance against Shahsuwār. It was, however, clear that he meant to exclude the Ottomans from all influence in the land, a policy which was successful until 1480 when Mehemmed, free to intervene once more, established 'Alā ad-Daula, a younger brother of Budak Beg, as prince of Albistan.

Ottoman relations with Egypt became worse after the death of Sultan Mehemmed, for Kā'it Bāy, as we have seen, aided Jem against Bāyezīd in 1481–2. The Ottomans complained, too, that the Mamluks were inciting the Turcoman tribes to make incursions into Karaman and that pilgrim caravans bound for Mecca were being molested in the Cilician passes.

Serious warfare did not begin until 1485 when Karagöz Pasha, the Ottoman governor of Karaman, marched into Cilicia and seized Adana and Tarsus. In retaliation, Kā'it Bāy had Karaman raided by the Turcomans and sent to Cilicia a force of Mamluks which took the Ottoman troops by surprise. Reinforcements came to their relief under Hersek-oghlu Ahmed Pasha, beglerbeg of Anatolia, now appointed to be general in command of the campaign. Karagöz failed to co-operate with the beglerbeg, stood aloof from the fighting and thus by his inaction caused the defeat and capture of Ahmed Pasha. On hearing of these reverses, Bāyezīd made careful preparation for a new campaign. In 1487 the Grand Vizier Dā'ūd Pasha occupied Cilicia without resistance, the Mamluks withdrawing before his superior forces, and then, on the advice of 'Alā ad-Daula who had taken the Ottoman side, set out to punish the Varsak and Torghud Turcomans. In the next year 'Alī Pasha assumed command in Cilicia with a strong army which included the *sipāhīs*, i.e. the feudal cavalry, of Rumeli and Anatolia as well as a large contingent of janissaries. To repel this threat, a Mamluk army, reinforced by troops drawn from Damascus, Aleppo and Tripoli and by Turcoman warriors under the Ramazān-oghlü and the Torghud chieftains, advanced towards Adana. Near this town a battle was fought on 17 August 1488, after which 'Alī Pasha had to retire from Cilicia. This further Ottoman defeat caused 'Alā ad-Daula to desert to the Mamluks; whereupon his brother Budak Beg, since 1480 an exile in Damascus, fled to Istanbul. Bāyezīd ordered the troops of Amasia, Kaysari, and Karaman to restore him to the throne of Albistan; but this attempt failed in 1489, Budak Beg being captured and sent to Egypt. In 1490 'Alā ad-Daula, supported by a powerful Mamluk army, invaded Ottoman territory and laid siege to Kaysari. Unable to take the strongly fortified town, the Mamluks ravaged the surrounding lands until lack of supplies and the approach of a large Ottoman force compelled them to withdraw.

Both sides were now willing to make peace. The attention of Bāyezīd was diverted once more to Hungary where Matthias Corvinus had died in April 1490; while Kā'it Bāy was eager to end an expensive war financed only by the imposition of harsh measures which aroused discontent in Egypt. In these circumstances, an agreement was soon reached in 1491. After six years of inconclusive warfare, Egypt was recognised in her possession of Cilicia but the revenues of Adana and Tarsus were to be devoted to the sanctuaries of Mecca and Medina.

To all appearance, Sultan Bāyezīd had met with a major reverse in failing to take Cilicia. And yet in no phase of the war had he exerted the full weight of his military power—for Jem was still alive. The forces which he had sent to Cilicia had consisted, for the most part, of *sipāhīs* from the provinces of Anatolia, with detachments of janissaries and *sipāhīs* from the Balkan lands to aid them when need arose. Compared with this limited use of the Ottoman might, the Mamluks, in their war effort, had gone to much greater lengths. The campaigns of 1488–9 had absorbed a large proportion of their resources. Even so, the situation on the Taurus frontier in 1491 was in no wise more favourable for the Mamluks, despite their victories in Cilicia, than it had been before the war. One fact was clear: the time was approaching when the Ottomans would seek in earnest to solve the problems of this frontier. When the critical moment came, the Mamluks would have to meet all the formidable strength of the Ottoman war machine.

The death of Jem in 1495 set Bāyezīd free at last to pursue a more enterprising policy; but before he could make use of this new freedom he had to meet a threat from Poland. The Polish king Jan Olbracht (1492–1501), unwilling to accept the fact that from the Crimea to the Danube the Ottomans and the Krim Tatars together blocked Poland's access to the Black Sea, hoped to break this barrier with Moldavian aid. The *voivode* of Moldavia, Stephen, who had sworn allegiance to Poland in 1485 after the loss of Kilia and Akkerman but, disappointed by Poland, had later paid tribute once more to the sultan, had no wish to be a Polish vassal in fact as well as in name. Moreover, the Hungarians, too, claimed a protectorate over Moldavia and might be expected to resent Polish intervention.

These complications did much towards the failure of the Polish campaign of 1497 which aimed at the conquest of Kilia and Akkerman but became, in fact, an invasion of Moldavia when the *voivode*, doubting the true intentions of Jan Olbracht, appealed for aid to the sultan. The Poles, after an unsuccessful assault on the Moldavian fortress of Suceava, were compelled to retire through lack of supplies and the approach of winter. Their withdrawal became a wild retreat when the Moldavians defeated them at Kozmin in the Bukovina (26 October 1497).

Bāyezīd, angered by this Polish attack on his vassal, ordered the great frontier warrior Malkoch-oghlü Bali Beg, the governor of the Danubian province of Silistria, to invade Poland. In the spring and summer of 1498 Bali Beg, reinforced by Moldavian and Tatar horsemen, laid waste Podolia and then Galicia as far as Lemberg; but a second incursion launched against Galicia in the late autumn of the same year came to grief in bitter snowstorms on the Carpathians. Abiding memories of Bali Beg's terrible retreat have survived in Roumanian folk ballads. The door was closed against further raids when in April 1499 Jan Olbracht made peace with the *voivode* of Moldavia. Bāyezīd, however, being now on the verge of war with Venice, had no desire to prolong hostilities and therefore consented to renew the former truce with Poland.

After the death of Jem, Bāyezīd could not ignore the growing pressure from those of his advisers who urged that it was time to renew the assault against the Christians. In the end, it was Venice which had to face a major Ottoman offensive, despite the fact that relations between the sultan and the *signoria* had remained tranquil since 1482 when Bāyezīd, anxious to maintain peace in the west during his conflict with Jem, had confirmed on more favourable terms than before the Venetian trade privileges within the Ottoman empire. The war, when it came, arose not so much from precise and determinable grounds of dispute as from tensions inherent in the general alignment existing between the two Powers. Ottoman domination on the Adriatic shore would remain incomplete so long as Venice held, in Dalmatia and Albania, important territories like Sebenico and Spalato, Zara, Budua, and Antivari, Dulcigno and Durazzo. The same was true of the Morea where Venice was mistress of Lepanto, Modon, and Coron, Navarino, Napoli di Romania, and Monemvasia.

To defend these possessions, Venice made use of Greek, Cretan, and above all Albanian mercenaries, who were no less bent on plunder than the Ottoman frontier warriors whom they opposed. 'Incidents' were therefore common enough. Moreover, there was friction at sea where Christian pirates using Venetian harbours and Muslim corsairs from the Ottoman coasts and islands were both numerous and active. Venice was alarmed at the growth of the Ottoman fleet, for in the years after 1496, at ports in the Aegean and the Adriatic, the sultan built many vessels of war and manned them by recruitment among the corsairs.

War became imminent in 1498–9 when hostilities flared out with a growing intensity along the frontiers from Dalmatia to the Morea. Venice complained of Ottoman raids on Sebenico and Spalato; while Bāyezīd was angered to learn that Venetian mercenaries had ambushed 500 Ottoman soldiers near Napoli di Romania. In November 1498 Venice had decided to send Andrea Zanchani to Istanbul with the tribute which she owed for the island of Zante and with the assurance that she had no desire for war. Zanchani's mission of March 1499 failed, however, to avert the approaching conflict. The sultan was apprehensive about the alliance which Venice had just made with Louis XII of France against Lodovico Sforza, duke of Milan. Sforza had sent emissaries to Istanbul with the information that France, if the invasion of Milan were successful, intended to prepare a crusade against the Ottoman empire, an argument which other Italian states hostile to Venice also urged on the sultan. Bāyezīd, believing that the Venetians would be gravely hindered by their Italian commitments, began the war in the summer of 1499.

On 12 August the Venetian fleet was defeated off the island of Sapienza, not far from Modon, when attempting to prevent the Ottomans from sailing to Lepanto in the Gulf of Corinth. Although reinforced by a French squadron, the Venetians fared no better in further minor engagements off Belvedere and Chiarenza (23–5 August) and withdrew to shelter under the guns of Zante, leaving the mouth of the gulf unguarded. Lepanto, besieged by the sultan on land and now deprived of all relief from the sea, surrendered on 29 August. Meanwhile, in order to divide the Venetian forces, Mikhāl-oghlü Iskender Pasha led the frontier warriors of Bosnia on a great raid into the Friuli. In June he laid waste the lands between Trieste and Laibach and then, reinforced after the fall of Lepanto, crossed the Isonzo and the Tagliamento in the last days of September and ravaged the Venetian lands as far as Vicenza.

In 1500 the Venetian fleet, ill-manned and ill-equipped owing to the financial difficulties of the *signoria*, failed once more to defeat the Ottoman naval forces operating off the coast of the Morea, where the great fortress of Modon, invested by land and sea, fell to the sultan on 9 August. Six days later Coron and Navarino surrendered to the Ottomans. Throughout this campaign the frontier warriors raided the Venetian territories in Albania and Dalmatia. Venice, desperate for allies, sought to win the aid of the Hungarians through the offer of large subsidies and at length succeeded in bringing them into the war, although a formal alliance, which also included Pope Alexander VI, was not completed until May 1501. In the meantime the Venetian fleet, with the help of a Spanish squadron which carried a force of veteran soldiers under the command of the famous Gonzalo de Córdoba, seized the island of Cephalonia in December 1500. The league between Venice and Hungary failed to check the Ottoman raids along the Adriatic shore, where, in the summer of 1501,

Mehemmed Beg, the governor of Elbasan, took Durazzo. In October of the same year Venetian and French ships sailed to the Aegean and made an unsuccessful attack on the island of Lesbos. This, however, was almost the last notable event of the war; for Venice found the conflict too expensive and was longing for peace, a desire which the sultan was the more inclined to welcome since affairs in Anatolia were beginning to demand his close attention. None the less, desultory warfare continued for most of 1502. Venice won a last victory when she captured the island of Santa Maura on 30 August; while the Hungarians, whose share in the war had been limited to ineffectual raids into Serbia and Bosnia, made an incursion into the Ottoman provinces of Vidin and Nicopolis.

Peace was now in sight. The main articles were approved on 14 December 1502, although the formal ratifications were not completed until August 1503. Venice abandoned all claim to Lepanto, Modon, Coron, Navarino and Durazzo; agreed to continue the payment of tribute for Zante; and promised to evacuate Santa Maura. In return, she retained Cephalonia and recovered her commercial privileges in the Ottoman empire. The delimitation of the frontiers on the Adriatic was reserved for further discussion, as the result of which Venice yielded to the sultan certain disputed lands near Cattaro in 1504, and, in 1506, the fortress of Alessio in Albania. The war, if unspectacular, had been a great triumph for Bāyezīd. On the Adriatic, and in the Morea where Venice now held only Napoli di Romania and Monemvasia, he had brought the consolidation begun by Mehemmed II much nearer to completion. Still more notable, since it foreshadowed their future mastery of the Mediterranean, is the fact that the Ottomans, aided by the Muslim corsairs, were becoming a formidable Power at sea. The peace was not confined to Venice alone. On 20 August 1503 the Hungarians obtained from the sultan a truce for seven years which embraced the other Christian states implicated directly or indirectly in the war. Bāyezīd was eager to be free of all complications in Europe, since he had to deal with threatening events in the east.

During the years of the Ottoman war with Venice a new power had arisen in Persia. Shaikh Safī ad-Dīn (1252–1334), who claimed descent from 'Alī, the son-in-law of the prophet Muhammad, had founded a religious order, known after him as the *Safawiyya*, at Ardabil in Azerbaijan. This mountainous region had long been a refuge for followers of the Shī'a, i.e. of various sects which all claim the caliphate for one or the other amongst the descendants of 'Alī. The *Safawiyya*, led by the family of its founder, had developed, from the time of Shaikh Khoja 'Alī (1392–1429), a widespread religious propaganda with the result that Ardabil became a much frequented centre of pilgrimage. Shaikh Junaid (1447–60), ambitious to add political power to his religious authority, forged out of the *Safawiyya* a military instrument which earned for him the enmity of neighbouring princes, so that he had to flee to Anatolia. In the years 1449–56 he taught and preached with great success in Karaman and in the province of Tekke around Antalia, in the Jebel Arsūs in northern Syria among the Varsak and Torghud Turcomans of Cilicia and the Taurus, and in Janik and Kastamuni, a mountainous area in northern Anatolia. From 1456–9 he disseminated his propaganda intensively from Diyarbekir where he found shelter with the ruler of the Ak Koyunlü, Uzun Hasan (p. 55), whose sister he married in 1458. The son of this marriage, Shaikh Haidar, later received the hand of Uzun Hasan's daughter, 'Ālemshah Begüm, who became the mother of Ismā'il, the future shah of Persia. Events continued to favour the rising power of the *Safawiyya*, for after the death of Ya'kūb Beg (1478–90), the son and successor of Uzun Hasan, dynastic quarrels brought about the rapid collapse of the Ak Koyunlü régime. There was now in western Persia and Azerbaijan a political vacuum which the *Safawiyya* alone was strong enough to fill. In 1499 Ismā'il, by this time the head of the order, set out on a war of conquest which, through his victories at Shurur (1501) and Hamadan (1503) over the divided princes of the Ak Koyunlü, made him the master of Persia.

The Safawid propaganda in Anatolia, pursued with unbroken vigour after the death of Shaikh Junaid, had won a success so remarkable, especially amongst the Turcomans, that it was the Anatolian followers of the *Safawiyya* who formed the main military strength of the new state in Persia. In this connection, the names given to some of the most powerful Turcoman tribes in the service of Shah Ismā'il are illuminating, such as the Rūm-lü (i.e. men from the Amasia-Sivas region, which was called Rūm), the Karaman-lü, and the Tekke-lü.

The Ottomans, who were sternly orthodox Muslims, abhorred the teaching of the *Safawiyya* as heretical. They rightly regarded the movement, however, as far more than a religious danger: for them it was also a grave political menace. Even in normal times, the authorities in the Anatolian provinces had difficulty in restraining the Turcoman tribes who were ever prone, as nomads always are, to bring trouble to the settled populations in the villages and towns. The tribes won over by the Safawid propaganda had become the blind and fanatical servants of a foreign master held by them to be endowed with divine attributes. There was a real danger that the *Safawiyya*, if it were allowed a free hand to organise the Turcomans, might undermine Ottoman rule over entire provinces in Anatolia. Nor was this all. The Shī'a beliefs were strong in those regions where Mamluk and Ottoman pretensions were in conflict. How, then, would the Mamluks react if the Ottomans sought to crush the Safawid movement in the Taurus lands? Intervention of this kind would mean a radical alteration in the balance of forces along the frontier and might drive the Mamluks, despite their adherence to the orthodox faith, into an alliance with the Shī'a State in Persia. If this were to happen, the Ottomans would be confronted with a major crisis.

Even before the peace with Venice, Bāyezīd had been alarmed at the progress of the *Safawiyya*. In 1502 he ordered numerous followers of the Shī'a to be deported from Tekke to his recent conquests, Modon and Coron, in the Morea and rejected a protest from Shah Ismā'īl who complained that his adherents in the Ottoman lands were being hindered from going to Persia.

Once he had established his power in western Persia, the shah began to intervene on the Taurus frontier. 'Alā ad-Daula, prince of Albistan, had given refuge to Murād, the Ak Koyunlü lord of Fars and Persian Iraq, whom Ismā'īl had routed near Hamadan in 1503. Moreover, he had tried to seize the region of Diyarbekir, which Ismā'īl claimed for himself as the successor of the Ak Koyunlü, and had refused to bestow his daughter in marriage on the shah. In 1507–8 Safawid forces defeated 'Alā ad-Daula, conquered Kharput and Diyarbekir, and occupied Kurdistan. Ismā'īl had been careful to assure the Mamluks and the Ottomans that he had no hostile intentions towards them. None the less, both Bāyezīd and the Mamluk sultan Kānsūh al-Ghaurī (1501–16) garrisoned their frontiers in strength to restrain the shah and keep the border Turcomans under control.

The danger of a conflict with Persia receded in 1510, for Ismā'īl had to turn his attention to the east where the Uzbeg Khan of Transoxania had overrun the Persian province of Khorasan. This diversion brought little relief to the Ottomans, since in the next year a great revolt broke out in Tekke amongst the adherents of the *Safawiyya*. Their leader, a certain Shah Kuli, who had long been active in Tekke, preached the end of Ottoman domination, declaring that Ismā'īl was the incarnation of the Godhead, and he himself the Mahdī or 'rightly guided one' who would restore the rule of the true believers. In the spring of 1511 the rebels defeated the beglerbeg of Anatolia near Afiun Karahisar, plundered Kutahia, and then advanced towards Brusa. The Grand Vizier 'Alī Pasha, with an army which included 4000 janissaries, joined the forces of Amasia commanded by Bāyezīd's son, Ahmed, and drove Shah Kuli towards Kaysari. Near this town, in June 1511, a battle was fought in which both 'Alī Pasha and Shah Kuli were slain. The rebels, routed and leaderless, fled to Ismā'īl, who had some of them put to death for excesses committed during their escape to Tabriz. The shah sought in this manner to disclaim responsibility for the revolt, since he could not afford to provoke the Ottomans while the Uzbeg war was still in progress. Bāyezīd, however, was not free to attack Persia, even had he wished to do so, for, owing to the quarrel between his sons over the succession to the throne, the Ottoman empire was on the verge of civil war.

Three sons of Bāyezīd were alive in 1511, each of whom, in accordance with the Ottoman custom, had been given charge of a province in Anatolia.

Korkūd, the eldest son, had been appointed governor of Tekke. Alarmed at the growing influence of his brothers and worsted in a dispute with the Grand Vizier 'Alī Pasha over certain lands in Tekke, he had sailed to Egypt in 1509, hoping to find there support for his claim to the throne. Although well received at Cairo, he was unsuccessful, for the Mamluk sultan Kānsūh al-Ghaurī, being then at war with the Portuguese in the Red Sea and the Indian Ocean, had no wish to offend Bāyezīd. Korkūd, therefore, had no choice but to seek reconciliation with his father who in 1510 restored him once more to Tekke. Each of the princes desired a province as near as possible to Istanbul, since, in the event of a conflict for the throne, to arrive there first might mean the difference between success and failure. In this respect, Korkūd won the advantage over his younger brothers when, in exchange for Tekke, he obtained from Bāyezīd the province of Sarukhan, centred around Manisa, which was much closer to Istanbul. Nevertheless, despite the fact that he had been sultan for some days after the death of Mehemmed II in 1481 (p. 56), he had little chance of succeeding Bāyezīd. Amongst the great officials of state and the janissaries he had the reputation of being a scholar and poet ill-fitted for the Ottoman throne, an impression which his undistinguished share in the quelling of Shah Kuli's revolt did nothing to diminish. In the events which now ensued Korkūd had but a minor role.

The issue was, in fact, to be fought out between Ahmed, the governor of Amasia, and the youngest of the three princes, Selīm, who had charge over the remote province of Trebizond. To all appearance it was Ahmed who would, in due course, become sultan. Bāyezīd seemed to incline towards him rather than towards Selīm, a predilection shared by a powerful group of high officials. Selīm, however, had one great advantage over Ahmed: because of his warlike and resolute character he was beloved of the janissaries. In the end, it was their approval, even more than the boldness of his own schemes, which brought him to the throne.

Selīm had prepared with great foresight for the hour of crisis. In Trebizond he had built up an armed force which he led on raids into Safawid territory with such effect that the shah had complained to Bāyezīd in 1505 and again in 1508. In spite of these protests, Selīm made further incursions in the region of Erzinjan, whereupon Ismā'īl, in 1510, threatened to retaliate but was placated when an envoy arrived bearing gifts from Bāyezīd. Not content with securing troops well trained in warfare and loyal to his person, Selīm made good use of his influence at court to arrange the appointment of Iskender Beg, reported to have been his son-in-law, as commander of the Ottoman fleet; if the course of events were to favour Selīm, Iskender Beg might be able to prevent Ahmed from crossing the straits to Istanbul. To create a further obstacle for Ahmed, Selīm had his own son, Sulaimān, made governor of Boli, a province in north-west Anatolia controlling the communications between Amasia and the capital; but the plan failed, for Ahmed, seeing the danger to himself, induced the sultan to revoke the appointment. Selīm now made the daring resolve to transfer his activities from Trebizond to the Balkans. He prepared for this enterprise by requesting and obtaining for his son, Sulaimān, the province of Kaffa in the Crimea, an excellent point of departure for a campaign across the Danube, all the more since he succeeded at the same time in winning the alliance of Menglī Girāi, the khan of the Krim Tatars, who promised to provide him with horsemen.

The time for action had come. Without seeking Bāyezīd's consent, Selīm sailed with his troops from Trebizond to Kaffa where he enrolled more men and increased his fleet. He ignored his father's command that he should return to Trebizond, declaring that he had left it because of his desire to make war on the Christians and, for this purpose, wished to be given a province in Europe. The extent of his request is not clear. He seems to have asked for Semendria, but Bosnia and Silistria are also mentioned in some of the sources. When Bāyezīd rejected this demand, Selīm sent his ships to the Danube estuary and, with an army composed largely of Tatar horsemen, crossed the river in March 1511.

At Adrianople, where the court was then in residence, the partisans of Ahmed strove to impress on the sultan the gravity of Selīm's offence; but Bāyezīd, loath to begin a war against his son and worried over the revolt of Shah Kuli which had broken out in Anatolia, resolved in the end to grant what Selīm desired. In a formal agreement he conferred on Selīm the province of Semendria and promised furthermore that he would not abdicate in favour of Ahmed. This concession of a great government on the middle Danube to a prince reputed to be himself a warrior and an avowed advocate of war against the Christians was in full accord with the wishes of the border chieftains of Serbia and Bosnia, for example the Malkoch-oghlu, who were resentful of the peaceful attitude which Bāyezīd had maintained towards the Christian states since 1503.

For the moment Selīm was content with his success; but while he was moving towards Semendria, news arrived that Shah Kuli had defeated the beglerbeg of Anatolia and that the Grand Vizier 'Alī Pasha, who was a staunch friend of Ahmed, had been ordered to lead a strong force of janissaries and other troops against the rebels. Selīm suspected, and with good reason, that 'Alī Pasha, if he were able to crush the revolt, would use the powerful army under his command to secure the throne for Ahmed. Even before attacking Shah Kuli, the grand vizier had tried to win over to such an enterprise the forces which he himself had brought from Istanbul, an attempt which had failed, however, before the determination of his janissaries not to be dissuaded from their preference for Selīm. In the meantime, to forestall the danger which would arise when Ahmed and 'Alī Pasha had united their armies, Selīm marched once more on

Adrianople which yielded to him without resistance, for Bāyezīd, thinking his son meant to dethrone him, had withdrawn in haste towards Istanbul. When Selīm continued his pursuit, the sultan, under the urgent pressure of his advisers, made a stand at Tchorlu. Here, on 3 August 1511, the janissaries of Bāyezīd, however strong their inclination towards Selīm, fought loyally for their lawful master and by their discipline proved more than a match for the Tatar horsemen who swarmed around them. Selīm, completely defeated, had no choice but to flee to his ships on the shore of the Black Sea and to sail back to Kaffa. Some sources relate that he had not intended to give battle to his father and that only the rumour of Bāyezīd's death had made him hasten towards Istanbul in order to secure the throne. Whether he was the victim of a deception and believed this rumour, or else started it himself from motives of policy is not clear; but there can be no doubt that Ahmed's followers were doing their utmost to bring about his downfall. A Venetian observer wrote at this time that it was the great dignitaries who 'dominate and lord it over the land' and that few of them wanted Selīm as their master, since he was a man who would pursue his own road and not submit to their control.[1]

Meanwhile, both Shah Kuli and 'Alī Pasha had fallen in the battle fought near Kaysari in June 1511. Ahmed, though deprived of his surest advocate, could still count on the aid of numerous and powerful friends at court. Moreover, the death of the grand vizier had left him in command of the strong forces which had suppressed the rebellion in Anatolia. He therefore led them towards the capital, hoping that he would be able to cross the straits despite the possible resistance of the Ottoman fleet now under Iskender Pasha. When, however, in September 1511, his allies at court sought to bring him across the water to Istanbul, the janissaries, more than ever ill-disposed towards him because of the ineptitude which he had shown during the campaign against Shah Kuli, rose in revolt and sacked their houses. The warning was unmistakeable: the janissaries would not have Ahmed as sultan.

This event was decisive. Now that his partisans were silenced, Ahmed had but one course left to him: to strengthen and extend his power in Anatolia and prepare for armed resistance. He brought much of western Anatolia under his own control and proceeded to take over Karaman as well, and this without asking for his father's consent. It was in fact an open revolt made manifest when he defied the order of the sultan to withdraw at once from Karaman to his own province of Amasia.

Angered by Ahmed's behaviour, Bāyezīd agreed to restore Semendria to Selīm who, since his defeat at Tchorlu, had been gathering new forces

---

[1] Marino Sanuto, *Diarii* (Venice, 1879–1903), XIV, 293 (Andrea Foscolo to Piero Foscolo, Pera, 28 March 1512): '...loro son quelli che domina e signorizano el paexe'; also *ibid.* XII, 515–16 (the same to the same, Pera, 21 July 1511): 'Pochi da conto voria veder dito Selim signor, perchè è di sua testa e faria quello li paresse; ma le persone di bassa man e homeni armigeri tutti lo desiderano...'.

68

at Kaffa. For a time his alliance with the Krim Tatars had seemed to be in danger as a result of the intrigues which Ahmed instigated at the court of the khan but, in the end, Menglī Girāi proved faithful to his word. Tatar horsemen rode once more with Selīm when he crossed the Danube in the last days of January 1512. His cause was already won. Ahmed was reported to be seeking an alliance with Shah Ismā'īl. This alone, by arousing the fear of a possible Safawid intervention, was enough to bring Selīm to the throne. It was evident that a campaign in force would have to be made against Ahmed without delay. In March 1512 the janissaries demanded that Selīm be recalled to lead them. To acquiesce meant to abdicate, but the old sultan was compelled to agree. At this moment, Prince Korkūd, the governor of Sarukhan, made his own bid for the throne. He came to Istanbul and went to the barracks of the janissaries, hoping to win their aid on the plea that he had once been their sultan. They refused to help him. Meanwhile Selīm was approaching with all haste and on 19 April encamped outside the capital. One week later he became sultan. Bāyezīd was allowed to retire to the town of his birth, Demotika, but died on 26 May 1512 before he reached his destination. Of him Machiavelli wrote that, benefiting by the great achievements of Mehemmed II, he was able to maintain the empire by the arts of peace rather than war; but that, if Selīm had been a sultan like Bāyezīd, the Ottoman State would have been ruined.[1]

Selīm could not feel secure as long as his brothers and their sons were alive. To do away with them was, therefore, his first concern. The danger was urgent, for news arrived that Ahmed's son, 'Alā ad-Dīn, had seized Brusa. In the summer of 1512, while the fleet watched the shores of Anatolia, lest one of the princes should seek refuge abroad as Jem had done, Selīm drove Ahmed's forces from Brusa back to Amasia and thence towards the Persian and Syrian frontiers. On his return to Brusa he ordered the death of five nephews who lived there (November 1512). Soon afterwards the same fate befell Korkūd who was captured in Tekke whither he had fled from Sarukhan in the hope of escaping across the sea. Meanwhile Ahmed had recovered Amasia where he passed the winter in preparing for a new advance against Selīm. His cause, however, was desperate, since Shah Ismā'īl, still occupied by his war against the Uzbegs (p. 65), could give him no effective aid. In the spring of 1513 Ahmed began his last effort to win the throne. Although he defeated the vanguard of Selīm's forces at Ermeni Derbend, the end came on 24 April when at Yenishehir not far from Brusa he risked all on a decisive battle. His men broke and fled before the might of the janissaries and the wild

---

[1] Machiavelli, *Discorsi sopra...Tito Livio*, Lib. I, cap. 19: 'Baiasit...potette godersi le fatiche di Maumetto suo padre; il quale...gli lasciò un regno fermo, e da poterlo con l'arte della pace facilmente conservare. Ma se il figliuolo Sali, presente signore, fosse stato simile al padre, e non all'avolo, quel regno rovinava.'

assault of Selīm's Tatar horsemen. Ahmed was taken in the rout and killed at once on the order of Selīm.

Ahmed's death did not diminish the tension between the Ottomans and the Safawids. In 1512 Ismā'īl had commanded the governor of Erzinjan to lead several thousands of the Anatolian followers of the *Safawiyya* into Persia. This action had given rise to frontier hostilities in the course of which the forces of Erzinjan had seized the town of Tokat. Now in 1513 the shah welcomed at Tabriz a son of Ahmed, Prince Murād, who had escaped from the battle at Yenishehir. These events convinced Selīm that war against Ismā'īl was unavoidable. As a precaution lest revolt should break out in his rear, while he himself marched against Persia, he ordered punitive expeditions to be made throughout Anatolia, in which 40,000 adherents of the Shī'a faith are said to have been slain or imprisoned.

On 24 April 1514 Selīm began the long march to Persia, advancing through Yenishehir and Akshehir to Konia and then to Kaysari. Here he asked for supplies of food and reinforcements of men from 'Alā ad-Daula, prince of Albistan, who returned an evasive answer and did nothing to restrain his Turcomans from molesting the Ottoman columns. From Kaysari the sultan moved to Sivas where he held a muster of his entire army and left behind a strong force to garrison the frontier regions. As he advanced through Erzinjan and Erzerum, he found the lands before him ravaged of all fodder and provisions by the Persian commanders, so that his men suffered severe privations which were only partially alleviated through the arrival of stores transported by sea to Trebizond and thence laboriously overland on camels. Despite the grumbling of the janissaries, Selīm pressed forward until at last the shah was constrained to give battle in defence of Tabriz. The two armies met at Tchaldiran on 23 August 1514. On the Ottoman right were the Anatolian horsemen under Sinān Pasha, the beglerbeg of Anatolia, and on the left the cavalry of Rumeli commanded by their own beglerbeg, Hasan Pasha; while at the extremity of each wing were the guns linked together by iron chains. The janissaries, protected by the baggage and the camels, held the centre, the sultan himself standing behind them with his viziers and his household cavalry. The Ottomans, exhausted after their arduous march, had to face what must have been a maximum concentration of the Safawid forces. In the number of his horsemen the shah was probably not inferior to Selīm; but he had no artillery and no infantry comparable to the janissaries. Hoping to overrun the Ottoman guns and take the janissaries in the rear, Ismā'īl attacked on the extreme left and right of the battlefield. His cavalry broke through the *sipāhīs* of Rumeli, only to be decimated by the fire-arms of the janissaries; while the assault against the horsemen of Anatolia was shattered because Sinān Pasha ordered his forces to fall back behind the guns which thus obtained a clear field of fire.

This crushing victory opened for Selīm the road to Tabriz which he entered on 5 September. He intended to winter in the neighbouring region of Karabagh where ample fodder and supplies could be found; but the janissaries threatened to revolt and compelled him to withdraw, through Kars and Erzerum, to winter quarters around Amasia and Ankara, where the army was dispersed in November 1514. Tchaldiran did not lead to the conquest of Persia but was none the less a decisive battle. Never again, not even when Selīm was involved in his perilous war with Egypt, did Shah Ismā'īl dare to attack the Ottomans.

Tchaldiran had made Selīm the master of Erzinjan and Baiburd which he now united with Janik, Trebizond and Karahisar to form, under the command of Biyikli Mehemmed Pasha, a strong frontier province in the north-east of the empire. To consolidate his hold on this region, Selīm, while still in winter quarters at Amasia, ordered Mehemmed Pasha to besiege the great fortress of Kamakh not far from Erzinjan. It did not fall, however, until May 1515, after the sultan himself had arrived there to hasten the siege. The conquest of Kamakh meant that the hour of reckoning had come for 'Alā ad-Daula, whom Selīm had not forgiven for his hostile behaviour during the campaign of Tchaldiran. Already in November 1514 Selīm had appointed as governor of Kaysari a nephew of 'Alā ad-Daula, Shahsuwār-oghlü 'Alī, and sent him to raid into his uncle's territories. In June 1515 Sinān Pasha, at the head of 10,000 janissaries, defeated and slew 'Alā ad-Daula together with four of his sons. The principality of Albistan was now conferred on Shahsuwār-oghlü 'Alī, who was to rule over it as an Ottoman vassal.

At the same time Selīm was extending Ottoman control over Kurdistan where the native feudal lords, jealous of their independence, resented Shah Ismā'īl's attempt, since 1508 (p. 65), to rule them through governors chosen amongst his own Turcoman chieftains. After Tchaldiran, Diyarbekir had revolted of its own accord against the shah. Moreover, twenty-five of the Kurdish begs had appealed for aid to Selīm who had thereupon sent a prominent Kurdish noble, Idrīs, later famous as an Ottoman historian, to receive their homage and organise the resistance against the Safawids. Idrīs and the Kurds, although not unsuccessful in the field, were unable, without further assistance, to relieve Diyarbekir, which was closely besieged by the main Safawid forces in Kurdistan. Once the campaign against 'Alā ad-Daula had ended, Biyikli Mehemmed Pasha, then at Baiburd, was sent with several thousand men to join Idrīs and raise the siege, a task which he achieved in October 1515. Nevertheless, the Safawid commander in Kurdistan, Karakhan, continued to resist stubbornly until at last he too was defeated in 1516 at Koch Hisar, after Mehemmed Pasha and Idrīs had been reinforced by Khusrev Pasha, the governor of Karaman. Urfa, Mardin, and Mosul now fell to the Ottomans, so that almost all Kurdistan was in their hands. Idrīs, receiving from Selīm full authority to regulate the future status of the new conquests, wisely refrained from any attempt to impose everywhere direct Ottoman control. He divided the land into twenty-four governments, of which five were to be completely autonomous under Kurdish chieftains, and a further eight likewise under native families, but with the right of supervision reserved to Ottoman officials; the other eleven areas becoming Ottoman provinces of the normal kind. This far-sighted policy secured for the sultan the continued allegiance of the Kurds.

The events of 1514–15 had altered profoundly, and to the detriment of Egypt, the balance of forces along the Taurus frontier. The Mamluk sultan Kānsūh al-Ghaurī had hoped in 1514 for an Ottoman defeat which would enable him, at little cost to himself, to improve his position on the Taurus. If he had not instigated 'Alā ad-Daula's hostile behaviour towards the Ottomans, he had clearly approved of it; for when Selīm, while on the march to Persia, sent an ambassador in all haste to Cairo, with the urgent request that Egypt should restrain 'Alā ad-Daula, Kānsūh had given a polite but unsatisfactory answer. Later it emerged that he had secretly congratulated the prince of Albistan, bestowing on him a robe of honour and urging him to persevere in his unfriendly attitude towards the Ottomans. Alarmed at the danger which threatened 'Alā ad-Daula after Tchaldiran, Kānsūh al-Ghaurī complained to Selīm about the appointment of Shahsuwār-oghlü 'Alī as governor of Kaysari, alleging that this province was a part of Albistan and therefore within the Mamluk sphere of influence. This protest, delivered to Selīm in April 1515, as he was marching to the siege of Kamakh, had no effect. As we have seen, once Kamakh had fallen, 'Alā ad-Daula was defeated and slain in June of the same year. Kānsūh al-Ghaurī was now compelled to take decisive action. When emissaries from the shah arrived in Cairo to ask for Mamluk aid against a possible renewal of the Ottoman attack on Persia, he promised, in such an event, to appear on the Syrian frontier with all his forces.

The belief that a mere demonstration in force would set a limit to the Ottoman advance and that no actual warfare would ensue was nothing but wishful thinking. The Mamluks indeed must have been aware of their own weakness compared with the Ottomans. The feuds of the great amirs amongst themselves and with their sultan, feuds in which their respective Mamluks were involved, were bound to have a disastrous effect in a time of crisis. As soldiers, too, the Mamluks, now less well trained than of old, had lost much of their former excellence. Moreover, their contempt for the use of fire-arms and their blindness to the value of artillery, so vividly shown at Tchaldiran, revealed them as a force which, in military technique, had already become rather obsolete. Equally grave was the fact that the populations of Egypt and Syria were wholly estranged from the Mamluk regime, indeed even hostile to it—and with good reason.

The contemporary historian, Ibn Iyās, emphasises time and again the rapacity of the Mamluks. Exorbitant taxation and unbridled licence amongst the soldiery had long been normal evils of their rule. Kānsūh al-Ghaurī, having lost the large revenues of the Indian trade because of the Portuguese blockade in the Red Sea, had to resort to harsh financial measures, with the result, as Ibn Iyās wrote, that each day of his reign seemed to the common people to be like a thousand years.[1] The Mamluks, in their hour of need, could expect no aid from their subjects.

Although aware of Kānsūh al-Ghaurī's intention to support the shah, Selīm was determined to resume the offensive against Persia, which he regarded as the more dangerous foe. He therefore sent Sinān Pasha, now grand vizier, to Kurdistan. Sinān set out on 28 April 1516 and, at Kaysari on 13 June, joined forces with the beglerbeg of Rumeli and the agha of the janissaries. He was compelled, however, to halt in Albistan when, on 4 July, spies brought him the news that Kānsūh was advancing towards Aleppo and that the Mamluk governor of Malatia had been instructed to deny the Ottomans passage through his province.

Already on 21 April Kānsūh had issued orders for a campaign on the Taurus frontier. From 9 May Mamluk detachments marched daily into Syria, the sultan himself, with the main force, moving out of his camp at Ridaniyya near Cairo on 24 May. He took with him almost all the funds available in the state treasury and most of the valuable war material gathered by his predecessors. Arriving at Gaza on 5 June and at Damascus two weeks later, he reached Aleppo on 10 July. Here emissaries whom Selīm, still hoping that the Mamluk intervention might be averted or at least deferred, had dispatched from Istanbul on 4 June, awaited him with the assurance that their master had no wish for a conflict with Egypt. Kānsūh reproached them vehemently for the seizure of Albistan and threw them into prison.

Meanwhile, Selīm had crossed from Istanbul to Scutari on 5 June. Marching through Kutahia (20 June) and thence through Afiun Karahisar and Akshehir to Konia (1 July) and Kaysari, he joined Sinān Pasha with strong reinforcements on 23 July. At this moment, an ambassador sent by Kānsūh al-Ghaurī from Aleppo arrived, warning Selīm not to proceed against Persia and, as one Ottoman source relates, requesting that Albistan be restored to Egypt. Selīm's answer was brief: insistence on these demands would leave him no choice but to invade Syria.

This unexpected defiance must have brought sudden disillusionment to Kānsūh al-Ghaurī. In a last effort to avoid war, he ordered the Ottoman emissaries imprisoned at Aleppo to be set free and sent one of his amirs, Mughul Bāy, to Selīm. It was already too late. On 28 July Selīm had entered the plain of Malatia where he was well placed to move

---

[1] Ibn Iyās, *The Ottoman Conquest of Egypt*, transl. W. H. Salmon (Oriental Translation Fund, New Series, vol. xxv), London (1921), p. 58.

towards either Aleppo or Diyarbekir, as need should arise. Here he was joined by the troops of Kurdistan led by Biyikli Mehemmed Pasha. When, on 3 August, it became known that Kānsūh al-Ghaurī had asked the shah for aid, Selīm was forced to make an immediate decision. On 4 August, in consultation with his viziers, he resolved to leave Persia alone and to turn at once against Syria. Some days later he must have received in audience the Mamluk envoy Mughul Bāy. In his anger that Kānsūh had chosen a soldier as ambassador, Selīm had the amir's retinue slain and sent the amir himself ignominiously back to Aleppo. Advancing from the north-east the Ottomans reached 'Aintab on 20 August, the day after the Mamluks had marched out to meet them, leaving most of their baggage and treasure in the citadel of Aleppo, since it was evident that the decisive battle would be fought somewhere near the city. The two armies met at Marj Dābik on 24 August 1516.

There is no good evidence for the total strength of the Ottoman forces, but their battle order is clear: in the centre stood Selīm with the grand vizier and the janissaries; on his right were the Anatolian cavalry and, beyond them, Turcomans from Albistan and Cilicia commanded by Shahsuwār-oghlü 'Alī and by Mahmūd Beg, a prince of the Ramazān-oghlü; on his left, the horsemen of Rumeli and then the Kurds under Biyikli Mehemmed. To oppose the Ottomans, Kānsūh al-Ghaurī had perhaps 60,000 men, of whom 12,000 to 15,000 were Mamluks. The rest were contingents from Egypt and Syria composed in part of Bedouin, Turcoman, and Kurdish horsemen. The Mamluk order of battle is not known in detail, but the sultan himself held the centre, the troops of Aleppo being on his right, and those of Damascus on his left wing.

Even now, Kānsūh al-Ghaurī could not refrain from acting as a partisan in the feuds which divided his forces. Wishing to spare his personal Mamluks, he ordered those who had belonged to his predecessors to make the first assault. These veterans, about 2000 in number, followed by the horsemen of Aleppo and Damascus, drove back the Kurds and the Turcomans on the extreme left and right of the Ottoman formation, only to be cut down by the fire of the enemy guns and of the janissaries. At this critical moment when a resolute advance might yet have won success, Kānsūh al-Ghaurī and his own Mamluks remained inactive. As the Ottomans launched a violent attack on the Mamluk centre, Khā'ir Beg, the governor of Aleppo, who had long been in traitorous communication with Selīm, spread the rumour that Kānsūh was slain. The Mamluks wavered and, after a brief resistance, fled. In the turmoil Kānsūh al-Ghaurī met his death. At Aleppo, where in the weeks before the battle their excesses had aroused bitter resentment, the fleeing Mamluks found the gates closed against them, a disaster which meant the loss of the state treasury and all the war material lodged in the citadel. Syria could no longer be defended. Nothing was left to them save to continue their flight first to Damascus and then to Egypt.

Syria yielded to the Ottomans without further resistance. Selīm entered Aleppo on 28 August. One month later he reached Damascus where he decided to rest his tired army. Ottoman governors were now appointed to each of the more important cities like Aleppo, Tripoli, Damascus, and Jerusalem; while a strong garrison was stationed at Gaza to watch the route into Egypt across the Sinai desert. As yet Selīm was uncertain about the wisdom of continuing the war. His main purpose had been achieved. No more need he fear an alliance between Egypt and Persia, now widely separated by a Syria firmly held in Ottoman hands. It was true that he could count on enough time to invade Egypt, for Shah Ismā'īl would not attack during the harsh Anatolian winter but wait at least until the spring of 1517. Nevertheless, an assault on Egypt would be a dangerous enterprise. There was first the desert to be crossed where water would be scarce and the Arab tribes eager to harass the Ottomans; and then, no doubt, the Mamluks would resist desperately in defence of their last stronghold. After much thought and despite Khā'ir Beg's plea for continued war, Selīm sent an ambassador to Cairo, offering peace if the new Mamluk sultan, Tūmān Bāy, who had been raised to the throne on 16 October, would consent to govern Egypt as an Ottoman vassal.

Before the result of this mission could be known, it was learnt that Tūmān Bāy, though hard pressed by the discontent of the Mamluks and by lack of funds and equipment, had dispatched about 10,000 men under the amir Jānberdi al-Ghāzālī to reconquer Gaza. To meet this threat, the Grand Vizier Sinān Pasha marched from Damascus on 1 December with 5000 men, including a contingent of janissaries, and joined the garrison of Gaza just as the Mamluks were emerging from the Sinai desert. Feigning a retreat, he moved northward by night, turned swiftly to the south, and forced Jānberdi to stand and fight on 21 December. The fire of the janissaries drove the Mamluks from their strong position on the edge of a steep wadi. Sinān Pasha crossed, re-formed his men, and launched a fierce assault which ended in the rout of the Mamluks.

Meanwhile, Selīm, with all his forces save for the garrisons left in Syria, had moved southward from Damascus on 14 December. The Mamluk attempt to recover Gaza and the news, received towards the end of the month, that his ambassador to Cairo had been slain convinced him that Egypt would have to be conquered. He joined Sinān Pasha at Gaza on 3 January 1517 and six days later began the march through the desert. Although repeatedly harassed by the Arab tribes whom Tūmān Bāy had roused against them, the Ottomans were on Egyptian soil by 17 January and, after a further march of two days, reached Belbeis about thirty miles to the north-east of Cairo. Through the treachery of the Mamluk amir Jānberdi al-Ghāzālī it was discovered that Tūmān Bāy had constructed at Ridaniyya a fortified emplacement defended by ditches and by all the guns which he could muster. On 23 January Selīm took these defences in the rear and destroyed them by artillery fire. None the less, the battle was not won until the repulse of a desperate Mamluk assault, during which the Grand Vizier Sinān Pasha was killed. Four days of stubborn street fighting ensued in Cairo (27–30 January), before the Mamluk resistance was broken. On the night of the 27th Tūmān Bāy, with about 7000 men, surprised and overcame the Ottoman detachments stationed in Cairo after the battle of Ridaniyya; but defeat was inevitable when, in the following night, Selīm brought his artillery into the city in order to batter down the Mamluk barricades. After a last stand near the citadel, Tūmān Bāy escaped with a mere remnant of his forces. With some aid from the Arab tribes he continued to harass the Ottomans until at last he was beaten once more on the banks of the Nile in March 1517. Soon afterwards he fell into Ottoman hands and on 13 April was executed in Cairo.

The conquest of Syria and Egypt meant a great increase in the prestige of the Ottomans, already renowned as the foremost warriors of Islam in war against the Christians. Now for the first time an Ottoman sultan was honoured as the Servitor of the two Sacred Cities, Mecca and Medina, a title which made him pre-eminent amongst the rulers of the Muslim world. In Egypt, Selīm contented himself with leaving an Ottoman pasha and a strong garrison at the head of affairs, the old Mamluk order with its own laws and its own system of military fiefs and administration being allowed to continue; whereas in Syria he created provinces organised on the lines found elsewhere in the empire, although here, too, Mamluk laws and local customs were confirmed to a large degree. At the same time he recognised the privileges of the Arab chieftains, of the Druze and Christian lords of the Lebanon, and of the Turcoman dynasties on the Taurus frontier, for example the Ramazān-oghlü. Nevertheless, despite these arrangements, there was unrest for some years in the former Mamluk dominions, until in the reign of Selīm's son, Sulaimān, the Ottoman regime was reorganised in a more stable and permanent manner.

On 10 September 1517, having appointed the former Mamluk amir Khā'ir Beg as pasha of Egypt because of his intimate acquaintance with conditions there, Selīm began the long march from Cairo back to Anatolia. By 7 October he was outside Damascus, where he spent the winter in making further arrangements for the administration of Syria and in dealing with the revolt of an Arab chieftain, a certain Ibn Hanush. While Selīm was still at Damascus, he received an ambassador from Persia, who had come to compliment him on the conquest of the Mamluk realm. Throughout the Ottoman campaign Shah Ismā'īl had remained quiet, in part because he feared to risk another defeat, but also because troubles in eastern Persia had claimed his attention. His dispatch of an ambassador to Syria implied that he had no wish for further hostilities with the Ottomans. Nevertheless, around Tokat in Anatolia, adherents of the Shī'a, led by a certain Shah Welī, had started a new rebellion which was crushed in 1518 by Shahsuwār-oghlü 'Alī, the Ottoman vassal prince of Albistan. In the meantime, Selīm, having entrusted Damascus to the former Mamluk Jānberdi al-Ghazālī, had arrived at Aleppo in March 1518. Here he received the news that the new pasha of Damascus had defeated and killed the Arab chieftain Ibn Hanush. After remaining in Aleppo for two months the sultan resumed the march towards Istanbul which he reached on 25 July, just over two years since he had left it in 1516.

With the Christians there had been peace since 1503. Venice, in 1513, had obtained the renewal of her commercial privileges in the Ottoman empire. After the conquest of Syria and Egypt she sought from Selīm a confirmation of the rights which she had secured in those countries under the Mamluk sultans. This was achieved in the agreement of 17 September 1517, Venice promising to pay to the Ottomans the annual tribute of 8000 ducats which she had given to the Mamluks for the possession of Cyprus. The Hungarians and the Poles were also able to remain at peace with the sultan despite the ceaseless unrest along the frontiers. In 1519 Selīm renewed with them the truce which had been extended on several occasions since 1503. This maintenance of peace in the west cannot be taken to mean that Selīm had no aggressive intentions for the future. In 1515 he had begun the creation of a great arsenal at Istanbul. Now, in the years 1518–20, he pressed forward with the building of a new and more powerful fleet. It seems that he had in mind an attack on Rhodes which Mehemmed II had failed to take in 1480; but before he could set out on such an enterprise, he died on 20 September 1520 near Tchorlu while travelling from Istanbul to Adrianople.

Even in his own time his character gave rise to widely differing judgments. To the superficial observer he was, by reason of his severity, little more than a tyrant. Yet, with all his warlike ardour and fierce anger which earned for him the name, compounded both of fear and admiration, of Yavuz Sultan Selīm, i.e. the Grim Sultan, he was also a patron of learning and literature, himself writing poetry in Persian. The Venetian Luigi Mocenigo who saw him victorious in Cairo at the summit of his fame and splendour retained an abiding impression of his greatness.[1] In five years of relentless warfare Selīm had solved the grave problems which his father had bequeathed to him. Now he handed to his own son Sulaimān an

---

[1] Paolo Giovio, *Commentario de le cose de Turchi* (Venice, 1541), fol. 25v–26r: '...mi diceva il clarissimo Miser Luigi Mocenigo...che essendo lui al Cairo Ambasciadore, appresso à Soltan Selim, et havendo molto ben pratticato, che nullo huomo era par ad esso in virtù, iustitia humanità, et grandezza d'animo, et che non haveva punto del Barbaro....'

empire vastly increased in size, enriched with new resources, and able to resume the offensive against the Christians on a scale more formidable than ever before. The Ottoman poet and historian Kemālpashazāde, Selīm's companion on the Egyptian campaign, wrote, with no exaggeration, in a lament on the death of the great sultan, that in a brief space of time he had achieved much and, like the setting sun, had cast a long shadow over the face of the earth.[1]

[1] See E. J. W. Gibb, *A History of Ottoman Poetry*, vol. III (ed. E. G. Browne, London, 1904), p. 19.

3

THE REIGN OF SULAIMĀN THE MAGNIFICENT, 1520–66

TOWARDS the end of his reign Selīm I had been preparing for a new offensive, but no one could be sure where the blow might fall. Now, in September 1520, the great sultan was dead. As the news became known in Christendom, men felt that a dark shadow had been banished, an imminent peril suddenly dispelled. Sulaimān, the only son of Selīm, was said to be ill-versed in affairs and of a quiet nature, a prince, therefore, who would be little inclined to war. Seldom has prediction been more rash or doomed to swifter disillusionment. In 1521 Sulaimān marched against Hungary.

The campaign had been organised with meticulous care: the *beglerbeg* of Rumeli moved towards Sabacz, the sultan following with most of his household regiments; the grand vizier Pīrī Pasha, with a strong contingent of janissaries and ample provision of siege guns, made for the main objective, Belgrade, which Mehemmed II had tried but failed to capture in 1456. At the same time the Akinjis[2] rode out in two columns, the one to effect a diversion against Transylvania, the other to devastate the lands between the Sava and the Drava. The fall of Sabacz and Semlin severed the routes leading to the north and west of Belgrade, so that Sulaimān was now free to assail the great fortress. Guns bombarded the walls from an island in the Danube, a fierce assault drove the garrison into the citadel, an Ottoman flotilla, sailing upstream, cut off all relief by water. The end came when dissension broke out between the Hungarians and their Serbian mercenaries, the former wishing to prolong, the latter to abandon the defence. Belgrade surrendered on 29 August 1521.

Sulaimān turned now to the conquest of Rhodes. The Knights of St John had long harassed Muslim commerce, plundered vessels bearing pilgrims towards Mecca, slain and enslaved the subjects of the Ottoman sultan, their depredations being so severe that in 1480 Mehemmed II had tried to seize the island, though without success. The fate of Rhodes had in fact been decided in 1517 when Selīm I conquered the Mamluk sultanate: thereafter the Ottomans could not suffer the continued existence of this 'pirate-stronghold' athwart the sea-routes from Istanbul to their new provinces of Syria and Egypt. Yet the fortress was almost impregnable, and Sulaimān was well aware that the knights were making elaborate preparations to defend it. The bitter fighting of 1522 was to

---

[1] For an analysis of the structure of the Ottoman state, cf. chapter 4.

[2] I.e., raiders, volunteer light-armed horsemen serving for the reward of plunder and captives.

underline how much the sultan owed in this campaign to his father, Selīm, who in the last years of his reign had strengthened and improved the naval resources at his command, with the intention, as it would seem, of subjugating the island.

The invasion fleet arrived at Rhodes on 24 June 1522. More than a month passed in the landing of troops and munitions, in work on trenches and on sites for the siege artillery. Sulaimān, marching through Asia Minor with strong reinforcements, crossed over to Rhodes late in July. Attempts to storm the fortress made it clear that mining and bombardment of the walls alone offered a prospect of success. There now ensued a stubborn and protracted conflict, the Ottomans, in their intermittent assaults, losing heavily in men and material. With the onset of winter, rain and cold so hindered the conduct of the siege that the sultan was induced to hold out generous terms of capitulation, but it was not until 21 December that the knights, worn down to the limit of their endurance, yielded on promise of freedom to withdraw unmolested to Europe.

There were grave events, too, in Syria and Egypt during the first years of the new reign. Memories of their former splendour still survived amongst the Mamluks whom Selīm I had incorporated into the Ottoman régime, and now, with the accession of Sulaimān, the more dissatisfied elements believed that the time had come to regain their independence. The pasha of Damascus, Jānberdi al-Ghazālī, once a Mamluk amir, had risen in revolt in 1520-1, had besieged Aleppo in vain and then suffered defeat and death while resisting a punitive force sent against him from Istanbul. Unrest and intrigue were rife in Egypt, leading to disturbances on the death of the pasha, Khā'ir Beg, in 1522 and thereafter to a more serious rebellion in the winter of 1523-4 when the new Ottoman pasha Ahmed, in alliance with some of the Mamluk begs and Arab chieftains, tried to crush the janissaries stationed at Cairo and so make himself the real master of the land. His ambition was doomed to failure, for in view of the rivalries amongst the Mamluks and also between the various tribal confederations there could be no question of a united resistance to Ottoman rule. The revolt, although suppressed without undue trouble, convinced Sulaimān of the need to modify the settlement improvised at the time of the conquest. He entrusted the task to his grand vizier Ibrāhīm who in 1524-5 carried out in Egypt an extensive reform of justice, finance and administration, reshaping the government on lines that it was to retain, in essentials, until the rise of Muhammad 'Alī almost three centuries later. Ibrāhīm created a balance of power and privilege between the pasha, the janissaries, the Mamluk begs and the Arab tribes. Henceforth, the alignments and tensions among them were to exert a dominant influence on the course of events inside Egypt. In time, the delicate equilibrium now established would break down in favour of the Mamluks and to the disadvantage of the pasha; but this change was as yet far in the future, and in the meanwhile the reforms ensured to Egypt a long interval of firm and beneficial rule.

It was three years since Sulaimān had gone to war. Amongst the janissaries inaction bred resentment which, in March 1525, flared out in a sudden tumult, warning the sultan not to defer too long the preparation of a new campaign. The grand vizier, recalled from Cairo, arrived at Istanbul in September and the decision was made to launch a great offensive on the Danube. Sulaimān marched against the Hungarians in April 1526. Progress was slow and difficult because of bad weather, and it was late August before he crossed the Drava near Eszék. The advance continued through a region of marshes and swollen streams, under persistent rain and occasional mist, until the Ottomans reached the plain of Mohács.

The Hungarians faced a desperate crisis. Bitter rivalries ruined all prospect of a prudent and united resistance.[1] No effort was made to hold the line of the Drava, nor would the Hungarian nobles agree to withstand a siege in Buda in the hope of prolonging the defence until the approach of winter should compel the sultan to retreat. The critical weeks of mid-August were wasted in acrimonious debate, and the final choice fraught with extreme danger: to risk a field battle against a foe much superior in numbers and armament, and this before the men of Zápolyai, before all the Croatian levies and the troops summoned from Bohemia had arrived.

To the east of Mohács flowed the Danube, to the south and west of the plain were low wooded hills, which masked the advance of the Ottoman columns: in the van, the frontier warriors of Semendria; next the *sipāhis* of Rumeli and then, of Anatolia; behind them, Sulaimān with the janissaries and the regiments of household cavalry; and in the rear, the warriors of Bosnia. It was 29 August 1526. The Hungarians had no intention of fighting on the defensive behind their waggons and carts. Their heavy cavalry, in a first violent charge, hurled back the troops of Rumeli against those of Anatolia, but was itself halted when the begs of Bosnia and Semendria, who had moved to the left through the hills, came down from the west into the right flank of the Christian advance. King Lewis now led the rest of his horsemen in a second assault, cut through the *sipāhis* of Anatolia and rode headlong into the janissaries and the guns ranged around the sultan. A terrible artillery fire shattered the Hungarians, massive flank attacks drove them in rout towards the Danube. Soon the king and most of his nobles were either dead on the field or else drowned in the river marshes, only a few remnants of the broken army escaping under cover of rain and darkness. Sulaimān reached Buda on 10 September. One week later the Ottomans began to cross the Danube to Pest. The Akinjis, who had ravaged far and wide in the direction of Raab (Györ) and Komorn, were recalled, the rich booty and all the guns

[1] Cf. *NCMH*, vol. II, p. 348.

found at Buda shipped downstream. Swiftly the sultan retreated, first to Szegedin and thence to Peterwardein and Belgrade, after a campaign resplendent with the most famous of all his victories.

During the return march news had arrived of revolt amongst the Turcomans in Cilicia who were angered at the conduct of Ottoman officials sent out to make a register of their lands and wealth for purposes of finance and administration. There was trouble, too, in Karaman, where a certain Kalender-oghlu and his dervish adherents roused the Turcoman tribes against the Ottoman régime. For almost two years the troops of Anadolu, Karaman, Amasia and Diyarbekir, with the aid of reinforcements from Damascus and Aleppo, were engaged in a fluctuating war, so serious as to demand at last the personal attention of the grand vizier, Ibrāhīm Pasha. By tactful diplomacy and the bestowal of fiefs he induced the Turcoman begs to abandon their alliance with Kalender-oghlu. Thereafter, the defeat and death of the rebel were soon achieved, but, even so, a further outbreak occurred in the Taurus region, and it was not until the summer of 1528 that the last embers of revolt were extinguished.

Meanwhile, a fateful conflict had arisen beyond the northern frontier. Lewis, king of Hungary and Bohemia, had married a Habsburg princess, Maria, sister of the Archduke Ferdinand and the Emperor Charles V, while Ferdinand himself had taken as wife Anna, the sister of Lewis, and had then received from the emperor the government of Austria and its dependencies. When Lewis died at Mohács, leaving no child to succeed him, Ferdinand laid claim to the rich inheritance. If he could realise his ambition, Hungary and Bohemia might be welded, with Austria, into a formidable barrier against Ottoman aggression. The sultan would then be confronted, not with a mere Hungarian king, independent yet weak, as Lewis had been, but with a prince who belonged to the greatest dynasty in Europe, to a house tenacious in the extreme of its rights and privileges and, despite vast commitments elsewhere, able to muster on the Danube, in time of dire need, resources far above those which Sulaimān had overcome at Mohács. Although Ferdinand soon acquired the Bohemian Crown, no facile success awaited him at Buda. He had first to defeat a rival candidate, the *voivode* of Transylvania, John Zápolyai, whom the native faction amongst the nobles had raised to the throne in November 1526. One year later Ferdinand was acclaimed king at Stuhlweissenburg, his troops having driven the Transylvanian to take refuge on the border with Poland. Zápolyai now turned to Istanbul for aid.[1]

The sultan, though regarding the Hungarian realm as his own by right of conquest, knew that indirect control, comparable with that which he wielded in Wallachia and Moldavia, would be far less arduous to win and maintain than a permanent and direct occupation. If he were to establish a dependent prince at Buda, a cordon of vassal states would then cover

[1] For the way in which the issue appeared to Ferdinand, cf. *ibid.* pp. 348, 470.

the northern frontier of his empire from the Black Sea almost to the Adriatic. He therefore welcomed the appeal of Zápolyai, bestowed on him the kingdom of the dead Lewis, and swore to guard him against the enmity of Austria. Soon ambassadors arrived from Vienna demanding that the Ottomans relinquish all the fortresses which had fallen to them along the Sava and on the Croatian border during and since the campaigns of Belgrade and Mohács. In bitter scorn Ibrāhīm, the grand vizier, wondered that Ferdinand did not ask for Istanbul, while the sultan, in a final audience, gave to the envoys the ominous message that he himself would come to Vienna and restore what the archduke demanded: 'Bid him therefore have all in readiness to receive me well.'

A major offensive on the Danube was a stern test of Ottoman military skill and resource. The campaign season extended, in the Hungarian wars of Sulaimān, from mid-April to the end of October, but the distance to Belgrade alone was so great that the sultan could seldom cross the Sava in force before the first days of July. The march was often slow and laborious, for the weather seems to have been bad even in summer, the official war diaries of Sulaimān referring constantly to storms, cold winds and relentless rain.[1] Problems of supply and transport were especially hard to solve. Rivers had to be spanned by means of pontoon bridges, a feat that required high technical ability; roads had to be made over difficult ground—and Hungary was a land of many streams and marshes. The Danube flotilla could only share to a limited degree in the movement of guns and munitions, most of which were needed for immediate use in the field and had therefore to be loaded on waggons and carts, on camels and other beasts of burden; yet, owing to the harshness of weather and terrain, the loss of animals was not infrequently severe. Ample reserves of food were essential, since the retreat might lie through territories swept bare of sustenance by the Akinjis during the forward march or else waste and barren from the devastation wrought, by Christian and Muslim alike, in the raids of former years; and always, in the last phase of a long campaign, a new danger might arise—the premature and sudden onset of winter.

Never were these difficulties more evident and more formidable than in 1529. Sulaimān left Istanbul on 10 May, did not reach Belgrade until mid-July and only on 27 September stood at last before Vienna. Because of incessant rains and flooded rivers, he had lost a vital month in which Ferdinand was able to garrison the city with a powerful force of veteran soldiers. Time was short, food already becoming scarce, and the Ottomans were far from their nearest base. If they were to take Vienna, it would have to be quickly or not at all, but the Christian defence held out against every assault. On 14 October the sultan gave the order to retreat. 'Snow from evening until noon next day', 'much loss of horses and men

---

[1] Cf. the diaries in J. von Hammer, *Geschichte des Osmanischen Reiches*, vol. III (Pest, 1828), pp. 621–25, 639–44, 647–52, 665–71.

in swamps', 'many die of hunger'—so ran the story of the grim march to Belgrade. And yet the campaign was not a complete failure, for it achieved one important result: Zápolyai ruled again at Buda.

The Archduke Ferdinand had not the means to launch a vigorous counter-offensive. His troops were ill-paid and discontented, his need of money acute. The German princes, though prepared to aid him in the hour of danger, would never fight a long and costly war on the Danube for the benefit of the Habsburgs. Nor could he depend on receiving prompt assistance from the Emperor Charles V, now deeply preoccupied with the conflict between Catholic and Protestant. Ferdinand tried, therefore, to make peace with the sultan, offering tribute in return for the possession of all Hungary, but the attempt met with no success. He himself would not abate in the least his claim to the whole kingdom, while Sulaimān was adamant in his refusal to abandon Zápolyai.

The sultan left Istanbul in April 1532, his declared aim being to seek out and crush the combined forces of Ferdinand and Charles V. He crossed the Sava in the last days of June, followed the Danube route as far as Eszék, and then turned to the north-west through Babocsa and over the river Raab, until he came to the little town of Güns. Here, in a desperate and brilliant defence sustained for almost three weeks, a small garrison resisted the full weight of the Ottoman assault, yielding at last on 28 August. Most of the summer was now gone, the rains were frequent and prolonged, and meanwhile, as the sultan must have known, German, Italian and Spanish veterans had been able to join the troops of Ferdinand at Vienna. Sulaimān, having no mind to renew the bitter experience which he had suffered three years before, abandoned his original purpose and, from this moment, the campaign assumed the character of an immense razzia. The Akinjis rode far into Austria, while the main army moved through the mountain valleys of Styria towards Graz where the Tatars of the Krim Khan were let loose along the river Mur. It was a march 'wearisome as the Last Judgment'. The sultan now retreated across the Drava and then swept with fire and sword down the whole length of Slavonia to the Bossut, an affluent of the Sava. Here the raids came to an end, for beyond this stream lay Sirmium, a region under Ottoman control. On 12 October Sulaimān arrived once more at Belgrade.

After two exhausting but indecisive campaigns against Austria the sultan realized that time and distance were enemies at least as formidable as the power of the Habsburgs and that, unless he committed himself to the conquest of a permanent base far to the north of the Sava, he would have little chance of inflicting on Ferdinand a sudden and catastrophic defeat. He therefore granted peace to the archduke in June 1533. The 'king of Vienna' was to retain what he then held of the Hungarian realm. He could also make a separate agreement with Zápolyai subject to the approval of the Porte. Sulaimān had in fact conceded little more than a truce without time limit. A prince dependent on his favour would continue to be master of Buda; his own word would still shape the future course of events on the Danube. Meanwhile, he had obtained an immediate advantage: freedom to deal with urgent affairs in the east.

The Ottoman frontier with Persia was ill-defined. The direct rule of the sultan extended, in the north of Asia Minor, only to Erzinjan and Baiburd, the lands beyond these fortresses remaining under the control of Turcoman begs who gave allegiance, as their need dictated, now to Istanbul and now to Tabriz; in the south, it embraced western and most of central Kurdistan, but not the region around Lake Van, where the forces of the shah were still active. The war of 1514–16 had died down into a smouldering tension along the frontier. No formal peace had been made between the sultan and the shah. Feuds and incursions continued to disturb the border zones, and the odium which divided the orthodox or Sunnī Ottomans and the Shī'ī Persians was no less fierce than before.[1]

While Sulaimān was marching towards Güns, the troops of Karaman, Amasia and Diyarbekir, with detachments from Syria, were fighting in Kurdistan against the khan of Bitlis, who had gone over to the shah. The defection of this border chieftain brought home to the sultan the need to consolidate and strengthen the unstable frontier in Asia Minor. There was a further ground for war, in that the Persian governor of Baghdad had offered submission to the Porte, only to be murdered before Ottoman aid could be sent to him. Sulaimān did not intend to forego so opportune a pretext for the conquest of Iraq.

As soon as peace had been concluded with Austria, the Grand Vizier Ibrāhīm hastened towards Kurdistan, but on receiving news that Bitlis was once more in Ottoman hands, he retired into winter quarters at Aleppo. In the spring of the next year he moved against Persia and by mid-July had taken Tabriz. Shah Tahmasp, mindful of the crushing defeat which his father, Ismā'īl, had endured at Tchaldiran in battle with Sultan Selīm (August 1514), preferred to abandon the city rather than face the janissaries and the Ottoman field artillery. Sulaimān left Istanbul only in June 1534. During his advance he traversed almost the whole of the frontier zone, passing through Erzinjan to Erzerum, then south to Lake Van and eastward to Tabriz, where he joined Ibrāhīm Pasha on 28 September. There now ensued a most formidable march across the mountains of western Persia. 'Snow as in deepest winter' beset the land, food was scarce, the loss of transport animals severe, but at last, on 30 November, the sultan entered Baghdad. He remained there until April 1535 and then, having provided for the defence and administration of Iraq, withdrew northward through Kurdistan to Tabriz. The shah was still determined to avoid all risk of a great battle. To these tactics of evasion the sultan

[1] On the rise of the Shī'ī Safawids and the danger of this movement to Ottoman rule in Asia Minor, cf. chapter 2.

could find no effective answer. Tabriz was in the heart of Azerbaijan, a mountainous area far removed from the nearest Ottoman base. An attempt to hold this region would be a most doubtful venture, as long as the army of the shah remained intact—yet the prospect of destroying that army, rapidly and at one blow, was almost negligible. In late August Sulaimān gave the order to retreat. The campaign had achieved two notable results: the formation of a new province at Erzerum on the eastern frontier, and the conquest of Iraq.

In 1536, soon after his return from the Persian war, the sultan bestowed on France commercial privileges similar to those which Venice had long held in the Ottoman empire. This agreement was the visible symbol of the growing friendship that united the king of France and the sultan. In the years following his defeat and capture at the battle of Pavia (1525) Francis I had striven to bring about a sustained Ottoman assault against Austria, hoping thus to relieve the Habsburg pressure on his own realm.[1] Sulaimān, aware of the benefit to be won from an understanding with a Christian state hostile to the Emperor Charles V and the Archduke Ferdinand, welcomed an appeal so close to his desire for effective control of the Hungarian kingdom. And yet, as the campaigns of Vienna and Güns had shown, the war on the Danube ensured to Francis I no decisive gain and even worked to his disadvantage, in so far as it rendered the German Protestants less willing to join him in overt resistance to the emperor and forced them, for their own interest, to make common cause with Austria against the sultan.

There was, however, a second front which offered a prospect of more favourable co-operation. The maritime resources of Charles V had been much increased in the Mediterranean. Genoa, dissatisfied with the conduct of her French allies, deserted to the emperor in 1528—an event of the first order, for the republic possessed the sole fleet which might have secured to France an effective command of the sea. Moreover, in the same year and with the approval of Charles V, the Knights of St John established a garrison at Tripoli on the African shore and in 1530 accepted from the emperor the task of defending Malta. Spain, which had long aspired to the conquest of the Muslim principalities in North Africa, seemed now to be on the verge of achieving her desire. The vital issue was one which Sulaimān, as the greatest of all Muslim rulers and also as the overlord of Algiers, could in no wise disregard: was North Africa to be preserved or lost to Muslim rule? Only a bold offensive at sea could avert the danger of Christian domination. At the same time, if the Ottoman fleet were sent against the emperor, it would serve, in respect to France, as an admirable substitute for the galleys of Genoa. To Sulaimān, no less than to Francis I, war in the Mediterranean appeared to be of more immediate advantage in their conflict with Charles V than further campaigns on the Danube.[2]

[1] Cf. *NCMH*, vol. II, pp. 343, 352 f.   [2] Cf. also *ibid.* p. 351.

The sultan had great arsenals at Istanbul and Gallipoli, good harbours along the Aegean and Levantine coasts, abundant timber in Asia Minor and ample supplies of labour for his shipyards. The main defect of his naval organisation was a lack of competent sea-captains and of an efficient high command able to match the skill and experience of the Venetian and Genoese admirals. One event, above all, warned Sulaimān of the urgent need to eliminate this weakness. The ministers of Charles V had advised their master to strengthen the defences on the Italian coast, especially in Apulia, and at the same time, as the best means of deflecting the sultan from the Danube, to begin a vigorous sea offensive in the eastern Mediterranean. In September 1532 the Genoese commander, Andrea Doria, led his fleet, reinforced by papal, Maltese and Sicilian squadrons, to the conquest of Coron in the Morea. Ottoman troops recovered the fortress in April 1534, but only after a wearisome siege prolonged by the aid that Doria was able to bring to the Spanish garrison which he had left there. Sulaimān was preparing to march against Persia, yet he could not leave the sea unguarded in his absence. The danger of a new raid by Doria to the east of Malta, no less than the growing threat to North Africa and the problem of co-operation with France, demanded immediate measures to ensure that the naval forces of the sultan would be reorganised and then employed with the greatest energy and effect. A splendid instrument was available for this purpose in the community, or tā'ife, of corsairs at Algiers, veteran sailors trained and hardened in ceaseless forays against the Christians. Their famous leader, Khair ad-Dīn, came to Istanbul at the sultan's bidding[1] and brought with him his own captains and naval technicians. He built new ships, sailed forth at the head of the Ottoman fleet and in August 1534, eight months after his arrival at the Porte, captured Tunis, thus neutralising the hold which Charles V had won over the narrow waters of the central Mediterranean. It was only a transient victory, for in July of the next year the emperor conquered the town and restored its Muslim ruler as a vassal prince supported and controlled by Spanish troops stationed in the fortress of La Goletta. Khair ad-Din, however, escaped to Algiers and in the autumn raided the Balearics and the coast of Valencia.

Francis I, in the hope of regaining Milan and Genoa, made war once more on the emperor in 1536. The sultan was willing to co-operate against the common foe, but did not move until his naval preparations were complete. In the summer of 1537 he marched to Valona on the Adriatic, while Khair ad-Dīn sailed with a much enlarged Ottoman fleet to Otranto and laid waste the adjacent lands. The king of France had found the war expensive and unprofitable and, far from invading Milan, was even now negotiating with the emperor for a truce on the Italian front. Sulaimān

---

[1] Khair ad-Dīn had made submission to Selīm I (1512–20) in return for aid against the Christians.

declined, therefore, to run the risk of crossing the Adriatic in force. Doria was cruising in the Ionian sea, and, having no reason to fear a French attack on Genoa, might yet concentrate his warships and attempt to wrest from Khair ad-Dīn command over the strait of Otranto. In August the sultan abandoned the raid on Apulia and struck at the Venetian island of Corfu.

Sulaimān had no need to look far for grounds of accusation against Venice. The Christian corsairs who preyed on Muslim shipping in the eastern Mediterranean had long been accustomed to sell their plunder and obtain supplies in the Venetian harbours of the Adriatic and the Aegean. In Dalmatia and the Morea the Cretan, Greek and Albanian mercenaries of the Signoria were often involved in local conflict with the Ottoman begs. The tension had grown in the years since Khair ad-Dīn began to reorganize and improve the naval forces of the sultan. Now more than ever before, Venice felt the need to strengthen her squadrons in the waters near Corfu, each time that the Ottoman fleet sailed out from Istanbul. The republic acted thus from mere precaution, but there was a real danger that her captains, although warned to behave with the utmost forbearance, might fail in self-control under the strain of constant watchfulness and restraint. A serious 'incident' could well bring disaster to Venice, for she had lost much of her former influence at the Porte. Ibrāhīm Pasha, throughout his career a staunch friend of the Signoria, had been executed in 1536, and now, amongst the officials and ministers who were high in the favour of Sulaimān, no one enjoyed more prestige than Khair ad-Dīn—and he was the advocate of a ruthless offensive at sea. If trouble came, Venice would find it difficult to appease the anger of the sultan. Venetian patrols did in fact seize a number of Ottoman ships at the time of the raid on Apulia and then committed the fatal mistake of attacking a small squadron which had on board an ambassador bearing letters of complaint from Sulaimān to the Signoria.

In reprisal Ottoman troops laid waste Corfu, but withdrew in September 1537 on discovering that the main fortress could not be taken save at the cost of a prolonged siege. Venice, realizing that all hope of peace was now dead, welcomed the prospect of an alliance with the pope and the emperor. Articles of agreement were signed in the spring of 1538, yet it was not until the autumn that the naval forces of the league at last assembled for a joint campaign against the Ottomans. The decisive moment of the war came on 28 September when Khair ad-Dīn defeated the Christians off Prevesa in the Gulf of Arta, a success due in no small measure to the conduct of Doria, who was resolved to maintain his fleet intact and therefore left the brunt of the fighting to the Venetian and papal commanders.[1] The battle was in itself only a minor affair, the allies losing but few of their ships. None the less, it marked a more ominous phase of the conflict for

[1] For a different interpretation of Doria's action, cf. *ibid.* p. 507.

naval supremacy: the Ottomans had met and repulsed the combined strength of the two fleets alone capable of thwarting their ambition to win control of the Mediterranean. From this time forward until Lepanto in 1571 the initiative at sea was to rest largely with the sultan.

Venice obtained no real advantage from her league with the emperor. Indeed, the sole achievement of the allied fleet was to take Castelnuovo on the Dalmatian coast in October 1538, but even this modest gain was soon erased, for Khair ad-Dīn recovered the fortress in August of the following year. The republic viewed the alliance as a means of protecting her dominions in the Adriatic and the Levant, whereas Charles V, concerned above all with the defence of the western Mediterranean against the raids of the Algerian corsairs, regarded it as no more than a limited commitment and would not risk the destruction of his naval forces for the benefit of the Signoria. Venice, despairing of effective aid from the emperor, now sought to end the ruinous conflict. Her need of peace was the more urgent in that she drew from the Ottoman lands indispensable supplies of grain, a traffic which the war had so restricted that in 1539 she was suffering from a grave dearth of corn and found it difficult to feed her citizens. A truce arranged in this same year led, after long discussion, to the settlement of October 1540. Venice paid a high price for the renewed favour of the sultan, ceding her last strongholds in the Morea (Napoli di Romania and Monemvasia) together with the islands which she had hitherto controlled in the Aegean Sea.

Meanwhile, Sulaimān had begun a naval offensive against yet another foe, the Portuguese, who, in the distant waters of the Indian Ocean, were attempting to sever the trade routes along which the spices of the East flowed to Syria and Egypt, there to pass into the hands of merchants from the great commercial centres on the northern shore of the Mediterranean. The Portuguese conquered Goa in 1509, thus securing in western India an admirable base from which their fleet could dominate the sea-lanes leading towards Arabia. Sokotra, guarding the approach to the Bab al-Mandab, had been taken in 1507. Thereafter, although never successful in their efforts to capture Aden, the Portuguese were able to penetrate deep into the Red Sea—indeed, in 1541, Estevão da Gama carried out a daring raid even as far as Suez. An alliance was also sought with Christian Abyssinia which had long been in conflict with the Muslim amirs of the Sudan. In the Persian Gulf, too, the Portuguese were no less active, Ormuz (occupied in 1515), Maskat and Bahrain being the chief harbours under their control.

The Mamluk sultan, Kānsūh al-Ghaurī, anxious to retain the large revenue that he derived from the transit trade, sent to western India a small fleet which overcame a Portuguese squadron off Chaul in 1508, but was itself defeated at Diu in the next year. Despite this reverse, al-Ghaurī, with the aid of timber, guns and naval stores obtained from the

Porte, built new ships at Suez and in 1515–16 tried to gain effective command of the coastal towns in the Yemen, a campaign brought to a premature end when Selīm I conquered Syria and Egypt (1516–17), although local warfare continued on land between the Mamluk troops disembarked from the fleet and the Arab chieftains of the region.

The Ottomans now had a direct interest in the defence of the Red Sea, yet were for a long time so preoccupied with Balkan affairs as to give little heed to the danger from the Portuguese. The grand vizier, Ibrāhīm Pasha, during his visit to Cairo, reorganized the naval administration at Suez, with the result that the old Mamluk fleet sailed out in 1525 to exact from the Yemen a more than nominal obedience to the Ottoman sultan. The venture led to no great success. Not until after the conquest of Iraq, an event which indicated that to the conflict in the Red Sea there would soon be added war between the Ottomans and the Portuguese in the Persian Gulf, did the sultan at last decide to begin a vigorous counter-offensive.

The governor of Egypt, Sulaimān Pasha, was ordered to build a new fleet at Suez, a task which he began in 1537 and, impressing into his service Venetian sailors whom he found at Alexandria, completed in the spring of the next year. In August 1538 he captured Aden and in September, having crossed the sea to India, joined the forces of Gujarat in their attempt to seize the fortress that Nuño da Cunha had erected at Diu in 1535–6. The pasha, now far from his base, had not the means to undertake a prolonged siege, and the Christians at Diu held out in a stubborn defence. On 6 November Sulaimān Pasha abandoned the enterprise and withdrew to the Yemen, organised there a new Ottoman régime, of which the main centres were Aden and Zabid, and then returned to Egypt.

At the end of 1538 the Portuguese were still in control of the trade routes to Arabia and the neighbouring lands. The initial effect of their blockade had been severe, for Venetian merchants often found that almost no spices were for sale in the markets of the Levant. Indeed, the Signoria was compelled at times to obtain cargoes of pepper and other eastern commodities from Lisbon. And yet the old traffic, although disrupted and much reduced in volume, had continued despite all adversities. The Portuguese were able to restrict but not obliterate the Muslim commercial interests so long established on the coasts of Malabar and Gujarat. Their squadrons could enter yet had failed to win command of the Red Sea and might soon be confronted with a strong challenge to their domination in the Persian Gulf. If the sultan chose to persevere in a more active resistance to the Portuguese, the trade to Basra and Suez would no doubt regain much of its past splendour.[1]

The peace with Austria did not end local hostilities on the Danube frontier. The border warriors of Bosnia, Semendria and the adjacent

---

[1] For these Portuguese activities, cf. also *ibid.* pp. 596 f., 599 f., 604.

regions were *ghāzīs*, soldiers devoted to the *jihād*. To them the *ghazā* or razzia into the non-Muslim lands—the Dār al-Harb, that is the Abode of War—was an obligation of their faith as well as a means of material benefit in the form of plunder and of captives who could be sold as slaves. The Hungarian and Croat marcher lords in the service of Austria had, too, a code of behaviour not unlike that of the *ghāzīs* and fought no less in conscious defence of Christendom than in the desire to safeguard the territories under their immediate control. No decree from Istanbul, no edict from Vienna, could have halted the unceasing strife in the border zones where the razzia constituted, as it were, an entire mode of life with its own peculiar patterns of conduct and belief.

Along the Drava Ottoman raids became so troublesome that in 1537 a force of about 24,000 men—German and Bohemian troops, levies from Carniola, Styria and Carinthia—advanced southward against the fortress of Eszék. The frontier begs hemmed the imperialists into their laager near Valpó, cut them off from all supplies of food and fodder, and slew or stole most of the animals which had drawn their carts and guns. It was now late November. The Christians began to retreat, moving between lines of waggons and light field-pieces chained together. Snow-storms hindered the march and at last the long columns broke under the pressure of a fierce pursuit, the men of Carinthia, with the German and Bohemian regiments, being almost annihilated in a desperate battle fought on 2 December.

There was conflict, too, on the lower Danube. Moldavia retained, even at this time, a certain degree of independence in relation to the Porte, for the sultan, in 1529, had confirmed to the nobles the right of naming their own prince, subject to Ottoman approval of the candidate thus elected. The *voivode* of the moment, Peter Rareş, was suspected of intrigue with Vienna. His eviction, therefore, was considered at Istanbul to be desirable and indeed urgent. In September 1538 Sulaimān occupied Suceava, then the capital of Moldavia, raised a new *voivode* to the throne and annexed southern Bessarabia, henceforth to be a *sanjak* the revenues of which would maintain the Ottoman fortresses of Akkerman and Kilia. The sultan had reason to be well satisfied with this achievement. Moldavia would in future come under more effective restraint, and the land-route from the Crimea to the Danube, which the Tatar horsemen of the Krim Khan followed when summoned to the Hungarian wars, would be much safer than before.

It was now five years since peace had been made between the sultan and the Archduke Ferdinand. In the meantime, despite frequent missions from Vienna to Istanbul, no method had been found of reconciling the rival claims of Zápolyai and the archduke to the Hungarian Crown. Sulaimān defined his own attitude in the clearest terms when he told the Austrian ambassador, Schepper, in 1534:

...this realm belongs to me and I have set therein my servant....I have given him this kingdom, I can take it back from him, if I wish, for mine is the right to dispose of it and of all its inhabitants, who are my subjects. Let Ferdinand, therefore, attempt nothing against it...What Janos Kral[1] does there, he does in my name....

In 1538 Zápolyai made a compact with the archduke: each was to have the title of king and each to retain what he then held of the Hungarian realm, but on the death of Zápolyai (at this time unmarried and childless) his lands would pass to Ferdinand, with the proviso that due recompense be assigned to his queen and her issue if he should ever take a wife. To be effective, the compromise required the approval of Sulaimān—and his consent had not been asked. Moreover, a strong faction amongst the Hungarian nobles, with Martinuzzi, the bishop of Grosswardein, at their head, viewed with disfavour the prospect of Austrian rule. In 1539 Zápolyai married Isabella of Poland. His death in July next year, just after his queen had given birth to a son, led at once to a crisis of the first magnitude.

Martinuzzi, knowing that Ferdinand would seek to enforce the compact of 1538 and himself confronted with dangerous rivals at home, appealed to the sultan for immediate aid. Sulaimān realised that, in regard to the Hungarian problem, no return was possible to the solution of indirect control. The kingdom, torn by bitter feuds, could not be left to the nominal rule of Isabella and her infant child, John Sigismund, nor could a substitute be found for the young prince, the sole claimant around whom the 'native' faction might be expected to gather in defiance of Ferdinand. A new approach was needed, strong enough to curb the designs of the archduke. The sultan must have weighed in his mind the harsh lesson, learned before Vienna and Güns, of the difficulties involved in protracted warfare on the remote Danube. None the less, his final choice was one of permanent conquest. War, indeed, had become unavoidable, for in the meantime imperial troops were marching towards Buda. Sulaimān ordered the beglerbeg of Rumeli to reinforce its garrison and, in his furious anger, stormed at the ambassador who had arrived from Vienna: 'Have you...told your lord...that the kingdom of Hungary is mine? Why does he send an army into my kingdom? What is your purpose here and where is your honour? Your king wants only to deceive me...it is winter now, but summer will come again.'

In August 1541 the sultan encamped at Buda, the begs of Bosnia and the Danube, together with the partisans of Isabella, having earlier cut to pieces the Christian troops opposed to them. Of the ambassadors now sent to him from Ferdinand, Sulaimān demanded that their master return all the fortresses taken since the death of Zápolyai. The archduke was also to give tribute to the Porte for the Hungarian lands under his control before that event. John Sigismund and his mother were escorted to

[1] 'King John', i.e. John Zápolyai.

Lippa, there to rule over Transylvania as vassals of the sultan. Buda itself would be the centre of a new Ottoman beglerbeglik on the Danube. The next campaign was organised with minute care. In the summer of 1543 Sulaimān marched northward from Belgrade with an army of unexampled power and splendour. Long camel trains carried food and munitions, the river flotilla bore the siege guns and also large supplies of grain and other stores, the janissaries and the mounted regiments of the household, the corps of engineers and the artillery had been mobilised in full strength. The fall of Valpó, Siklos and Pécs to the beglerbeg of Rumeli cleared the road to Buda. Gran, the sultan's main objective, yielded on 10 August; Stuhlweissenburg was stormed on 4 September. Now that he had won a firm basis for Ottoman rule on the Danube, Sulaimān returned to Istanbul. The campaign of 1544 was entrusted to the frontier begs. Mehemmed Pasha, the commander at Buda, took Nógrád, Hatvan and also Visegrád, a strong fortress which hindered the movement of the river fleet to and from Gran. Meanwhile, the Bosnians captured Velika in Slavonia, raided into the region of Varaždin and, at Lonska, routed the levies of Styria, Carinthia and Croatia. The Archduke Ferdinand, seeing no hope of effective aid either from the German princes or from his brother, sought and obtained a truce in 1545. Sulaimān was not unwilling to end the war, his attention being now drawn towards the Persian frontier. After long debate, articles of peace, valid for five years, were signed in June 1547. Ferdinand, for the lands still under his direct control—the far northern and western areas of the kingdom—agreed to send annually to the Porte the sum of 30,000 Hungarian ducats.

There had been no serious conflict with Persia since 1536. None the less, local hostilities flared out from time to time in the border regions; the sultan and the shah still vied with each other for the uncertain allegiance of the chieftains, Muslim as well as Christian, of Armenia and the Caucasus. The flight to Istanbul of Elkāss Mīrzā, a brother of Shah Tahmasp, gave Sulaimān a favourable prospect of strengthening the eastern frontier. In the summer of 1548 he marched to Tabriz but found that the shah had chosen once more to abandon it, rather than fight a decisive battle. The sultan now withdrew westward to besiege the great fortress of Van which he had taken in 1534 and then lost to the Persians in the following year. After a brief resistance Van surrendered on 25 August and, with the adjacent lands, became the nucleus of an Ottoman frontier *vilayet*. Having wintered at Aleppo, Sulaimān moved to Erzerum and in September 1549 sent the Vizier Ahmed Pasha against the Georgians of Akhaltzikhé who, with the Safawid begs, had been raiding in the border zones between Kars, Oltu and Artvin. The vizier, in the course of a razzia which lasted for six weeks, brought the district around Tortum under more effective Ottoman control. In the meantime, Elkāss Mīrzā, engaged in a vain attempt to foment revolt inside Persia, had fallen into the hands of the shah. Being thus denied all hope that Tahmasp might be overthrown, the sultan returned to Istanbul, arriving there on 21 December.

The shah was now free to recover, if he could, the territories which had just been taken from him. In 1551 Safawid horsemen laid waste the region of Akhlat and 'Adiljevaz on the northern shore of Lake Van and also defeated the troops of Iskender Pasha, the beglerbeg of Erzerum. Sulaimān ordered the grand vizier, Rustem Pasha, and Mehemmed Sokollu, the beglerbeg of Rumeli, to recover the ground lost in Armenia. The campaign, planned to begin in 1552, was deferred until 1554, the sultan being confronted meanwhile with a grave crisis in the relations between himself and his son Mustafā. When at last the Ottomans did move against Persia, Sulaimān, and not the grand vizier, was in command. He set out from Aleppo in April 1554 and marched through Diyarbekir and Erzerum to Kars. The Persian border defences, especially at Erivan and Nakhjivan, were now subjected to a ruthless destruction and the rich lands of the Karabagh behind them devastated with fire and sword. If he could not destroy the army of the shah—withdrawn, as in former years, far ahead and to the flank of the Ottoman advance—Sulaimān meant at least to wreck the forward zones which had long been the main point of departure for Persian raids into Asia Minor. With his aim largely achieved, the sultan retired to Erzerum and there, in September, agreed to a truce with the shah. A formal peace, the first to be made between the Ottomans and the Safawids, was signed at Amasia in May 1555. Sulaimān abandoned all claim to Tabriz, Erivan and Nakhjivan, but retained Iraq, together with most of Kurdistan and western Armenia.

The conflict with Persia had been fought in a region so remote from Istanbul that, as a rule, it was June before the sultan could enter the territories of the shah. Problems of transport were hard to overcome, for, with Safawid horsemen harassing the Ottoman columns in the mountainous terrain of Armenia and Azerbaijan, the loss of camels and other beasts of burden tended to be severe. Each campaign, in terms of actual warfare, had to be carried out and finished within three to four months, a sudden onset of the long, harsh winter and the rigour of a snow-bound retreat being of all dangers the most to be feared. The shah, remembering the lesson of Tchaldiran, avoided all risk of a great battle, swept the mountain valleys bare of food and fodder, then withdrew, leaving his frontier begs to watch and hinder the Ottoman advance. To these tactics of evasion and the irremediable difficulties of remoteness, terrain and climate there was indeed no simple and effective answer. The victories of Sulaimān had brought the Ottomans to the extreme limit of valid and enduring conquest in the east. A war to annex Georgia, Persian Armenia and Azerbaijan would be certain to involve the state in a vast and onerous expenditure of men and material. Success might be even more harmful than defeat—for numerous forts and garrisons would be needed to hold back the Safawids and, at the same time, control the Turcoman tribes and the Christian peoples of the Caucasus. The campaigns of Sulaimān had made the issue clear: to rest content or to go forward? The hour could not be far off when a fateful decision would be taken at Istanbul.

Two years after his return from Persia in 1549 the sultan found himself once more at war with Austria. Martinuzzi, the bishop of Grosswardein, had long been the real master of Transylvania, despite the continued efforts of Queen Isabella and her partisans to end his domination. Aware that he himself was held in no great esteem at the Ottoman court—in 1548 Sulaimān had warned him not to disregard the interests of Isabella and her son—he began to intrigue with Ferdinand of Vienna. In 1551 he forced the queen to surrender Transylvania to the archduke and accept in exchange certain territories in Silesia. Ferdinand now sent Spanish and Italian soldiers, under the command of Giam-Battista Castaldo, to assume control of the main fortresses. The raid which Mehemmed Sokollu carried out against Lippa and Temesvár in the autumn of this same year convinced Martinuzzi that Sulaimān would unleash a massive campaign against the imperialists, as soon as the winter had gone. He sought therefore to act as mediator between the sultan and the archduke, hoping thus to maintain his own power in Transylvania, whatever the ultimate course of events might be. His conduct led the imperialists to believe that he was a traitor to their cause. Castaldo, armed with permission from Vienna to follow his own judgment, made a fatal error when, on 18 December 1551, he brought about the murder of Martinuzzi. By this deed Ferdinand lost all prospect of winning the Transylvanians to his side.

The war went badly for the archduke in 1552. At Szegedin 'Alī Pasha, the beglerbeg of Buda, routed a force composed of Spanish and Hungarian troops, took Veszprém in April and at Fülek, in August, won a second battle against the imperialists. Mehemmed Sokollu and the vizier Ahmed Pasha conquered Temesvár in south-west Transylvania (henceforth to remain under direct Ottoman rule) and then swept northward along the river Theiss to attack the fortress of Erlau. The Christian garrison fought, however, with such desperate courage that in October the Ottomans abandoned the siege. Although the war lasted until 1562, it led to no further change of real importance in the Hungarian scene, for neither the archduke nor the sultan could afford to launch a sustained offensive; the one because he lacked the means to do so, and the other because he was soon involved in a new campaign against Persia and in a prolonged and dangerous conflict over the succession to the Ottoman throne. The archduke, knowing that he would not be able to evict John Sigismund, the son of Zápolyai, through force of arms, made use of diplomatic manoeuvre at the Porte in order to achieve his aim. Ambassadors sent from Vienna to Istanbul strove to draw the maximum advantage from the difficulties of the sultan and insisted that Transylvania should be ceded to their master. Sulaimān had no great desire to continue the war; yet, despite his deep concern in regard to the internal crisis, he was adamant in his refusal of this claim. When, in 1561, the sultan at last recovered his freedom of action, Ferdinand was left with no valid resource. The peace of 1562 renewed, in substance, the terms of 1547. Austria paid tribute to the Porte, and to the same amount as before—30,000 ducats. Transylvania was still a vassal state under Ottoman control.

The campaigns of 1541–62 had brought about the emergence of three distinct Hungaries: Austrian, in the extreme north and west, Transylvanian, east of the Theiss, and, between them, the territories which the sultan had conquered along the middle Danube. The Ottomans did not attempt to 'colonize' their new province *en masse* but created 'islands' of effective occupation in the neighbourhood of great fortified towns like Belgrade and Temesvár, Buda, Gran and Stuhlweissenburg, the begs and their *sipāhīs* moving in armed columns from fortress to fortress and living in fact as a garrison in an alien land. The imperialists, too, evolved a military régime centred around their own strongholds, for instance, Kanizsa, Raab, Komorn and Erlau. Moreover, on the one side as on the other, minor forts, of the type known as 'palanka' (constructed from timber and earth and enclosed in wooden palisades), were raised to guard the main routes and river crossings. In the course of time, therefore, the fluid frontier zone where Christian marcher lord and Muslim beg waged unceasing guerrilla warfare tended to harden on more or less stable lines. The Archduke Ferdinand, although he lacked the means to fight a major campaign of reconquest, could and did find the resources to erect a formidable barrier against the Ottomans. Throughout his reign he devoted much care to the rebuilding and improvement of the Hungarian fortresses in his possession and often entrusted them to Italian, Walloon, Spanish and German troops, that is, to professional soldiers expert in the most advanced military techniques of the age. This effort to organise an elaborate defence in depth was far from complete when Ferdinand died in 1564, yet its effect was becoming apparent long before this date. The Ottomans, committed to the assault against a strong defensive armature and a foe resolved not to run the risk of a great field battle, had to conduct a war of sieges, laborious and wasteful in men and material—a war, in short, which could not fail to heighten the basic difficulties confronting them, of time, remoteness and terrain, of transport and logistics. The years of rapid conquest would soon be gone; victories now cost more and brought less reward than in the past. As in Armenia, so too on the Danube, the Ottomans had almost attained the farthest limit of valid and justifiable expansion.

It was the Ottoman custom that a sultan, on ascending the throne, should kill his brothers and their male children in order to dispel the danger of civil war. Princes of the blood lived, therefore, under a dire constraint, the more compulsive and intense as their father grew old, to prepare for the critical hour which would mark the commencement of a new reign. Of the sons still left to Sulaimān in 1552[1] the eldest was Mustafā, born of Gulbahār, a prince well aware that in Khurrem, the consort whom the sultan cherished with an abiding love, he had an implacable foe determined to achieve his ruin and thus win the throne for one of her own children. Khurrem had drawn to her side the astute Rustem Pasha who received the hand of her daughter, the princess Mihr-u-māh, and in 1544 became grand vizier, an office which he was to hold, save for one brief interval, until his death in 1561. The pasha strove to form and maintain a faction hostile to Mustafā, raising to power men who were dependent on himself.[2]

In their youth the sons of a sultan went out from Istanbul to administer provinces in Asia Minor, each of them having a small court, with officials and tutors to instruct him in a practical knowledge of how the empire was ruled. At this time Mustafā held the *sanjak* of Amasia. To counter the intrigues of Khurrem and the grand vizier, he had long sought to gain the trust of his personal entourage and to acquire favour with the Turcoman tribes, with the *sipāhīs* or 'feudal' horsemen under his control and also with the janissaries and the great dignitaries of the Porte. His endeavours were crowned with notable success, for in 1552, when Rustem Pasha came to Anatolia as *serdār* (general-in-chief) of the new offensive against Persia, there arose among the soldiers an ominous murmur that Sulaimān had grown too old for service in the field and that it would be better to set a young and vigorous sultan on the throne. Sulaimān had no choice but to assume command of the troops destined for the Persian campaign. He left Istanbul at the end of August 1553, having summoned his eldest son, with the *sipāhīs* of Amasia, to join him during the outward march. In October, near Eregli in Karaman, Mustafā appeared before his father and was at once executed.

It would seem that the sultan had good reason to act in this drastic manner. There existed a definite and increasing tension between the *sipāhīs* or 'feudal' class within the empire, and the *kullar*, the 'men of the sultan', that is, the janissaries, the mounted regiments of the imperial household and the numerous personnel educated in the palace schools. The *sipāhīs*, Muslim born and in general of Turkish descent, formed the main weight of the armed forces, yet had no access to power and privilege through the higher ranks of the provincial administration. The *kullar*, recruited from captives of war and from the *devshirme* or child-

---

[1] The sultan was now past the prime of life, for he had been born in November 1494 or, according to other sources, in April 1495.

[2] Sinān Pasha, the brother of Rustem held the office of *kapudan*, i.e., high admiral, in the years 1550–54. The grand vizier knew that, if the fleet were in safe hands, it would be difficult for Mustafā to cross the straits to Istanbul.

tribute levied in the Balkans, were converts to Islām, a *corps d'élite* trained to wield an almost exclusive control over affairs of state and to fill the great commands and appointments in the provincial as well as in the central régime. Now, in the reign of Sulaimān, social and economic stresses began to affect the status and attitude of the feudal class, rendering more burdensome the strain of frequent and remote campaigns and making the *sipāhīs* more aware and envious of the superior role accorded to the *kullar*. Distress in the rural areas also gave rise to the so-called *levends*, men uprooted from the soil, who had recourse at times to brigandage, often with the connivance of the feudal warriors, and welcomed a prospect of service in a cause as desperate as their own. Mustafā became, as it were, the focus and symbol of this unrest. To spare him meant in effect to run the risk, not of a mere revolt in Anatolia, but of a formidable rebellion founded on grave discontent and, still worse, fought with the aid of the *sipāhīs*, that is of soldiers expert in the art of war. How real the danger had been was made clear in the camp at Eregli, for among the troops assembled there the death of Mustafā evoked a reaction so tense that Sulaimān deemed it wise to dismiss the grand vizier Rustem Pasha, reputed to be the prime author of the tragic deed.

A bitter conflict was now to be waged between Selīm and Bāyazīd, the sons of Khurrem. The portents of a further crisis became visible in 1555, when Ahmed, the grand vizier, lost his life as a result of court intrigue designed to discredit him and so bring about the recall of Rustem Pasha. A brief revolt, also in this year, in the name of a 'false' Mustafā, was symptomatic of continuing disaffection within the empire. No irreparable breach occurred between Selīm and Bāyazīd as long as their mother remained alive. Khurrem, with the aid of Rustem, controlled among the dignitaries of the Porte a faction able to exert a strong and perhaps decisive influence on the course of affairs. Her ultimate purpose is still a subject for conjecture rather than categorical statement. Western observers at Istanbul inclined, however, to the belief that she favoured Bāyazīd.

The death of Khurrem in April 1558 hastened the onset of civil war. Selīm and Bāyazīd, profiting from the unrest in Anatolia, recruited armies of their own among the Turcomans, the *levends* and the *sipāhīs*. Aid was indeed forthcoming, yet only at a price fraught with grave consequence to the Ottoman régime and, in itself, indicative of the resentment which the 'feudal' class and its allies felt for the 'men of the sultan': the princes had to confer on large numbers of their troops the status of janissaries, thus promising them entry into the privileged ranks of the *kullar*. The storm broke in the autumn of 1558. Bāyazīd, no less than Selīm, had long striven to obtain from the sultan a *sanjak* close to Istanbul. A geographical advantage might well decide the conflict, for, if Sulaimān should die, the throne would no doubt go to the son who first arrived at the Porte and there seized the *khazīne* or state treasury. The sultan now transferred Bāyazīd from Kutahya to the more remote Amasia, Selīm being moved at the same time from Manissa to the more distant Konya in Karaman. Bāyazīd, fearing that compliance would mean the ruin of his cause, rose in overt rebellion and thus left Sulaimān no choice but to intervene in favour of Selīm. Defeated in battle near Konya in the summer of 1559, Bāyazīd withdrew to Amasia and then, despairing of success, fled into Persia.

The sultan assembled troops along the eastern frontier and sought to induce the Uzbeg khan of Transoxania and the chieftains of the Caucasus to prepare for war against the Safawids. He was, however, loath to begin yet another Persian campaign. The shah, too, although determined to profit from his good fortune, had little desire to become involved in a new and dangerous conflict with the Ottomans. He agreed, therefore, after two years of diplomatic manœuvre, to surrender the ill-fated prince in return for a large financial reward. Bāyazīd was executed in September 1561. The long crisis had come to an end. There is no means of knowing how much of private anguish it had inflicted on the old sultan, but a glimpse of the truth can perhaps be discerned in the tragic words which the Venetian Donini ascribed to him: that he was glad to see the Muslims freed from the miseries of civil war between his children and to feel that he himself could live out the rest of his life in peace and not die in despair.[1]

Meanwhile, since the campaign of Diu in 1538, there had been spasmodic warfare against the Portuguese along the shores of Arabia and in the Persian Gulf. The Ottomans, having brought Basra under their direct control for the first time in 1546, established there a small fleet and an arsenal. Pīrī Re'īs, sailing from Suez with a large squadron in 1551, raided Maskat and Ormuz, made for Basra and then returned to Egypt, leaving most of his command to be blockaded in the Shatt al-'Arab. A new admiral, Murād Beg, tried in vain to break out of the Gulf in 1552. Sīdī 'Alī Re'īs, a seaman who had fought at Prevesa under the great Khair ad-Dīn, left Basra in 1554, lost some of his vessels in action with the Portuguese and, after suffering severe damage in a storm off the coast of Makran, found refuge at Surat in western India where the remnant of his fleet was disbanded. On the African shore of the Red Sea the Ottomans had long held Sawakin and now, as a further safeguard against the danger of an effective alliance between the Christians of Abyssinia and the Portuguese, occupied Masawwa' in 1557. The war at sea continued, although on a minor scale, far into the reign of Murād III (1574–95) when

---

[1] Cf. the Relazione of Marcantonio Donini (1562) in Alberi, *Relazioni degli Ambasciatori Veneti*, 3rd Series (Florence, 1840), vol. III, pp. 178–9: '...dicesi comunemente che...al cielo disse queste o altre simili parole, cioè: Sia laudato Iddio, che sì come ho sommamente desiderato di vivere tanto tempo che io avessi potuto vedere li musulmani liberi dalla tirannide che loro soprastava senza che venissero all'armi tra di loro, così mi sia felicemente ora succeduto, che da qui innanzi mi parrà di vivere vita veramente beata; che s'altrimenti mi fosse occorso, sarei vissuto e morto disperatissimo....'

a certain 'Alī Beg, with a squadron based on the Yemen, carried out raids to Maskat in the 'Uman and to Malindi and Mombasa on the coast of Africa.

The effort to maintain, in the Red Sea and in the Persian Gulf, a fleet able to resist the Portuguese demanded of the Ottomans a vast expenditure in men and material. Stores and equipment, guns and timber had to be brought overland to Suez or else down the rivers of Iraq to Basra. Construction methods valid in the Mediterranean would not serve in Arabian waters. Technicians and crews must therefore be found with the skill needed to build and man ships of an appropriate type. And yet, despite these and such other difficulties as the lack of good harbours in Arabia, the Ottomans achieved no small measure of success. It was clear, even before Sulaimān's death, that the Portuguese had not the strength to win absolute command of the Indian Ocean. As the Muslim counter-offensive gathered weight and momentum, the ancient traffic through the Red Sea and the Persian Gulf began to revive. A rich commerce flowed once more to Egypt, Alexandria receiving in the years around 1564 cargoes of pepper equal and perhaps superior in volume to those which were then arriving at Lisbon. Aleppo, the terminus for caravans from Iraq and Persia, was now to flourish as one of the great spice and silk markets of the Levant. A precarious equilibrium had been established between the old traffic and the new. The balance would incline at last irremediably in favour of the sea route around Africa, but only when maritime nations far stronger than the Portuguese—the Dutch and the English—broke into the waters of the Indian Ocean and won for themselves a dominant share of the eastern trade.

In the Mediterranean, too, there had been prolonged warfare since the battle of Prevesa in 1538. Charles V, knowing that he would soon be in conflict once more with France, struck hard at Algiers in October 1541, hoping thus to forestall the danger of renewed co-operation between the corsairs and the French naval forces. A splendid armada sailed from the Balearics to the African coast and there, in a sudden storm, suffered damage so severe that the campaign was abandoned. Khair ad-Dīn took his revenge in 1543 when he burnt Reggio in Calabria and, uniting with a squadron under the Duc d'Enghien, captured the town, though not the citadel, of Nice. The Ottoman fleet, to the great disgust of Christendom, wintered at Toulon, the port, with most of its people removed to make room for the Muslims, becoming, as it were, a second Istanbul. There now ensued a period of relative calm, for the emperor signed a peace with France in 1544 and was moreover included in the armistice that Sulaimān granted to Austria in 1547. Meanwhile, Khair ad-Dīn had died in the summer of 1546, leaving behind him a number of captains well qualified to continue his work, among them the famous Dragut (Torghūd Re'īs) who conquered Tripoli in North Africa from the Knights of St John in

1551 and thereafter so harried the western Mediterranean that Philip II of Spain resolved at last to crush him. A powerful force sent against Tripoli, where Torghūd now ruled in the name of the sultan, met, however, with disaster, the Ottoman fleet, commanded by Piyāle Pasha, surprising and routing the Christians at the island of Djerba in May 1560. This brilliant success encouraged Sulaimān to attempt the conquest of Malta. The *kapudan* Piyāle left Istanbul with a splendid fleet on 1 April 1565, the corsair squadrons of Algiers and Tripoli being also summoned to the campaign. Most bitter fighting marked the course of the siege, but the Knights of St John held out with desperate valour until at last, in September, strong reinforcements came to their aid and so compelled the Ottomans to withdraw.

The Christian cause triumphed at Malta and again at the battle of Lepanto in 1571, five years after the death of Sulaimān, yet these celebrated victories led to no enduring advantage. A far more decisive campaign was waged in 1574, when the Ottomans conquered Tunis and so resolved in their own favour a vital issue of the sea war—whether North Africa would be saved or lost to Muslim rule. Algiers, Tripoli and Tunis now owed allegiance to the Porte and stood, moreover, on the threshold of a golden era as the three great corsair states of the Mediterranean. The threat of Christian domination had in fact been averted in North Africa for some two and a half centuries.

The agreement of 1562 with Austria became null and void on the death of the Emperor Ferdinand in 1564. Sulaimān, although willing to renew the peace, was angered at the outbreak of hostilities between the Emperor Maximilian II and John Sigismund of Transylvania. The refusal of his demand that the imperialists restore certain towns belonging to the *voivode* made war inevitable. The sultan marched once more to Belgrade in the summer of 1566. It was to be his thirteenth and last campaign. A powerful column under the Vizier Pertev Pasha had been sent off in advance to capture Gyula on the river Körös in western Transylvania. A much stronger force, with Sulaimān himself in command, moved towards Szigetvár. Of these fortresses the first yielded, and the second was stormed, at the beginning of September—but just before the fall of Szigetvár death had come to the old sultan.

The reign of Sulaimān owed its splendour to far more than the great campaigns of conquest. Administrators and statesmen of exceptional skill, like the grand viziers Ibrāhīm, Rustem and Mehemmed Sokollu, flourished at this time. Among the *'ulemā*—the theologians and jurisconsults trained in the *Sharī'a* or Sacred Law of Islām—none were more illustrious than Kemālpasha-zāde and Abu Su'ūd. Bākī, the prince of poets, and Sinān, a famous architect, gave lustre to an age resplendent with the rich unfolding of all that is most typical in Ottoman culture and civilisation. The sultan devoted large revenues to frontier defence, as in the repair of fortresses at Rhodes, Belgrade, Buda and Temesvár, and to the building of mosques, bridges, aqueducts and other public utilities, for instance at Mecca, Baghdad, Damascus, Konya and Kaffa. Above all, he strove to embellish his capital on the Golden Horn and, in pursuit of this aim, did much to complete the enormous task, begun by Mehemmed II, of transforming Constantinople, impoverished and depopulated during the last years of Byzantine rule, into Ottoman Istanbul, the proud centre of a vast empire.

To his people Sulaimān became known as Kānūnī, the law-maker. He could not alter or violate the *Shari'a*, a code embracing wide areas of human thought and conduct which in the Christian world belong to the realm of secular and not of religious affairs. The edicts bearing his name, although to the western mind somewhat narrow in range and in character more interpretative than original, represent none the less a long effort to improve and adapt to the needs of a new age the complex structure of the Ottoman state. Men of his own time emphasized his zeal for justice and the Venetian Navagero paid high tribute indeed when he wrote that Sulaimān, provided he were well informed, did wrong to no one.

Among those who saw the sultan in all his power and splendour not a few have left on record their abiding impression of his personal qualities and character. Navagero discerned in his face a 'marvellous grandeur'. To Andrea Dandolo he was a monarch wise and just, yet ruthless beyond measure when danger threatened his empire or himself. Busbecq, describing how the sultan went to the mosque soon after the return of the Ottoman fleet from its brilliant success at Djerba, read in his countenance no more than a stern and impenetrable reserve, 'so self-contained was the heart of that grand old man, so schooled to meet each change of fortune however great'. The historian confirms, refurbishes and sometimes corrodes the fame of the dead. A final verdict on the true role of Sulaimān in the triumphs and achievements of his reign must rest with future research, but there is little reason to think that he will not continue to be for us, as he was for the Christian world of his time, the Magnificent Sultan.

4

THE SUCCESSORS OF SULAIMĀN, 1566-1617

THE Ottoman empire had attained under Sulaimān the Magnificent (1520–66) the summit of its power and splendour. Now, during the period that followed his death, strains and stresses originating both within and without the empire gave rise to notable changes in the structure of the Ottoman state. The general trend of events after 1566 cannot be understood, therefore, without reference to some at least of the essential characteristics of the Ottoman régime as it was in the reign of Sultan Sulaimān.

The household of the sultan was far more than a domestic organisation designed to meet the private and personal needs of the monarch. It included also much more than the apparatus and adornments of an imperial court. The household embraced within itself the personnel of the central administration and of the great executive offices of state; of the higher ranks in the provincial administration; and also of the armed forces of the central régime—the Janissaries, the mounted regiments of the household (sometimes known as the Sipāhīs of the Porte) and the various specialist corps such as artillerists and engineers. The numerous personnel of this household had in general the status of *ghulām* (pl. *ghilmān*), a term better interpreted as 'man of the sultan' than as 'slave', since it in no wise implied, as the English word 'slave' might suggest, a position of inferiority, but was on the contrary a mark of privilege and prestige within the state. A basic principle observed in recruitment to the household was the exclusion of Muslim Turkish subjects[1] of the sultan from the ranks of the *ghilmān*. To be born non-Muslim and non-Turkish was an essential qualification for entrance into this dominant élite. There were several sources of recruitment available to the sultan: captives of war taken in the course of land or sea campaigns against the Christians; captives acquired by gift or by purchase; and, in addition, the children of the *devshirme*, the child-tribute levied at intervals from the subject Christian—and, in respect of ethnic origin, above all from the Slav and Albanian—populations of the empire. The recruits drawn from these sources, being as a rule no more than children or youths in point of age, became converts to Islam, not simply as the result of direct compulsion, but also by the pressure of their new environment, by force of example, and by the prospect of advancement in the service of the sultan. The actual road that a recruit might follow would depend, in large degree, on his possession or lack of high

---

[1] To the Muslim-born subjects of the sultan was reserved, however, exclusive control of the Muslim religious, legal and educational institutions of the empire.

intellectual and physical qualities. Of the recruits the best endowed went into the palace schools, there to be instructed in the Muslim faith and in the arts of war, statecraft and administration. After long years of training, and in the prime of their young manhood, the most gifted amongst them would be sent out as governors (*sanjak-begi*) of provinces. Some of them might rise in the course of time to the rank of governor-general (*beglerbegi*) over a number of sanjaks and then, if fortune favoured them, to the status of vizier, with a seat in the Diwān, that is, the Council of State which controlled the great affairs of the empire. The most exalted office—the grand vizierate—would now be within their reach. Few, however, amongst the recruits chosen for education in the palace schools attained to high eminence. Service in the subordinate offices of the court and of the central administration or in the mounted regiments of the household was the lot which awaited most of these more favoured recruits.

The captives of war and the *devshirme* children not selected for the palace schools underwent some years of hard physical labour on lands belonging to the state, above all in Asia Minor. These recruits—known as the '*ajemioghlanlar* ('foreign youths')—would be recalled in due course to Istanbul, a large proportion of them being now destined to enrolment in the corps of Janissaries after a rigorous training in the profession of arms. The household of the sultan also included the Sipāhīs of the Porte,[1] the mounted regiments, six in all, two of them numbering in their ranks men born Muslim, but hailing from lands outside the confines of the Ottoman empire, the other four regiments being composed of recruits drawn in general from the palace schools. Amongst the personnel of the specialist corps, the armourers, artillerists and engineers, could be found captives of war, children from the *devshirme*, and also renegades of Christian origin.

Two notable characteristics of the system must be stressed here. First, that the status of *ghulām* was not heritable, children of men who belonged to the imperial household being in general excluded from the system and absorbed into the Muslim population of the empire; and second, that the *ghilmān*, with some exceptions, received as their means of subsistence not landed estates, but fixed salaries paid to them in cash at regular intervals out of the revenues of the central régime.

The sultan had at his command, however, a warrior class far more numerous than the armed forces of the imperial household and distinct from them in status—the 'feudal' horsemen known as sipāhīs and located in most, but not all, of the provinces of the empire. These horsemen came to war at the call of the sultan and, in reward for their fulfilment of this obligation, held fiefs adequate to maintain them as efficient soldiers. A fief

[1] The term 'Sipāhīs of the Porte' is an expression of convenience used to designate the mounted regiments of the imperial household—the *spahi di paga* (paid sipāhīs) of the Italian sources, who are not to be confused with the 'feudal' horsemen, also known in general as 'sipāhīs' (on whom see below, pp. 128–30).

consisted of a nucleus called *kilij* (sword) and of further allocations of land described as *terakki* (increase). The *kilij* gave the minimum of revenue considered to be sufficient for the maintenance of the sipāhī himself, grants of *terakki* being added one at a time to the *kilij* in order to augment the total revenues of the fief as a reward for long and meritorious service. Each sipāhī had to provide his own equipment of war—arms, tents, beasts of burden and the like. Moreover, as his fief grew in value, he was obliged to bring with him on campaign, in proportion to his revenues, one or more mounted soldiers (*jebeli*) maintained and furnished with arms at his own expense.

There were, in relation to the 'feudal' horsemen known as sipāhīs, two main grades of fief: (i) the *tīmār*, yielding from between 2,000 and 3,000 to 19,999 akçes[1] per annum; and (ii) the *ziʿāmet*, ranging in value from 20,000 to 99,999 akçes per annum. The right to grant tīmārs and ziʿāmets had rested, in former times, with the beglerbegs. The central régime, in the course of time, reserved to itself, however, the assignment of all such fiefs save the lowest grades of *tīmār*, appointment to which was allowed to remain within the competence of the beglerbegs. Each sipāhī might hope, through good service, to rise from the lower to the higher grade of fief.

The sipāhī had no absolute right of possession in respect of the lands which constituted his fief—such lands belonged in law to the state. He enjoyed only the usufruct of the land, the right to receive certain defined dues, in cash and in kind, from the peasants who lived and worked on the soil. The status of sipāhī was, within limits, hereditable. A fief would be granted in normal circumstances to one of his sons—sometimes, indeed, more than one son might be given a small fief. If a sipāhī died childless or left sons not competent to perform the duties of a soldier, the *kilij* of his fief might go to the most deserving of the *jebeli* men-at-arms who had fought in the retinue of the dead sipāhī. Enrolment within the 'feudal' class was not restricted, however, to members of old-established sipāhī families and to the *jebeli* warriors associated with them: for example, the sons of some amongst the high dignitaries who belonged to the household of the sultan and held the status of *ghulām* had the right to receive a *tīmār* or a *ziʿāmet*, the size of the grant depending on the rank of the father; a Muslim volunteer, too, might be given a fief in reward for exceptional valour on the field of battle; and, not infrequently, personnel from the palace schools also passed into the 'feudal' system.

The sipāhīs in each province of the empire where the 'feudal' system was in being had their own officers chosen from amongst themselves. Of these officers the most important was the *alay begi*,[2] who, amongst other duties, mustered the sipāhīs of the province at the beginning of a

---

[1] The akçe, or asper, was a small Ottoman coin of silver. According to the rate of exchange operative in the time of Sulaimān the Magnificent 60 akçes equalled one Venetian gold ducat.

[2] *Alay* (Turkish) = an array of troops.

campaign. The rank of *alay begi* was the highest that a sipāhī could attain. Appointment to the great offices in the provincial administration—of *sanjak begi* and *beglerbegi*—was reserved to members of the privileged élite who had the status of *ghulām*. The sanjak begs and beglerbegs, in addition to the performance of the executive and administrative duties inherent in their office, also commanded the sipāhīs of their province in time of war. These high officials enjoyed the revenues of large fiefs known as *khāss* (special), which gave 100,000 akçes and more per annum. It was laid down that sanjak begs should receive not less than 200,000 and beglerbegs not less than 1,000,000 akçes a year—moreover, the longer their service the higher were the revenues assigned to them, additional lands being allocated as *terakki* to their fiefs. The minimum *khāss* granted to a *sanjak begi*, or to a *beglerbegi*, on the occasion of his first appointment to such a rank, corresponded therefore to the *kilij* of a sipāhī holding a *tīmār* or a *zi'āmet*. Each *sanjak begi* and *beglerbegi* had to furnish and bring to war *jebeli* warriors in proportion to the value of his fief—some of these great officials indeed maintained retinues much larger than was in fact demanded of them. There was, however, in relation to the fiefs called *khāss*, no right of inheritance, even to a limited degree, as in the case of the *tīmār* and the *zi'āmet*. The *khāss* fiefs pertained not to the individual, but to the office of *sanjak begi* or *beglerbegi* and thus changed hands as one incumbent succeeded another.

It will be evident that in such fields of action as war, politics and administration a preponderant measure of power and privilege in the Ottoman state rested with the *ghilmān*, the 'men of the sultan'. The 'feudal' sipāhīs, although constituting in effect a privileged aristocratic element in the life of the provinces, found themselves excluded from the highest levels of power and prestige within the state—an exclusion which, again in relation to war, politics and administration, embraced indeed the great mass of the Muslim-born subjects of the sultan.[1] A line of division so paradoxical in character might obtain a more or less general acceptance as long as all went well with the empire and the system as a whole worked to the obvious advantage of its members, whether of Muslim or of non-Muslim birth. It was to become blurred, however, and to an increasing degree obliterated, when the tide of Ottoman affairs began to take an adverse course. The years 1566–1617 saw the Ottomans confronted with new and unfavourable circumstances which brought about a profound transformation in some of the institutions of their empire. This transformation marked, in fact, the first phase in a long and slow process of decline.

There were amongst the Ottomans themselves men who sought to discover the reasons for the decline. One of the *'ulemā* (the Muslim theologians and jurists learned in the *sharī'a*, or sacred law of Islam), a

---

[1] See, however, p. 103 n. above.

Bosnian named Hasan al-Kāfī, lamented in his small treatise on the art of government, written in 1596–7, that justice was becoming ill administered in the empire, that incapable men untested in long years of service rose to the highest offices of state and that the Ottóman armies had lost much of the obedience and discipline, the courage and skill, which distinguished them in former times; the sultans had fallen into a life of ease and self-indulgence, viziers intrigued one against the other, the influence of women had become marked in the conduct of affairs; there was no regular muster-ing of the armed forces and their equipment, the soldiers often committed grave excesses against the subject populations of the empire, and failure to adopt the latest techniques of warfare had led to defeat in battle with the enemies of Islam; negligence, corruption, favouritism and greed now bade fair to ruin the Ottoman system of government. A similar diagnosis of the ills that beset the empire can be found in the famous *Risāle* or memorandum which Koçu Beg submitted to Sultan Murād IV (1623–40)— a memorandum wider in scope, however, and more elaborate than the little treatise of Hasan al-Kāfī. Some of the arguments that Koçu Beg advanced can be summarised thus: the sultans have ceased to lead their armies in war and to attend the Diwān or Council of State; favourites attain to high office over the heads of able and experienced men; intrigue and corruption, now rife amongst the viziers and great dignitaries of the central régime, have filtered down through all levels of the administration; the harem exercises, all too often, a pernicious influence on the course of affairs; ostentation and luxurious living have done much to undermine the moral fibre of the dominant class in the empire.

The criticisms of such men as Hasan al-Kāfī and Koçu Beg contain a solid element of truth. It cannot be denied that, save on rare occasions, the sultans who followed Sulaimān the Magnificent neither led their armies in time of war nor overburdened themselves with a constant attention to the great affairs of state. Their negligence facilitated beyond doubt the growth of manifold abuses. The women of the harem, for example the *Wālide Sultan* (the mother of the sultan on the throne) and the *Khāsseki Sultans* (the consorts who had borne the sultan a male child), made and unmade the fortunes of the high officials who secured or lost their favour. Princesses of the Ottoman house, married to viziers or other dignitaries of exalted rank, strove to advance the careers of their husbands and the interests of their children. The spirit of faction and intrigue, grown strong amongst the great personalities of the central régime, determined all too often the policies of the government even in matters of serious concern. Abuses like the over-frequent appointment, dismissal or transfer of high officials meant that the Ottoman administration became less efficient than it had once been. To a modern historian, however, these factors, which have so large a place in the treatises of Hasan al-Kāfī and of Koçu Beg, will stand out rather as symptoms than as fundamental causes of the Ottoman decline. Koçu Beg, it is true, examines in some detail problems of a deeper significance—the increase in the number of the Janissaries, the introduction into their ranks of Muslim-born subjects of the sultan, the growing confusion evident in the 'feudal' system and in the financial affairs of the empire—and yet these factors, too, are in some measure the overt symptoms and not the basic causes of a decline the real origins of which must be sought elsewhere.

Of all the forces that now contributed to deform and break down the 'classical' institutions of the Ottoman state, thrusting them into new and unfavourable lines of evolution, none was perhaps more important than the strain arising out of prolonged and arduous warfare. The tide of Ottoman conquest, which had been so strong for almost three centuries, came to a virtual halt in Asia and above all in Europe during the years 1566–1617. It was an event formidable in its consequences. The Ottoman state had been founded on the frontier between Islam and Byzantine Christendom; its *raison d'être* was the *jihād*, or war against the Infidel, on behalf of the Sunnī or orthodox Muslim faith. To the Ottomans, whether men of the sword or men of religion, the advancing frontier had given, over and above the material rewards of conquest, a distinctive ethos and purpose which exercised a profound influence on the evolution of their political, religious and social life. The Ottoman war machine, the administration, the systems of land tenure and taxation had been geared to the needs of an expanding state. Now, as the onward tide of warfare slowed down—a process first visible in the later years of Sulaimān the Magnificent —these institutions failed to harmonise with the new and unfamiliar stresses of a frontier that was becoming static.

The main event in the reign of Selīm II (1566–74) was the conquest of Cyprus, an island which had been under Venetian rule since 1489. It was not difficult to discover arguments in favour of a new war against Venice— for example, the friction that existed along the borders of the Venetian enclaves on the eastern shore of the Adriatic, the failure of the Signoria to deal with the so-called Uskoks (a band of corsairs operating from Segna (Senj) in Dalmatia), or the harbouring in Cyprus of Christian corsairs who infested the waters of the Levant, assailing Muslim commerce and the sea-borne traffic of Muslim pilgrims bound for Mecca. The Grand Vizier Mehemmed Sokolli strove to avert the outbreak of war, but a number of influential personalities—amongst them Piyāle Pasha, Mustafā Pasha and Uluj 'Alī Pasha—convinced the sultan that Cyprus might be won without undue trouble and expense. Selīm II had renewed in 1567 the formal state of peace existing between the Porte and the Signoria at the time of his accession to the throne. The Mufti Abū'l-Su'ūd now issued a *fetwā* (a legal judgement based on the principles of the *sharī'a*, or sacred law of Islam), declaring that it was permissible to break treaties of peace when the purpose in view was to recover control of lands which, like

Cyprus, had once been under Muslim rule. Some members of the Venetian Senate urged that Cyprus be ceded in exchange for compensation in Dalmatia and Albania and new commercial privileges in the Ottoman empire; others proposed that an attempt be made to placate the sultan and the great dignitaries at the Porte with lavish gifts; but at Venice, as at Istanbul, the war faction gained the ascendant. The Signoria trusted indeed that, in the event of an armed conflict, assistance would be forth-coming from the other Christian states and was thus emboldened in the spring of 1570 to meet a formal Ottoman demand for the cession of Cyprus with a refusal so uncompromising that it closed the door to the prospect of further negotiation.

A powerful Ottoman force, under the command of Mustafā Pasha, landed in Cyprus during the month of July 1570. Meanwhile Pope Pius V had been labouring hard to bring about an alliance between Spain and Venice. A deplorable spirit of distrust, procrastination and intrigue marked, however, the course of the negotiations. It was soon made clear that, as in the years 1537–40,[1] so now the interests of Spain, preoccupied with her ambitions in North Africa and with the defence of the western Mediterranean against the corsairs from Algiers, and of Venice, intent on preserving the remnants of her old imperium in the Levant, did not coincide. Philip II of Spain, in answer to the pleas of Pope Pius V, agreed at last to send a squadron to the aid of the Signoria, but it was not until the end of August 1570, at Suda in Crete, that the Spanish and papal contingents joined the Venetian fleet. A vigorous prosecution of the campaign was not to be achieved, however, in the face of the dissension so rife in the high command of the Christian armada. On the arrival of the news that Nicosia in Cyprus had fallen to the Ottomans on 9 September, the entire force, then not far from Castellorizo on the southern shore of Asia Minor, sailed back to Crete and thence to Italian waters, having done nothing of importance.

There now followed, during and beyond the winter of 1570–1, a series of further negotiations between Spain, the papacy and Venice. A formal league signed on 15 May 1571 envisaged an extension of the war to include operations in North Africa as well as in the eastern Mediterranean. A new Christian armada assembled at Messina in September 1571—but it was too late to save Cyprus. Famagusta, the last major Venetian stronghold in the island, surrendered to the Ottomans on 1 August 1571 after a siege of almost eleven months. The Christian armada, under the command of Don John of Austria, did achieve, however, one notable success—the virtual destruction of the Ottoman fleet at the famous battle of Lepanto fought on 7 October 1571. Although it broke the initiative that the Ottomans had held at sea since the battle of Prevesa in 1538, Lepanto must be considered as a triumph symbolic in character rather than positive in its actual consequences. The season for naval warfare in the Mediterranean

[1] See above, pp. 88–9.

was now too far advanced for the Christians to undertake an immediate exploitation of their success, all the more since at Lepanto their own vessels and crews had suffered no small damage and loss. During the winter and spring of 1571–2 the Ottomans, making a supreme and sustained effort, built and equipped a large new fleet which, in 1572 off Cerigo, Navarino and Modon and under the able guidance of Uluj 'Alī Pasha, frustrated the attempt of the Christians to win a second and this time decisive battle against their Muslim foes. The Christian armada was in fact able to achieve nothing of importance in the campaign of 1572.

Venice, dissatisfied with the outcome of a war at once expensive and unsuccessful and burdened with the loss of her trade to the Levant and of the essential supplies of grain that she was accustomed to draw from the Ottoman empire, now sought peace from the sultan and in March 1573 obtained it in return for the cession of Cyprus and the payment of a large sum in war indemnities. Spain, left to fight alone against the Ottomans, turned her attention towards North Africa. The Emperor Charles V had established a protectorate over Tunis in 1535, the harbour fortress of La Goletta becoming the main instrument of Spanish control. Uluj 'Alī Pasha had marched overland from Algiers to Tunis in the winter of 1569–70, the Muslim prince whom Spain supported there had fled for refuge to La Goletta, and the Pasha had seized and garrisoned the town. Don John of Austria, sailing from Sicily, brought Tunis once more under Spanish domination in October 1573—a brilliant success, but one destined to be of no long duration. Uluj 'Alī Pasha appeared before Tunis with a large fleet in July 1574 and after a short siege took both the town itself and the fortress of La Goletta. The Ottoman conquest of Tunis in 1574 was an event of some significance. It marked in fact the virtual end of a long conflict waged between Spaniard and Ottoman to decide whether North Africa was to come under Christian or remain under Muslim rule. Algiers, Tunis and Tripoli, dependent on the sultan and now poised on the verge of their golden age as corsair states, stood as a visible sign that the issue had been resolved in favour of the Muslims and that the Spanish *conquista* along the African shore, begun in the time of Isabella of Castile and Ferdinand of Aragon, had terminated in failure.

The war of Cyprus exacted from the Ottomans a large expenditure and no inconsiderable loss of men and munitions at Nicosia, Famagusta and Tunis. It cost them, too, the almost total destruction of their effective naval forces at Lepanto and an enormous effort thereafter to build in haste a new fleet strong enough to meet the Christian armada on equal terms. An ample reward, none the less, had fallen to the Ottomans in the acquisition of Cyprus and Tunis. The long war against Persia, extending over the years 1578–90, demanded of them, however, a far more lavish expenditure of resources—and for a success ambiguous in character and brief in duration, as the future course of events was to reveal.

The campaigns of Sulaimān the Magnificent against Persia had brought within the Ottoman empire Iraq and also, in Asia Minor, the regions around Erzerum and Lake Van.[1] A peace concluded at Amasia in 1555 made over these conquests to the Ottomans. There was now little reason for the Porte to fear a revival in Persia of the drive towards religious and political expansion in Asia Minor which had distinguished the reign of Shah Ismā'il (d. 1524), the founder of the Safawid state. And yet the old causes of tension and distrust retained much of their earlier force—the odium dividing the Ottomans, as Sunnī or orthodox Muslims, from the Persians, who adhered to the Shī'ī form of Islam; the presence in Ottoman-controlled Asia Minor of numerous elements pro-Shī'ī in belief and therefore suspect to the government of the sultan; and the endless irritation arising out of local quarrels in the ill-defined frontier zones which separated the Ottoman and the Persian territories. Moreover, with the passing of the years, the antagonism between the two states had begun to assume a more complex character. The sultan and the shah vied with each other for the allegiance of the small principalities, Christian as well as Muslim, situated in the Caucasus, the western areas of this wide region falling under Ottoman and the eastern areas under Persian influence. Ottoman statesmen sought to establish and consolidate an effective *entente* with the Uzbeg Turks of Transoxania—Muslims of the orthodox belief and avowed enemies of the Safawid régime, which had wrested from them control over the great province of Khurāsān in north-east Persia. At the same time the conviction that in the armies of the shah an apt instrument might be found to hinder the Ottoman advance against Christendom became en-grained in the political consciousness of Europe. There was from time to time an exchange of ambassadors and of diplomatic correspondence between Persia and such states as Austria, Venice and Spain, but diffi-culties of communication made it almost impossible to organise a united front against the Ottomans.

A new factor which made itself felt within the broad context of the Ottoman/Safawid antagonism was the advance of the Muscovites towards the Black Sea, the Caucasus and the Caspian Sea. Ivan IV subdued Kazan in 1552 and Astrakhan at the mouth of the Volga four years later. Musco-vite forces thrust southward as far as the river Terek, which flows a little to the north of the High Caucasus. The tsar had thus created a situation that the Porte could not ignore. Muslim merchants and Muslim pilgrims to Mecca and Medina from the lands of the north often found it difficult to pass through Safawid Persia into the Ottoman empire. Now it seemed that the routes leading to the shores of the Black Sea might also become less accessible to them. The sultan, as *Khādim al-Haramain*, or protector of the two sacred cities, Mecca and Medina—a status which gave him a vast prestige in the world of Islam—was under the obligation to defend

[1] See above, pp. 85–6, 93–5.

the religious interests of the Muslims. He had, moreover, to take into account the obvious disadvantages, political and economic, that a continuation of the Muscovite advance would bring to the Ottoman empire. Ottoman forces tried to conquer Astrakhan in 1569, but without success. Among the unrealised objectives of the campaign was the construction of a canal between the Don and the Volga. Such a canal would have given to the Ottomans a continuous water route extending from the Black Sea along the Don and thence down the Volga to the Caspian Sea. There can be little doubt that the statesmen at Istanbul had much more in mind than the reduction to Ottoman control of the lands around the lower Volga. Access to the Caspian Sea would mean direct contact with the Uzbeg khans of Transoxania and freedom to transport men, guns and munitions into the heart of the Caucasus and into northern Persia. The failure of the Astrakhan campaign, it is true, denied to the Ottomans the use of the Don and the Volga in the event of a new war against the Safawids. It did not diminish, however, their preoccupations with the strategic possibilities of other routes to the north of the Caucasus. Ottoman forces would in fact march from the Crimea across the Kuban steppe to the shore of the Caspian Sea during the course of the great conflict with Persia which began in 1578.

The campaigns of Sulaimān the Magnificent had underlined the formidable nature of the difficulties confronting the Ottomans in their wars against Persia—the long distances to be traversed, the harshness of the climate and of the terrain, the brief duration of the campaign season, the serious problems of logistics to be overcome and the high rate of loss in men, animals and supplies.[1] To the Ottoman soldier such warfare, over and above the normal risk of death, wounds and sickness, brought exposure to extremes of heat and cold (a German travelling in the empire during the years 1553–5 saw at Istanbul men who had lost their feet as a result of frost-bite contracted on the eastern front); it also meant hunger in regions laid waste by the Safawids and at times, with most of the camels, mules and horses dead, the abandonment of arms, tents and munitions. Moreover, the prospect of a rich reward in the form of plunder was small, since the forces of the shah, pursuing their usual tactics of retreat, harassment and evasion, took care to denude the towns and the land itself of all that might assist or benefit the foe. It is evident from the historical sources of this time that the eastern campaigns had little appeal for the rank and file of the Ottoman armies, and this despite the efforts of the central régime to stimulate their morale, even to the extent of procuring from the Sunnī, or orthodox, 'ulemā legal pronouncements, i.e. fetwās, which equated the Shī'ī with the Christians as enemies of the true faith, and declared it lawful therefore to sell as slaves, Shī'ī Muslims captured in war—a measure so extreme that it was fated to evoke no effective response.

---

[1] See above, p. 95.

The forces of the shah made use of 'burnt earth' tactics, avoided in general all risk of a major engagement, harassed the Ottoman columns and withdrew deep inside their own territories. It was thus almost impossible to win a rapid and decisive success against them. To seize Tabriz and then abandon it, as the Ottomans had done on several occasions, was of little avail. The statesmen at Istanbul found themselves confronted in fact with a difficult choice: to rest content with the eastern frontier as it now was or to enlarge the range and character of their objectives in the event of a new war. There was but one real alternative to the frustrating sequence of hard-fought advance and laborious retreat experienced in earlier campaigns—a grand offensive mounted and sustained at whatever cost in Ottoman resources, human and material, to achieve the outright conquest and permanent occupation of the wide lands beyond Erzerum and Lake Van.

One factor which counted for much in the ultimate decision of the Ottomans to renew the conflict was the growth of a serious crisis inside Persia during the last years of Shah Tahmāsp (1524–76). The Turcomans from Asia Minor and northern Syria who rallied to the cause of Ismā'īl, the founder of the Safawid state, had obtained in Persia the position of a privileged military aristocracy.[1] As the religious fervour which gave a dynamic force and cohesion to the Safawid movement in the time of Ismā'īl began to decline, inter-tribal feuds made their appearance amongst the Turcomans. Moreover, during the reign of Tahmāsp, the son of Ismā'īl, various Caucasian elements, from Georgia and Circassia and from Shirvān and Dāghistān, became more and more important in the affairs of the court and in the armed forces of the state, thus constituting a new and dangerous threat to the predominance of the Turcomans. After the death of Tahmāsp the tensions existing within the Turcoman tribes and between them and the Caucasian elements in the régime erupted into open and embittered violence.

It was to be a conflict fought out under the guise of dynastic quarrels, each of the two main factions, Turcoman and Caucasian, using princes of the blood as pawns in the struggle for power. An attempt of the Caucasians in alliance with one of the Turcoman tribes, the Ustājlū, to raise their own candidate to the throne ended in failure when their protégé Haidar Mīrzā, a son of Tahmāsp, was slain in May 1576. Ismā'īl, also a son of Tahmāsp, now ascended the throne as the choice of the Turcoman faction. His brief reign of less than two years witnessed the execution of almost all the male members of the Safawid house and of some of the most powerful amongst the great amirs and dignitaries of the state. Such unbridled violence, productive of increased fear and distrust, together with the suspicion, abhorrent to his Shī'ī subjects, that he was inclined to favour the Sunnī form of Islam, brought about his downfall and death in November 1577.

[1] See above, pp. 63–5, for a brief account of the formation of the Safawid state.

The spirit of intrigue and dissension remained alive throughout the reign of Muhammad Khudābanda (1577–87), a prince, who, suffering from an ailment which had left him half-blind, was little more than a tool in the hands of the Turcoman chieftains. It affected also the small principalities of the Caucasus, Christian as well as Muslim, some of which, after long years of subjection to Safawid influence, had become identified with one or the other of the factions at the court of the shah, and this to such a degree that their resistance to the Ottoman offensive begun in 1578 tended—apart from the actual fortunes of the war—to fluctuate with the course of the feuds which still beset the Safawid régime. To some of the high dignitaries at Istanbul, prominent amongst them being Mustafā Pasha and Sinān Pasha, it seemed that a most opportune moment had come to settle once and for all the long contention with Persia. Sultan Murād III (1574–95) listened to their arguments and, despite the counter-advice of the grand vizier, Mehemmed Sokolli, who feared the conse-quences of so ambitious an enterprise, resolved to attempt the permanent conquest of the broad region between the Black Sea and the Caspian Sea.

Erzerum, to which men and munitions could be brought either along the land routes through Asia Minor or else by sea as far as Trebizond, was to be the main Ottoman base during the years of the Persian war. Here in the summer of 1578 the Ottoman commander-in-chief Mustafā Pasha concentrated a large number of Janissaries and of Sipāhīs of the Porte, and also the 'feudal' sipāhīs of Erzerum, Diyārbekir and Sivas, of Dhū'l-Kadr, Karamān and Aleppo. The Ottomans had chosen as their first major objective the subjugation of Georgia and the territories adjacent to it—a wide area divided at this time into the principalities of Kartli (including Tiflis), Kakheti, Imereti, Samtzkhé or Meskhia (including Akhaltzikhé, the Altun Kal'e of the Ottoman sources), Guria and Mingrelia. Mustafā Pasha, having defeated the Persians near Lake Çildir in August 1578, occupied and garrisoned Tiflis later in the same month. Moving now in the direction of the lands that border the Caspian Sea, Mustafā Pasha won a further battle against the Persians which enabled him to force a passage across the river Kanak (or Alazan) and then took Arash, a point of great strategic value, since it controlled the line of march from Tiflis towards Shamakhi in Shirvān and Derbend in Dāghistān and also the routes leading to the Safawid fortresses of Ganja, Erivan and Tabriz. At Arash Mustafā Pasha, before withdrawing to winter quarters at Erzerum, made arrangements for the administration of the territories thus far over-run and for the future conduct of the war: Kartli, with Tiflis, was to become an Ottoman province; Kakheti to remain under the rule of a Georgian prince dependent on the sultan; at Sukhum an Ottoman Pasha would have control of affairs in the lands along the eastern shore of the Black Sea; the reduction of Shirvān and Dāghistān, as yet unsubdued, was entrusted to a separate force under the command of Osmān Pasha. During the course of the Ottoman withdrawal towards Erzerum the princes of Imereti, Guria and Samtzkhé offered their submission to Mustafā Pasha. The Ottomans had achieved much in this first major campaign of the war, but their success was far from complete. The years 1579–84 saw them engaged in laborious and expensive operations designed to consolidate their hold on Georgia—operations which involved the construction of a great fortress at Kars in 1579, the capture and refortification of Erivan in 1583 and the establishment in 1584 of less elaborate defences on the routes leading into Tiflis, for example, at Gori, Tomanis and Lori. Moreover, the Ottomans had to undertake each year large and often hard-fought 'convoy' campaigns bearing reinforcements of men and material to the garrisons at Tiflis and elsewhere, which found themselves time and again blockaded and harassed by the Safawids and their Georgian allies.

Meanwhile, Osmān Pasha had fought a series of brilliant campaigns in the region bordering the western shore of the Caspian Sea. Although he was able to defeat the Persians on the river Kura in 1578, the forces at his command proved to be inadequate for the conquest of Shirvān. Withdrawing into Derbend, which controls the narrow coastal route, about six miles wide, between the mountains of Dāghistān and the inland sea, Osmān Pasha maintained himself there, almost isolated and against great odds, throughout the years 1579–83. At last he received, late in 1582, reinforcements sufficient for him to assume the offensive, the flower of the troops of Rumeli moving now from Kaffa in the Crimea across the Kuban and Terek rivers to Derbend—a formidable march that took almost twelve weeks under the repeated harassment and raids of the Kalmyk and Çerkes (Circassian) tribes to the north of the Caucasus. Osmān Pasha, on the river Samur in 1583, won a great battle which drove the Persians from Dāghistān and also out of Shirvān, where Shamakhi and Baku soon surrendered to the victorious general. Ordered now to reassert Ottoman control over the Crimea—the Tatar khan had evaded his obligations as a vassal of the sultan, refusing to send his horsemen to the war in the Caucasus—Osmān Pasha crossed the Kuban steppe, held Kaffa until a naval force under Uluj 'Alī Pasha came to his assistance, and then installed a new khan on the throne. Murād III welcomed the famous soldier at Istanbul with the highest tokens of esteem and favour and in July 1584 raised him to the grand vizierate in reward for his incomparable services.

The Ottoman campaigns of 1585–8 had as their main purpose the conquest of Azerbaijān. Osmān Pasha, in the face of a stiff resistance, broke through to Tabriz in 1585, seized and fortified the town and then died in the course of an arduous retreat under sustained pressure from the Safawid forces. Tabriz, Tiflis and Erivan had now to meet the weight of a Persian counter-offensive, but their garrisons, although reduced to sore straits, held out until the new Ottoman commander-in-chief on the eastern front, Ferhād Pasha, was able to relieve them in 1586. The last great campaign of the war, carried out in 1588, witnessed the fall of Ganja and of the fertile region of Kara-Bagh to the Ottomans. Meanwhile, in 1587, subordinate operations conducted from Iraq under the guidance of Çighāla-zāde Sinān Pasha, the beglerbeg of Baghdad, resulted in the occupation of two provinces—Luristān and Hamadhān—on the western borders of Persia.

The feuds that divided the Safawid régime flared out into renewed violence during the last years of the war. Hamza Mīrzā, a son of Shah Muhammad Khudābanda prominent in the resistance to the Ottomans, was slain and Muhammad Khudābanda himself forced in June 1587 to relinquish the throne in favour of another of his sons, 'Abbās (1587–1629). Moreover, in 1588 and 1589 the Uzbeg Turks of Transoxania invaded Khurāsān, capturing Herāt, Mashhad and Nīshāpūr. The urgent need to overcome the factions within the state and to drive out the Uzbegs convinced Shah 'Abbās that the war against the Ottomans must be brought to an end, whatever the cost might be. Under the terms of a peace concluded in 1590 the shah ceded to the sultan Tabriz and the territories dependent thereon in Azerbaijan, Ganja and the Kara-Bagh region, Shirvān, Georgia, Luristān, and Shahrazūr in Kurdistān.

As the war against Persia drew towards its close, a new conflict began to take form along the Ottoman frontier in Europe. A state of peace had existed between Austria and the Ottoman empire since 1568, but the endless raids and counter-incursions of Muslim *ghāzi* against Christian marcher lord continued unabated in the ill-defined zones along the border, giving rise to tensions ever liable to break out into more serious warfare.[1] The *Kleinkrieg* of the frontier was now assuming, e.g. in 1587 near Koppan, Buda and Kanizsa and in 1588 at Szikso, dimensions which threatened to undermine the suspect and unquiet peace. Hasan Pasha, the *beglerbeg* of Bosnia, raided into Croatia and besieged Sisak (Sissek) on the river Kulpa in 1591 and again in 1592. Meanwhile, some of the great dignitaries at Istanbul, most prominent amongst them being the influential Sinān Pasha, urged the sultan to make war on Austria. Murād III yielded at last to their insistence when the fateful news arrived that the ghāzis of Bosnia had been routed with great loss at Sisak in June 1593, Hasan of Bosnia being numbered amongst the slain.

A major offensive on the Danube was a severe test of Ottoman skill and resource in war. As in their Persian, so too in their Hungarian campaigns, the Ottomans had to meet and overcome formidable difficulties of time and distance, of climate, terrain and logistics.[2] Moreover, the actual warfare itself was now far less fluid in character than it had been in the earlier years of the reign of Sultan Sulaimān. The Habsburgs of Austria sought to erect a strong defensive barrier against the Ottomans. As archduke of

---

[1] See above, pp. 90–1.   [2] See above, pp. 83–4.

Austria and later as emperor (1558–64), Ferdinand I encouraged Germans and also Slav and Hungarian refugees from the lands under Ottoman rule to settle in the Christian border zones, granting to them religious and financial privileges in return for their services as guardians of the frontier. Out of these first tentative measures there emerged the Croat and Windisch marches, extending from the Adriatic along the Unna and Kulpa rivers and thence to the higher reaches of the Sava and the Drava—a defence system furnished in the course of time with a fully organised military apparatus of its own and financed after 1578 largely by revenues levied in Carniola, Carinthia and Styria. The more effective resistance thus made possible to the Christians, the progressive strengthening of their border defences, and the continuing recruitment of refugee Slavs and Hungarians as *limitanei* did much to evoke from the ghāzis of Bosnia the violent reaction that led to the war of 1593. The government at Vienna strove also to improve and strengthen the main fortresses still left in Christian hands— for example, Kanizsa, Raab, Komorn and Erlau. At the same time a network of small forts—palankas—came into existence, protecting the more important routes, the river crossings and the approaches to the large fortified towns. As the prospect of rapid conquest diminished with the passing of the years, the Ottomans perforce created for themselves a similar defensive armature based on a number of great fortresses like Belgrade, Temesvár, Stuhlweissenburg, Buda and Gran, each of them controlling minor strongholds situated at points of strategic value. Muslim and Christian now stood ranged one against the other behind the defences which marked out their respective zones of domination. The frontier in fact was hardening along more or less stable lines.

Not the least of the difficulties that the Ottomans had to face was the character of the troops opposed to them. The emperor, exploiting the international ramifications of Habsburg influence, was able to draw into his service some of the best soldiers of the time, the German, Walloon and Italian mercenaries, turbulent, it is true, and hard to control when ill paid, but none the less professionals expert in the most advanced techniques of warfare. Hasan al-Kāfī indeed noted with regret that the Christians, through their use of new types of hand-gun and cannon, as yet neglected by the Ottomans, had won a definite advantage over the armies of the sultan.

Moreover, despite the vast changes which the Reformation wrought in Europe, the modes of sentiment and belief deriving from the old ideal of a *Corpus Christianum* designed to unite in one common allegiance, regardless of race and language, all nations that held the true faith, retained even now some of their ancient force. At the call to arms against the Muslim foe numerous volunteers, Protestant as well as Catholic, still came to serve on the Hungarian front. One Christian was to describe the war of 1593 as a conflict fought *pro aris et focis, pro patria et religione*. The

Emperor Rudolf II, in declaring his armies to be the shield of all Christendom, but echoed the conviction of his contemporaries. The immense interest aroused amongst the Christians is reflected in the popular demand for works, old and new, analysing the strength and weakness of the Ottoman empire and in the appearance of innumerable *Zeitungen* and *Relationes* written in German, Latin and Italian and then translated into other languages and all of them narrating, often with much detail and on the basis of first-hand information, the events and fortunes of the war. A Venetian author of this time, Lazaro Soranzo, expressed indeed far more than a personal judgement when he stated that the conflict begun in 1593 was the greatest affair then happening in the world: *la presente guerra e il maggior negotio, c'hora corra nel Mondo*.[1]

The great Hungarian war which followed the rout of the Bosnian ghāzis at Sisak lasted for thirteen long and arduous years (1593–1606). Throughout most of this time the Ottomans had to face a grave situation on the lower Danube, where in 1594 Moldavia, Wallachia and Transylvania, hitherto dependent on the sultan, rose in revolt and made common cause with Austria. The defection of the three principalities constituted a serious menace to the lines of communication running from Istanbul to Belgrade, Buda and Gran, for the Danube was of high importance as a water-route much used in the transport of guns and munitions to the Hungarian front. It also denied to the Ottomans the rich supplies of grain and meat, of horses and other beasts of burden which came to them from Moldavia and Wallachia. A not inconsiderable portion of the Ottoman war effort was therefore directed perforce towards the defence of the river line, and this to the obvious advantage of the imperialist armies operating on the middle Danube. The entente now established between the three Danubian states and Austria rested, however, on a most insecure foundation. Sigismund Bathory, the prince of Transylvania, had acquired from the Jesuit influences surrounding his youth the ambition and zeal to lead a new resistance to the Ottomans. He also wished to reassert old Hungarian claims to control over Wallachia and Moldavia—a desire that ran counter to the aims of Michael, the energetic voivode of Wallachia. The Habsburgs, too, had their own objectives and, as heirs to the ancient Hungarian realm which came to an end at the battle of Mohács in 1526,[2] would miss no favourable occasion to bring Transylvania under their direct rule. A further complication was the interest and, at times in the course of the war, the armed intervention of Poland in the affairs of Moldavia. Sigismund Bathory, unstable of purpose, abdicated the throne of Transylvania in favour of the Emperor Rudolf II and then reassumed it, thus increasing the confusion which reigned north of the Danube. Michael of Wallachia, professing to act on behalf of the emperor, overran Transyl-

---

[1] L. Soranzo, *L'Ottomanno* (Ferrara, 1599), Proemio, VI.
[2] See above, pp. 81–2.

vania in 1599 and Moldavia in 1600. His success called forth a Polish intervention in Moldavia and also in Wallachia itself and, in addition, a combined resistance in Transylvania of the Hungarian elements there and of imperialist forces now sent to their aid. On the murder in 1601 of the Voivode Michael there followed in Transylvania some four years of imperialist control involving measures against the Protestant religion and the local estates, confiscations designed to break the influence of the great nobles and, in addition, the appointment of German and Italian officials as the instruments of a centralised Habsburg régime. The end result was that Transylvania, led by Stephen Bocskai, the ablest of the lieutenants of Sigismund Bathory, abandoned the alliance with the emperor and sought a new entente with the sultan. This change of alignment had a marked effect on the course of the long Hungarian war, since it so eased the situation of the Ottomans that their armies now recovered, during the last phase of the conflict, the territories lost earlier to the imperialist forces. It brought about also the emergence of a Transylvania soon to enter into a brief golden age as a state endowed with a large measure of independence in relation alike to the emperor and to the Ottoman sultan.

The first years of the Hungarian war went ill for the Ottomans. It is true that the great fortress of Raab fell to them in 1594, but this gain was more than counterbalanced when in 1595 Gran—the northernmost bulwark of Ottoman rule on the middlè Danube—surrendered to the imperialists and at the same time a full-scale campaign directed against Wallachia, now ranged on the side of the emperor, came to a disastrous end with the rout—at Giurgiu on the lower Danube—of the Ottoman forces under the command of Sinān Pasha. So grave was the outlook that Mehemmed III (1595–1603) was induced to take the field himself in the next year. As their main objective for the campaign of 1596 the Ottomans chose the Hungarian fortress of Erlau situated close to the narrow corridor of land through which ran the imperialist lines of communication with Transylvania. Erlau surrendered to the sultan on 12 October 1596, before the imperialists, who had brought together a powerful concentration of forces, could arrive to relieve it. There now followed the greatest field battle of the war. At Mezö-Keresztes on 26 October 1596 the Ottomans, at first driven back almost to the verge of disaster, routed the Christians in a final desperate assault. This battle, although it led to no immediate consequences of note (the campaign season was in fact far advanced), denied to the imperialists all hope of a rapid conquest which would evict the Ottomans from the Hungarian lands under their control.

The war became now a laborious conflict of sieges demanding of Muslim and Christian alike an exorbitant expenditure in men and material. The imperialists reconquered Raab in 1598, but failed in a determined attempt to seize Buda. This same year saw the Ottomans engaged in a vain effort to capture Varaždin. A notable success came to the Ottomans, however, in 1600 with their conquest of Kanizsa, a fortress almost impregnable in its encircling marshes. The Christians in 1601, though repulsed with severe loss in their endeavour to regain Kanizsa, besieged and took Stuhl-weissenburg, only to lose it to the Ottomans in the following year. The main operations of 1602–4 centred around Buda, which the imperialists strove in vain to reduce, and Pest, which the Ottomans sought to re-capture—it had fallen to the Christians in 1602. Not until 1605, when Transylvania aligned itself once more on the side of the sultan, did the conflict enter into a more decisive phase. The Ottomans, in the course of this year, fought the last major campaign of the war, recovering Gran, together with several lesser strongholds, amongst them Visegrád, Vesz-prém and Palota.

At Vienna, as at Istanbul, the desire for peace was now dominant. The revolt of Transylvania against Habsburg control had turned the tide of war in favour of the Ottomans. It was clear that Austria would gain little and might indeed lose much from a continuation of hostilities. An agree-ment negotiated in June 1606 resolved the differences existing between Stephen Bocskai and the Emperor Rudolf II. Bocskai—to whom the sultan in 1605 had promised Transylvania and also the Hungarian throne —was to retain Transylvania for himself and his heirs, the pretension to the title of king being allowed to lapse in silence. The sultan also was eager to end the long conflict on the Danube. Asia Minor had been aflame with rebellion since 1596. Moreover, in 1603 Shah 'Abbās of Persia had begun a new war against the Ottomans with the aim of reconquering the large territories ceded to the sultan in 1590. Until there was peace with Austria, the Porte would be free neither to stamp out the fire of insurrection nor to halt the Safawid advance.

Peace was made between the emperor and the sultan in November 1606. The long war brought into the foreground one basic fact—that the Ottomans, despite a most lavish expenditure of their resources, had failed to break the resistance of the Habsburgs. Their formidable war machine, extended beyond its effective range, was ground almost into exhaustion on the far-off plains bordering the middle Danube. The actual location of the peace conference, and still more the terms of the peace itself, revealed how much the relative balance as between Austria and the Ottoman empire had altered, since the golden years of Sulaimān the Magnificent, to the advantage of the emperor and to the detriment of the sultan. Hitherto Austria had been forced to send ambassadors to Istanbul when seeking agreement with the Porte. Now the conclusion of peace was not to have the appearance of an act of grace and favour from the sultan to a sup-pliant foe. The final conference took place on the Hungarian frontier between the Christian fortress of Komorn and the Muslim fortress of Gran, on neutral ground at Zsitva-Torok, where the river Zsitva flows into the Danube. Here the Ottomans assented to terms which reflected not so much their concern over the dangers confronting them in Asia Minor as their recognition that the war begun in 1593 was ending for them in virtual failure. The emperor, after a single and final 'gift' amounting to 200,000 gulden, was to yield no more tribute to the sultan, as he and his predecessors had done since the time of Sulaimān the Magnificent. Henceforth the sultan would accord to the emperor, in all future diplomatic intercourse, his full rank and titles, that is, was to accept him as an equal. Each side retained the territories then under its control. The Ottomans continued, therefore, to hold the Hungarian lands subject to their rule in 1593 and now added to them two fortresses, Erlau and Kanizsa—a meagre reward for thirteen years of arduous conflict.

The long wars against Persia and Austria had—over and above their immediate outcome—a disadvantageous effect on some of the basic institutions of the Ottoman state. One factor of great importance was the character of the warfare itself. The conquest, with a view to permanent occupation, of large territories in the region of the Caucasus demanded of the Ottomans the construction of numerous fortresses and the establishment of garrisons adept in the use of firearms and the arts of siegecraft. On the Hungarian front the Ottoman war machine was committed to a laborious offensive against fortresses often manned with expert professional soldiers skilled in the latest techniques of warfare. Under these conditions the role of the Ottoman sipāhīs, the 'feudal' warriors of the sultan, tended to become less significant than it had been heretofore. Now on the eastern and still more on the western front, the dominant need was for foot soldiers trained to use firearms and for specialist troops such as engineers and artillerists. The 'feudal' sipāhī, fashioned and moulded in accordance with the old traditions of the Ottoman state, was ill at ease in the new warfare. The changed circumstances of war made inevitable a large increase in the paid forces of the central Ottoman régime, in the Janissaries and the other specialised corps of the imperial household.

The forces of the central régime bore time and again the brunt of the severest hostilities. Under the difficulties of warfare on the eastern front the rate of loss, for example amongst the Janissaries, through death, wounds and sickness became high indeed. The conditions prevailing on the western front must have been still more harsh—one Christian was to describe the Hungarian war as 'a slaughter-house of men'[1]—and here too the élite troops of the imperial household had to endure grave losses.

The combined effect of the need to increase the paid forces of the central régime and the need to make good the high casualties suffered in the long wars of this time was disastrous. It soon became clear that the traditional sources of recruitment—captives acquired through war, gift or purchase

---

[1] A. Tarducci, *Delle Machine, Ordinanze et Quartieri Antichi et Moderni* (Venice, 1601), p. 38.

and, in addition, the *devshirme* or child-tribute levied from the subject Christian populations of the empire—would in no wise suffice to meet this twofold demand. Nor did the adoption of expedients—for example, the throwing into battle of the '*ajemioghlanlar* or 'foreign youths' (the young recruits to the corps of Janissaries), before their training was complete—offer more than a transient relief from the dire pressures of war. The Porte was therefore driven to countenance a solution which blurred and broke down the barrier hitherto existing between the *ghilmān* and the Muslim-born elements in the state: now began the inclusion, on a large scale, of Muslim-born subjects amongst the Janissaries and the other paid troops of the central régime and the creation of new bodies such as the *culcardasi*, or 'brothers of the *kul*' (that is, of the *ghulām*), recruited from the same Muslim sources and assimilated in privilege and status to the 'men of the sultan'. This departure from the 'classical' system of Ottoman rule brought in its train a serious impairment of that *esprit de corps*, that efficient skill and discipline amongst the *ghilmān*, which had contributed so much towards the greatness of the Ottoman state.

The years 1566–1617 saw the emergence, in relation to the Ottomans, of new factors and new influences—some of them markedly adverse in character—within the realm of commercial, economic and social affairs. To the south, in the distant waters of the Red Sea, the Indian Ocean and the Persian Gulf, the protracted if spasmodic warfare between the Ottomans and the Portuguese was drawing to its close. Ottoman vessels, under the command of 'Alī Beg, sailed from the Yemen in 1580 to raid the Portuguese-dominated Maskat in the 'Umān. 'Alī Beg in 1584 moved down the coast of East Africa as far as Malindi. He repeated the venture in 1589, this time reaching Mombasa, where his squadron succumbed, however, to the assault of a superior Portuguese fleet from Goa in western India. Thus ended the last Ottoman endeavour to challenge the domination of Portugal over the waters of the Indian Ocean. It had long since become clear that the Portuguese had not the resources to win for themselves a complete control of the ancient trade routes running from India through the lands of Islam towards Europe. Their penetration into the Indian Ocean in the wake of Vasco da Gama disrupted for some considerable time the rich transit trade through the Red Sea and the Persian Gulf to the harbours of the Levant. None the less, as the tide of events revealed more and more the limitations of Portuguese power and influence, this traffic began to revive: the spices and the other exotic products of the East now flowed both around the Cape of Good Hope and also, once more and on a large scale, through Suez and Basra towards the shore of the Mediterranean Sea. Aleppo, indeed, became after 1550 a flourishing emporium dealing in spices and in the much coveted silk of Persia, while Alexandria in Egypt, too, prospered to the extent that it recovered no small measure of its former wealth and importance. This revival, however, of the old transit trade had no long duration. The advance into the Indian Ocean of maritime nations much stronger than the Portuguese—the English and the Dutch—was to ensure in the not distant future the undeniable pre-dominance of the sea route around Africa.

The English and, after them, the Dutch now began to penetrate into the Mediterranean Sea. English merchant vessels had sometimes previously ventured into the waters of the Levant, sailing under the aegis of those Christian states, such as Venice and France, which possessed commercial privileges within the Ottoman empire. As yet the circumstances did not exist, however, which would favour the growth of close and profitable trade relations between London and Istanbul. The merchants of England had no grant of privileges from the sultan. Their voyages to the Mediterranean long continued to be precarious enterprises. There was no powerful organisation at home to foster their interests. Not until the middle years of the reign of Queen Elizabeth did a more auspicious state of affairs become evident. The merchants had now to hand an adequate financial mechanism in the form of chartered joint-stock companies, increased resources of capital and, arising from the obvious revival of the old transit traffic through the Middle East, a strong interest in the possibilities of trade with the Levant. William Harborne went to Istanbul in 1578 as the representative of the London merchants Edward Osborne and Richard Staper. He obtained from the grace and favour of Sultan Murād III in 1580 a grant of 'capitulations', of commercial privileges similar to the ones that France and Venice enjoyed in the Ottoman empire. Osborne, Staper and their associates received from Queen Elizabeth in 1581 a charter incorporating them as a company of merchants trading to the Levant. The privileges secured from the sultan in 1580 had, and would retain, a provisional character until England appointed and maintained a permanent diplomatic representative at the Porte. Harborne became the first accredited agent of the Levant merchants at Istanbul in 1583 and also, at the same time, the first 'orator', or ambassador, of England to the Ottoman empire—an office that he held until 1588.

Neither France nor Venice desired to see established in the Levant a new rival to their own interests. Moreover, if the sultan allowed England to conduct an independent trade within his dominions, the two Christian states would lose the valuable dues of consulage that Englishmen had hitherto paid for permission to traffic under the French or under the Venetian flag. The ambassador of France and the *bailo* (representative) of Venice at Istanbul strove with all the means at their command to ruin the negotiations of Harborne, but in vain, since Murād III confirmed in 1583 the grant of trade privileges that he had made to England three years before. The Ottomans realised no doubt the advantages, both economic and political, to be drawn from close contact with a Christian state powerful at sea and hostile, like themselves, towards the house of Habsburg. None the less, it is surprising that Harborne, within the brief space of two years (1578–80), should have surmounted all the difficulties which confronted him at Istanbul. One factor did much to facilitate his success.

The long years of conflict with Persia and later with Austria demanded of the Ottomans an enormous expenditure in munitions of war—so enormous indeed as to create a genuine shortage of such materials. English merchants had the means and also the will to make good deficiencies of this kind. The Spanish ambassador at London, Bernardino de Mendoza, noted in 1579 that the Ottomans received from England quantities of tin, a metal indispensable in the manufacture of bronze cannon. Other cargoes sent out from England to the Ottoman empire included broken bells and images (plunder from English churches despoiled in the course of the Reformation), iron and steel, lead, copper, arquebuses, muskets, sword-blades, brimstone, saltpetre and gunpowder. One Englishman—a captive of the Ottomans from 1603 to 1605—wrote that the Janissaries had 'not one corne of good powder but that whyche they gett from overthrone Christians, or els is broughte them out of Englande' and that the English 'keepe 3 open shoppes of armes and munition in Constantinople...Gunpowder is solde for 23 and 24 *chikinoes* the hundred; in Englande it costeth but 3 pounde. Tinne in Constantinople beareth the same price. Muskettes are solde for 5 or 6 *chikinos* the peyce; in Englande they buy ordinary ones for 2 markes, the best for 18 shillings.'[1]

Trade was no doubt the initial motive force that brought the English to the Levant, but political considerations also exerted a strong influence during the embassies of William Harborne, the first ambassador (1583–8) of England at the Porte, and of Edward Barton, his successor in that office (1588–98). Harborne and Barton, time and again, entreated the Ottomans to begin a naval offensive against Spain in the interests of England and the other Protestant states. Barton, moreover, seems to have welcomed the drift toward war between the Ottoman empire and Austria in the years before 1593. He revealed, perhaps, his true attitude when he wrote: 'In my small judgment I think it nothing offensive to God to set one of his enemies against the other, the Infidel against the Idolaters, to the end that whilst they were by the ears, God's people[2] might respite and take strength.'[3]

The trade in munitions of war brought the good name of England into much disrepute at this time. This traffic contravened the old canon law of the Christian Church Universal, which forbade the sale of war material to the Infidel. It is true that the ancient doctrine had lost almost all its

---

[1] *Calendar of State Papers, Spanish (1568–79)*, no. 609, and *(1580–86)*, no. 265; Sir T. Sherley, *Discours of the Turkes* (ed. E. D. Ross) Camden Misc., XVI (1936), 7, 9–10.

[2] I.e. the Protestants.

[3] I. I. Podea, 'A Contribution to the Study of Queen Elizabeth's Eastern Policy (1590–1593)', in *Mélanges d'Histoire Générale*, II (Cluj, 1938), 9.

compulsive force, but the modes of thought and sentiment deriving from it, although now in decline, still remained alive in Protestant as in Catholic Europe. Men of firm religious belief felt this commerce to be therefore 'a contraband hateful and pernicious to the whole of Christendom'. No less damaging to the reputation of England was the character of the political objectives that Harborne and Barton sought to achieve at the Porte. The propagandists who wrote on behalf of the Roman church, notable amongst them being such Catholic exiles from England as William Allen, Joseph Cresswell, Thomas Stapleton, William Reynolds, Richard Rowlands and William Giffard, had ample and, indeed, given their own particular point of view, valid reason to belabour the two ambassadors and their mistress, Queen Elizabeth, as traitors to the Christian faith. Thomas Stapleton declared, indeed, that the greatest of the impieties— *summum impietatis culmen*—attributable to the queen and her servants was their incitement of the Ottomans to attack Christendom. Propaganda of this kind achieved a cumulative effect so embarrassing to Queen Elizabeth that she was obliged to take active measures against the uneasiness and distrust that it aroused both at home in England itself and abroad in Europe. One of the most harmful of the accusations made against the queen laid at her door the blame for the outbreak of war between the Ottomans and the imperialists in 1593. The German Protestants might well remain silent while the English ambassadors at Istanbul urged the sultan to attack Spain, the most formidable of the Catholic powers. Their compliance was not, however, to be assumed in the case of manœuvres designed to bring about a great Ottoman assault on Austria—an assault that would perforce imperil their own interests, if it were successful. Queen Elizabeth, therefore, in order to counteract the discredit now gathering about her name, sent Christopher Parkins to Prague in 1593 with instructions to exculpate her before the Emperor Rudolf II. The mission of Parkins was in fact a success, since the emperor declared himself to be satisfied that the queen was not to blame for the imminent war in Hungary. None the less, the Catholic propaganda continued unabated during the years of the Hungarian conflict (1593–1606) and had repercussions even in distant Russia. The ambassador of England at the Porte, Edward Barton, accompanied Sultan Mehemmed III on the campaign of 1596 which brought disaster to the Christians at Erlau and at Mezö-Keresztes. His presence in the field with the sultan was of great advantage to the Catholic agents at Moscow. The Muscovites, under the influence of papal and imperialist propaganda (the astute intelligences at the Roman curia of this time saw in Russia a potential foe—and indeed the ultimate ruin—of the Ottoman empire), communicated to Queen Elizabeth their astonishment and alarm at the conduct of Barton and also at the traffic in munitions of war. Once more the queen was obliged to defend her good name, first in 1597 through one of her merchants trading in Russia, and again in 1600 through Sir Richard Lee, whom she sent to Moscow with specious assurances that the sultan had forced Barton to go on the campaign of 1596 and that Englishmen had sold to the Ottomans no arms nor other material of war. Not until the course of events made clear the impotence of Spain to conquer England and of the Ottoman empire to subdue Austria did the war of propaganda begin to die down and the more debatable aspects of English traffic in the Levant cease to be of some significance in the field of international relations.

The years of warfare against Persia and Austria saw the Ottoman government confronted with serious financial difficulties. Revenue and expenditure were calculated in terms of the silver akçe or asper, the basic unit of coinage in the empire. The Ottomans, like the peoples of Europe, had suffered hitherto from a recurring shortage of the precious metals, gold and silver—a shortage so acute that it threatened at times to disrupt their silver-based system of coinage. To overcome such moments of stress and strain the sultans controlled the silver mines, favoured the import and discouraged the export of coin and bullion, enlarged those sectors of the state business which involved transactions in kind rather than in cash, and also resorted at need to a measure of debasement in the coinage. This situation underwent a marked change, however, when the empire, from about 1580 onward, began to feel the effects of a severe inflation.

American silver has been regarded as a major cause of the 'price revolution' which was affecting Europe at this time. The great increase in the amount of silver available brought about, so it is argued, a prolonged inflation. Silver, flowing from the Americas into Spain and thence to Genoa and Ragusa, penetrated thereafter into the Ottoman empire. As it moved eastwards through the channels of international commerce, the flood of silver left in its wake similar consequences in each of the countries that it overran, that is, a rapid rise in prices, depreciation of the coinage and debasement, counterfeiting, speculation and the like. This quantitative view of the 'price revolution', this emphasis on the sudden large expansion of the circulating medium has been subject of late to much criticism. Recent analyses have suggested that the rise in prices was not due—or at least not alone due—to the influx of precious metals from the New World, but to other factors of equal or even greater effect. Attention has been drawn, for example, to the importance of an increase in population more rapid than the parallel expansion of the means of subsistence and thus productive of grave social imbalance—and there is indeed evidence to show that the population of the Ottoman empire, above all in Asia Minor, was increasing to a considerable degree at this time. The 'price revolution' should be attributed, no doubt, to the interaction of a number of different causes rather than to the action of one single cause. It is difficult to believe, however, that the eastward movement of silver had nothing to do with the inflation which now beset the Ottoman state. It constituted, at the lowest estimate, a factor of disturbance in the complex and adverse situation now facing the Ottomans. The inflation occurred, moreover, at a time when the Porte was obliged to find and disburse enormous sums in connection with the long wars, first against Persia and then against Austria, and when it had, also, to countenance a notable expansion in the paid forces and personnel of the central régime—an expansion which meant, for the state, a further and large increase of expenditure.

The Porte, in order to alleviate the fiscal troubles of the moment, decreed in 1584 a reduction in the silver content of the akçe or asper from one-fifth to one-eighth of a dirham. This debasement of the coinage brought great, though ephemeral, profits to a government hard pressed to meet the high cost of the Persian war. It was also fraught with serious consequences. The ratio of the akçe to the ducat declined from 60 to over 200. Foreign coins, of gold as well as of silver, began to drive the debased Ottoman issues even from the internal markets of the empire. The Porte, faced with vast expenses and with a depreciating coinage, became more and more exorbitant in its fiscal measures and demands and thus aggravated the distress felt amongst the mass of the population as a result of the rise in prices.

The inflation struck hard at all classes dependent on a fixed income. Among the civil, administrative and religious personnel of the state, numerous officials, often underpaid and with their salaries in arrear, found it difficult to maintain themselves and sought relief for their troubles in malpractice and corruption. There was unrest, too, and a dangerous spirit of turbulence amongst the paid troops of the imperial household. The inclusion within the Janissaries of elements hitherto debarred from their ranks no doubt did much to undermine the old standards of obedience and trustworthiness prevailing in this famous corps. None the less, a further and cogent reason for the marked growth of indiscipline among the Janissaries—and also among the other categories of paid troops—was the fact that their wages, allotted to them in cash and at a fixed rate, had become insufficient, in view of the rise in prices, to meet their normal needs: hence their demands for large donatives and for increased rates of pay—demands too menacing to be ignored, since behind them was the ultimate sanction of revolt against the sultan and his viziers. The Janissaries in 1589 rose in rebellion when the government wanted to give them their wages not in old and good, but in new and debased, coin. Three years later, in 1592, the Sipāhīs of the Porte mutinied, because their pay was not issued to them in full. More serious still was the revolt which broke out, again amongst the Sipāhīs of the Porte, in 1603. The Grand Vizier Hasan Pasha induced the Janissaries to crush this insurrection. Their readiness to intervene—a source of much embitterment for the future between themselves and the mounted regiments of the imperial household—reflected how fast and how far the *esprit de corps* heretofore uniting the 'men of the sultan' was crumbling under the impact of adverse circumstance.

The price revolution affected, too, the 'feudal' sipāhīs, dependent for their maintenance on a fixed income accruing to them from their fiefs. Even before this time, the 'feudal' horsemen had begun to feel the strain of distant campaigns expensive to themselves in respect of supplies and equipment and at the same time less and less rewarding in terms of plunder and captives of war. It is understandable, therefore, that the inflation hit the 'feudal' class hard, and above all those sipāhīs who had tīmārs of low or moderate yield—such fiefs being far more numerous, it would seem, in Asia Minor than in the Balkans. Moreover, with the growth of intrigue and corruption amongst the personnel of the central régime, palace favourites and large-scale speculators obtained tīmārs and zi'āmets. The government at Istanbul, in its search for additional sources of revenue, seized and—through its deliberate failure to regrant them—held for its own use numerous fiefs which fell vacant in the normal course of affairs. It is from this time forward that a progressive diminution began in the number of tīmārs and a parallel increase in extent of the *khāss-i shāhī*, the domain of the sultan.

A further and potent factor in the growing disruption of the 'feudal' system was the flight of the peasants from the land—a phenomenon which meant that fiefs often became less productive through lack of labour. Even in the reign of Sultan Sulaimān, at a time when the empire was at the apogee of its power and splendour, Lutfī Pasha, in the small treatise entitled *Āsafnāme* which he wrote after his dismissal from the office of grand vizier in 1541, felt obliged to warn against the danger of rural depopulation and to recommend that the peasants be subjected to no more than a moderate taxation and also be safeguarded from possible oppression at the hands of the provincial authorities.

The growth in the population of the empire tended to exceed the increase in the amount of land under cultivation. This factor, in conjunction with the prevailing inflation, the debasement of the coinage and the fiscal pressures now emanating from the central régime and from the provincial authorities, led to the gradual emergence, especially in Asia Minor, of a rootless class of men (known as *ghurbet tā'ifesi* or *levendāt*)—men torn from the soil, some of them finding relief for their distress in brigandage, others fleeing in their trouble to the local towns, there to form a restive proletarian element ripe for mischief, should a suitable occasion offer itself. Around Mustafā, a son of Sultan Sulaimān, had been focused in 1553 the malaise and dissatisfaction felt amongst the *levendāt* and also amongst the 'feudal' sipāhīs. After the execution, in that year, of Mustafā, the two remaining sons of Sulaimān, Selīm and Bāyazīd, came into conflict (1558–9) over the succession to the Ottoman throne. The princes, eager to build armies of their own, sought and obtained support from the 'feudal' sipāhīs and their *jebeli* warriors and also from the Muslim elements driven from the soil. A grave price was demanded, however, for this assistance. Selīm and Bāyazīd had to confer on a large number of the troops thus recruited a status which would assimilate the recipient, in rank and prestige, to the paid forces of the central régime, to the 'men of the sultan'.[1] The need to grant such a concession indicated that, under the pressure of hostile circumstance, the Muslim-born subjects of the empire had become more reluctant than ever before to acquiesce in their own exclusion from those areas of high power and privilege in the state hitherto reserved for the personnel of the imperial household. It will be evident that the onset of inflation, the harsh fiscal policies of the central government, and the increasing disruption of the 'feudal' system augmented and accelerated the flight of the peasants from the land, heightening even to the point of crisis the unrest so widespread in the provinces of the empire. There was now a real danger that, in Asia Minor, 'feudal' grievance might coalesce with agrarian discontent in the form of rebellion against the central régime and its privileged personnel—rebellion, moreover, of a most formidable kind, since it would be fought with the aid of the *levendāt*, large numbers of whom had acquired experience of warfare as irregulars serving in the campaigns against Persia and Austria. It would also be waged with assistance from the 'feudal' sipāhīs and their *jebeli* retinues expert in the art of war.

Such indeed was to be the issue of events. The 'feudal' horsemen summoned from Asia Minor for service in the Hungarian campaign of 1596 did not distinguish themselves at the battle of Mezö-Keresztes. Moreover, of the sipāhīs called to the war, no small number had failed to take the field. Çighāla-zāde Sinān Pasha, raised to the grand vizierate after the battle, introduced severe measures to deal with this situation. It is to the bitter resentment thus aroused amongst the 'feudal' sipāhīs and to the increasing turbulence of the *levendāt* that the Ottoman chronicles relating to this time ascribe the great wave of rebellion which swept across Asia Minor between 1596 and 1610. To the Ottomans the movement was known as the *Khurūj-i Jalāliyān*, the insurrection of the *Jalālī* rebels. The main architects of revolt were a certain 'Abd al-Halīm, called Kara Yaziji (the 'Black Scribe'), and his brother Deli Hasan. Their depredations extended from Ruhā (Urfa) to Sivas and Kaysari and from the region of Albistān in the south to the region of Jānīk in the north of Asia Minor. The government at Istanbul sought to separate one from the other two elements involved in the tide of insurrection—on the one hand the 'feudal' sipāhīs (most of them warriors endowed with fiefs which did not yield large revenues) and, with them, the personalities most prominent amongst the *levendāt* and on the other hand the mass of the rootless men

---

[1] See above, pp. 96-7.

whom economic and fiscal pressures had driven from the land. It was indeed obvious enough that the discontent so rife in Asia Minor would become much less dangerous to the central régime once the *levendāt* rank and file of rebellion lost the co-operation of the sipāhīs. The means chosen at the Porte to attain such an outcome indicated how resolute the Muslim-born subjects of the sultan had become to force an entrance into the exalted world of power and privilege belonging, until this time, to the men of non-Muslim and non-Turkish origin, who rejoiced in the status of *ghulām*. Kara Yaziji received from the sultan an appointment as *sanjak-begi*, that is, governor of a province; later, Deli Hasan, his brother, was raised to the rank of *beglerbegi* (governor-general over a group of provinces). On these occasions, too, some at least of the more important and more intimate adherents of Kara Yaziji and Deli Hasan obtained for themselves inclusion amongst the 'men of the sultan'. Measures of this kind won, however, but a transient and partial success. New rebel chieftains made their appearance in Asia Minor, for example, in Aidin and Sarukhan, in the region of Brusa, in Karaman and in Cilicia. The need—becoming more urgent with each passing year—to take decisive action against the rebels goes far to explain the readiness of the sultan and his viziers to seek peace with the imperialists, as soon as operations on the Hungarian front had assumed a trend favourable to the Ottoman cause. Murād Pasha, able and vigorous, prominent at Zsitva-Torok and, in reward for his valuable services there, appointed to be grand vizier, crushed the revolts through a combination of fraud, treachery and force in a series of relentless campaigns (1607–10). His merciless severity stamped out most of the resistance and imposed some degree of order on a land which had endured a decade and more of spoliation. The basic causes of economic and social discontent remained, however, untouched and would continue to be active in the future.

Meanwhile, in 1603 a new conflict had broken out between the Ottomans and the Safawids. Shah 'Abbās of Persia (1587–1629), during the first fifteen years of his reign, overcame and brought under his own ruthless control the Turcoman chieftains and their tribesmen, who had dominated so long the internal life of the Safawid state. He increased in number the paid troops recruited from the Caucasus, and above all from Georgia, and introduced amongst them a more extensive use of firearms. These forces, non-tribal in character and dependent on himself alone, formed the hard core of the armies that 'Abbās mustered in order to face (1587–97) the repeated and dangerous invasions of the Uzbeg Turks from Transoxania into Khurāsān and thereafter to drive the Uzbegs back (1598–1602) into their own territories. The shah, once he had made himself the real master of Persia and also had overcome the challenge of the Uzbegs, turned his attention to the reconquest of the lands yielded to the Ottoman sultan in 1590. His endeavour, through such emissaries as the Englishmen Anthony and Robert Sherley, to establish an offensive alliance with one or more of the states of Europe against the Ottoman empire ended in failure. The moment was ripe, however, for the revival, even without Christian aid, of Safawid domination in the countries situated between the Black Sea and the Caspian Sea. Ottoman rule in the Caucasus was in effect an armed occupation limited over wide regions to control of the main lines of communication and of the more important strategic centres—a rule, save perhaps in some of the western areas long exposed to the influence of the Porte, too new as yet to have grown deep roots and still alien therefore to the mass of the people, a large proportion of whom retained their earlier and close ties with the Safawid régime. The fact, too, that the Ottoman empire was involved in war against Austria and beset, moreover, with rebellion in Asia Minor gave to Shah 'Abbās a pronounced advantage. How great this advantage was became clear when, in the brief space of five years (1603–7), the precarious edifice of Ottoman rule in the Caucasus crumbled into almost total ruin, Tabriz, Erivan and Ganja, Derbend, Baku and Shamakhi, Tiflis and even Kars falling to the armies of the shah. Not until the war with Austria had been brought to a close and the fire of revolt subdued in Asia Minor was the Porte free in fact to prepare a real counter-offensive. Ottoman resistance during these years, therefore, was spasmodic in character and of small effect. Çighāla-zāde Sinān Pasha advanced towards Tabriz in 1605, but suffered defeat in battle and then retired with considerable loss to Van and Diyārbekir. Murād Pasha, having beaten down the rebels of Asia Minor, marched to Tabriz in 1610 and ravaged the town, which Shah 'Abbās had chosen not to defend. This event proved, however, to be the sole occurrence of note during the campaign, since the Pasha soon withdrew to winter quarters at Erzerum. The truth was that, bearing in mind the vast strain of protracted warfare abroad and of hydra-headed revolt at home, neither the sultan, Ahmed I (1603–17), nor his ministers felt much desire to wage against Persia yet another major conflict, which might well be no less arduous and long and no less impermanent in result than the war begun in 1578 had been. A peace was negotiated, therefore, between the two states in 1612, the Ottomans surrendering the large territories ceded to them in 1590. Disputes over the terms of this settlement led to a renewal of hostilities in 1615. The Ottomans, in 1616, besieged Erivan and also rebuilt the fortress of Kars. Two events—the death of Ahmed I in 1617 and the rout of an Ottoman force near Tabriz in 1618—hastened the end of the war. The peace of September 1618, ratified in September 1619, reiterated in effect the articles of agreement laid down in 1612: once more the Ottomans renounced the lands yielded to them in 1590 and thus accepted a reversion to the state of affairs which had existed in the last years of Sulaimān the Magnificent.

The Ottoman empire, under the impact of forces that it was almost powerless to control, fell during the years 1566–1617 from the summit of its strength and splendour into a condition of indubitable, though as yet incipient, decline. It was perhaps an Englishman who, in relation to the Ottomans, summarised best the essential lesson of these years. Sir Thomas Roe, ambassador of England at the Porte from 1621 to 1628, made a shrewd judgement when he wrote that the Ottoman empire might 'stand, but never rise again'.[1]

[1] *The Negotiations of Sir Thomas Roe in his Embassy to the Ottoman Porte from the Year 1621 to 1628 Inclusive* (London, 1740), p. 809.

5

THE PERIOD OF MURĀD IV, 1617–48

O N the death of Sultan Ahmed I in 1617 the problem of the succession to the throne assumed a particular importance. The Ottoman custom had been that the sons of a reigning sultan should be sent out, while still young, to rule over provinces in Asia Minor. A prince thus sent out with the rank of *sanjaq begi*, that is, governor of a *sanjaq* or province, would now receive, under the guidance of the dignitaries composing his household and of the officials controlling the local administration, a long and elaborate education in the *'adet-i 'othmaniyye*—the *mores* and the culture distinctive of the Ottomans. It was an education which embraced language and literature, physical training and the practice of arms and which inculcated, moreover, a close and practical knowledge of how the empire was run—in short, an education designed to fit a prince for the responsibilities of rule, if ever he should come to the throne.

At the same time it had been the custom of the Ottomans that a new sultan should order forthwith the execution of all his brothers and their male children. The pressures imposed on princes of the blood through the operation of this 'law of fratricide' were acute. Aware that to win the throne or to die was the ultimate choice offered to them, the princes strove with all the means at their command to strengthen their resources in expectation of the evil hour which would mark the death of their father. Each of them sought to create in his particular province a nucleus of armed force and, in addition, to establish at the Porte, amongst the high dignitaries and the troops of the imperial household,[1] a faction committed to his cause.

To the influence of these factors must be ascribed in no small degree the sustained excellence of the Ottoman sultans before and including Süleyman the Magnificent. The experience acquired in the government of a province was invaluable as a preparation for the throne. The 'law of fratricide'—whatever judgement be made of it on moral grounds—had at least one beneficial effect: it exerted a psychological pressure which tended to drive the princes towards the development of all their personal capacities in the face of the mortal threat hanging over them.

The accidents of birth and death within the imperial house brought about now a less favourable situation. Of the male children of Selim II (1566–74) one alone, the future Murad III, and of Murad III (1574–95) again one son only, the future Mehemmed III, attained an age suitable

---

[1] Cf. above, pp. 103–4.

for their assignment to a province in Asia Minor. Mehemmed III (1595–1603) was destined indeed to be the last prince sent out to act as a *sanjaq begi*.

The 'law of fratricide' was also to fall into desuetude. It had served to limit the dangers of dynastic conflict and of political fragmentation at a time when, in the fourteenth and fifteenth centuries, the Ottoman state, then rising towards greatness, was beset with numerous difficulties. These dangers receded, however, into remoteness after the long consolidation carried out during the reign of Mehemmed II (1451–81). Henceforward the 'law of fratricide' acted more to the detriment than to the benefit of the Ottoman state, as the violent rivalries over the succession to the throne made clear in 1481–2, 1511–13 and above all in 1553–61. A western source of this time declares that in 1574 Murad III, on ascending the throne, enforced the 'law' against the wishes of the mufti, who stressed the fact that of the brothers of Murad none was old enough to be a danger to the empire. This account reflects perhaps uncertainties present in official circles at Istanbul over the wisdom of continuing a usage which, it could be argued, had outlived its original purpose and value.

The year 1595 witnessed the most dire example of fratricide in the annals of the imperial house. Mehemmed III, on his accession to the throne, ordered the execution of his brothers, nineteen of them in all. This grim event, however, was to be the last enforcement of the old 'law of fratricide'. The death of Mehemmed III in 1603 confronted the great dignitaries at the Porte with a situation unparalleled heretofore. The dead sultan left two sons—Ahmed, then almost fourteen years of age, and Mustafa, about two years younger than Ahmed. As the elder of the princes Ahmed now came to the throne, but there was no order for the execution of Mustafa. Ahmed, as yet, was childless. If Mustafa were done to death and if Ahmed should die before he had a son, the House of 'Osman would be extinct. Mustafa, therefore, was allowed to live. He was confined in the imperial palace and did not go out to govern a province in Asia Minor. The birth, in 1604, of 'Osman, the eldest son of Ahmed I, brought no change in the situation. Sultan Ahmed was still a mere youth and the death rate amongst infants was high. To execute Mustafa was not in fact feasible, unless and until there existed an heir to the throne who had survived through the years of childhood.

The death of Ahmed I in 1617 made Mustafa the eldest prince of the imperial line—the only prince of adult years—and as such he was raised to the throne. Mustafa I, however, was a man of feeble intellect. His brief reign of about three months (1617–18) revealed his unfitness to rule. He was now removed in favour of 'Osman, the eldest son of Ahmed I. On the deposition of 'Osman II in 1622 Mustafa became sultan once more, reigning for some fifteen months (1622–23), until his incompetence brought about his deposition for the second time. Thereafter, of the remaining sons of Ahmed I, Murad IV (1623–40), who left no male heir, and Ibrahim (1640–8), held the throne in succession.

The particular sequence of birth and death within the imperial house had created a new situation. The sending out of princes to appointments as *sanjaq begi* in Asia Minor was now at an end. The 'law of fratricide', too, ceased to be operative. Henceforward the princes would spend their lives in the seclusion of the palace, until and if the course of events should call them to be sultan. In fact, a new principle had come to govern the succession to the throne—the throne passed now, in descending order of age, from one prince to another within a given generation, until that generation was exhausted, and then fell to the eldest surviving prince of the next generation. Brother followed brother on the throne—and not the son in succession to the father. On the death of Sultan Ibrahim the throne went to his sons in the order of their age—to Mehemmed IV (1648–87), to Süleyman II (1687–91) and to Ahmed II (1691–5). Only on the 'death of Ahmed II did it go to a son of Mehemmed IV, to Mustafa II (1695–1703).

These changes worked to the disadvantage of the Ottoman state. The system prevailing before the reign of Ahmed I had done much to ensure that a series of able sultans should stand at the head of affairs. No such favourable judgement can be made for the new mode of procedure, which condemned the princes, in general, to long years of idle and enervating confinement within the palace walls—to a life, in short, which failed to prepare them for the responsibilities of power and, indeed, tended to undermine the capacities innate in them. It was still possible that a prince who came young to the throne might develop into a capable sultan. The House of 'Osman could even now produce a vigorous and ruthless monarch like Murad IV—but Sultan Murad was to be henceforth the exception rather than the rule.

On a government highly centralized the accession to the throne of sultans incompetent to rule well had perforce a most adverse effect. The sultan was the source of power within the state, his will set the machine of government in motion. If he did not define and direct the exercise of power, there were others—the great dignitaries of the central régime—who would do it for him, seeking at the same time to manipulate him to their own advantage.

The period here under review can be described, not unjustly, as one of rule by courtiers and officials—a period of intrigue, of shifting alliances and of spasmodic violence at the centre of affairs. Of great importance were the women of the harem, and in particular the Walide Sultan (the mother of the prince on the throne) and the Khasseki Sultans (the consorts who had borne the sultan a child). Often their influence was wielded through the *Kizlar Aghasi*, the chief of the black eunuchs, who controlled the administration of the harem. Their rivalries on behalf of their children, their private and personal access to the sultan, their forging of bonds between themselves and the high officials of the government— all these factors had a marked effect on the conduct of state affairs. A notable example can be found in the years 1617–23, which saw three Walide Sultans involved in the conflict around the throne: the mothers of Mustafa I, of 'Osman II and of Murad IV.

There was faction and intrigue, too, amongst the officials of the central régime, especially amongst the viziers, the number of whom was to rise as high as nine. These dignitaries, striving to attain the highest office in the empire, the grand vizierate, often aligned themselves with other elements engaged in the quest for power. Some of them had received in marriage princesses of the imperial house. These exalted ladies, endowed as of right with access to the intimate circle around the sultan, often counted for much in the advancement of their husbands.

To the factors mentioned thus far must be added here the *'ulema*, the men learned in the *Shari'a*, the Sacred Law of Islam. The *'ulema*, as the guardians of the Sacred Law, enjoyed great influence and prestige. Now, in these years of confusion, that influence was sometimes used to legitimize the course of events or to further the interest of a given cause—as, for example, in 1648, when the mufti issued a *fetwa* or legal pronouncement approving the execution of Sultan Ibrahim.

A further element in the complex picture is to be found in the troops of the central government—above all, the janissaries and also the sipahis of the Porte, the mounted regiments of the imperial household.[1] These forces, swollen in numbers and far less disciplined now than of old, rose in revolt from time to time, either of their own volition in quest of increased remuneration, donatives and other privileges or as a result of instigation emanating from one or other of the rival factions amongst the high dignitaries.

The intrigues and feuds surrounding the throne were especially virulent and bitter in the years following the death of Ahmed I in 1617. Mustafa, the brother of Ahmed, as the eldest of the Ottoman princes, now became sultan. His unfitness to rule soon led, however, to his deposition in 1618, a number of the great officials—amongst them the *Kîzlar Aghasî*, the chief of the black eunuchs, and the mufti, Es'ad Efendi—reaching an agreement with Mah-Firuze, the mother of 'Osman, to bring her son to the throne. The new sultan, 'Osman II, then about fourteen years of age, was too young and inexperienced to dominate the situation before him. He failed, moreover, to retain favour with the troops of the central régime—a disadvantage arising in no small degree from the ill-success of the campaign that he conducted against Poland in 1621.[2]

The position of the sultan became precarious indeed when it was

[1] Cf. *loc. cit.*   [2] See below, p. 149.

known that he intended to make a pilgrimage to Mecca. Suspicion grew amongst the janissaries and the sipahis of the Porte that the pilgrimage was a stratagem concealing designs hostile to themselves—that 'Osman II, escaping from Istanbul to the provinces, meant to use the armed strength available there as an instrument to curb their own pre-eminence and indiscipline. On 18 May 1622 the troops rose in revolt, demanding the lives of the dignitaries held to be most influential with the sultan, amongst them the grand vizier, Dilawar Pasha. Members of the *'ulema* submitted these demands to 'Osman II, but the sultan was loath to yield and hesitated too long before sending Dilawar Pasha to his death. The rebels, meanwhile, broke into the imperial palace and, freeing Mustafa, the brother of Ahmed I, from his confinement, acclaimed him as their master. Some of the janissaries consulted with the mother of Mustafa about the appointments to be made and it was in fact her son-in-law, the Bosnian Da'ud Pasha, who now became grand vizier. The faction committed to the cause of Mustafa and of his mother, the Walide Sultan, could not feel secure while 'Osman II was still alive. Their uneasiness was well grounded, since some of the rebels wished to spare 'Osman, hoping no doubt to make use of him for their own ends at some future date. Da'ud Pasha had recourse, therefore, to the last extreme measure—on 20 May 1622 'Osman II was strangled in the prison of Yedi Kule at Istanbul.

The second reign of Sultan Mustafa was a time of confusion, during which the troops of the imperial household dominated the course of events. Da'ud Pasha, in 1623, lost his life in the fluctuation of intrigue and violence around the throne. The unbridled conduct of the troops—with the janissaries and the sipahis of the Porte often at odds amongst themselves—was at its worst in 1623 during the grand vizierate of Mere Hüseyn. It was now becoming difficult to achieve even the indispensable minimum of government. A 'revolt' of the *'ulema* led, however, to the fall of Mere Hüseyn and also to the deposition, for the second time, of Sultan Mustafa—an event which was the essential prerequisite of a return to some degree of order.

The new sultan, Murad IV, was a son of Ahmed I. His accession to the throne did not mean that the rule of courtiers and officials was at an end. Murad, when he became sultan, had not yet completed his twelfth year. He was to remain for some time yet little more than a tool in the hands of his mother, Kösem, and of the dignitaries aligned with or against her according to the circumstances of the moment. Moreover, from time to time, indiscipline amongst the janissaries and the sipahis of the Porte still flared out into open violence. The intrigues of Rejeb Pasha in 1626 constituted, it would seem, one of the factors responsible for a new turmoil which, despite all that Sultan Murad and the Walide Sultan could do, brought death to a loyal and trusted vizier—the eunuch Gurji Mehemmed Pasha, who was ninety-six years old, had served under

Sultan Süleyman and now, in the judgement of the English ambassador at Istanbul, Sir Thomas Roe, was still 'the most able and only wise man in this state'.[1]

More violent still was the spasm of revolt which occurred in 1631–2. The animosities dividing some of the most prominent amongst the great dignitaries—Khusrew Pasha and Rejeb Pasha as against Hafîz Ahmed Pasha and Mustafa Pasha—awoke once more the fires of revolt. Murad IV, with his own life in danger, had to sacrifice Hafîz Ahmed to the anger of the soldiers. His reaction to this moment of humiliation was prompt and vigorous. Convinced that Khusrew Pasha was responsible in no small measure for the renewal of violence, he gave orders for his execution. A further paroxysm of revolt ensued, in the course of which the sultan suffered a second humiliation, even more intimate and personal, in the death of his friend Musa. For some two months the janissaries and the sipahis of the Porte gave free rein to their licence and indiscipline at Istanbul. Murad IV waited until the time was opportune and then struck hard, removing from the scene Rejeb Pasha, whom he considered to be one of the most active personalities behind the recent troubles. The execution of Rejeb Pasha was carried out on 18 May 1632—a date which saw the sultan liberated once and for all from the tutelage of the great officials and which marked the real beginning of his reign. He had grown to manhood in a world of danger and duress. His character was tempered to the hardness of steel in the harsh and bitter experiences of his youth. A ferocious and inexorable resolve to be the master in his own house would henceforth dominate his actions. It is not surprising that in the eight years of life remaining to him he was to become perhaps the most feared and terrible of all the Ottoman sultans.

The long turbulence which followed the death of Ahmed I was not due to the spirit of intrigue and faction alone. One factor contributing towards the murder of 'Osman II was, as noted earlier, the belief current among the janissaries and the sipahis of the Porte, that under the guise of a pilgrimage to Mecca, he meant to set in motion a scheme contrived for their ultimate ruin. The main proponent of this scheme, according to the correspondence of Sir Thomas Roe, was Dilawar Pasha, raised to the grand vizierate at the time of the Polish campaign in 1621 and destined to lose his life in the revolt of 1622—a resolute man, who won over 'Osman II, in the words of Sir Thomas, to 'a brave and well-grounded designe and of great consequence for the renewing of this decayed empire'[2]—a project for raising in the provinces of Asia Minor and Syria forces powerful enough to give the sultan control over the troops of the central régime. A scheme so daring reflected, in the mere fact of its formu-

[1] Cf. J. W. Zinkeisen, *Geschichte des osmanischen Reiches*, Vol. IV (Gotha, 1856), p. 48, note 2.
[2] Cf. Zinkeisen, *Geschichte des osmanischen Reiches*, Vol. III (Gotha, 1855), p.745, note 1.

lation, the existence of a particular and grave situation confronting the Ottomans.

The wars against Persia (1578–90) and against Austria (1593–1606) imposed on the Ottomans the need to increase greatly their regiments of infantry equipped with firearms and their technical services (e.g. armourers, artillerists, engineers, etc.)—to increase in fact the paid troops of the imperial household. The forces of the central régime, amongst them the janissaries and the sipahis of the Porte, had been recruited thus far from Christian captives of war and from the child tribute levied on the Christian subjects of the sultan—from human material non-Muslim and non-Turkish in origin. These sources of recruitment did not suffice to meet the new circumstances of war. The Ottomans had, therefore, to incorporate in the regiments of the household—or at least to assimilate in status to those troops—recruits drawn from the Muslim-born population of the empire. One consequence of this radical change was a decline in the discipline of the janissaries and the sipahis of the Porte.[1]

This change came, moreover, at a time when the Ottoman government was faced with serious financial difficulties. The tide of conquest was far less rapid and the campaigns much less lucrative than before. Warfare in the Caucasus area and on the middle Danube had become inordinately expensive. Now, with the paid troops of the central régime vastly swollen in number, the strain on the revenues of the state was still more insistent and severe. To find the enormous sums required of it the government had recourse to expedients like the manipulation of the coinage or the reservation to itself of lands belonging to the fief system in the provinces, these lands being then transformed into tax farms [muqata'a] and leased out to tax contractors [mültezim]. It also raised additional revenues known as 'awariḍ-i diwaniyye [levies of the Diwan or Council of State]—taxes imposed formerly to meet exceptional needs, usually of a military character, but now exacted as a regular contribution, and at a rate which increased steadily throughout these years. These factors—allied to other causes, amongst them the pressure of a rising population on resources—combined to bring about a marked inflation unfavourable to all classes enjoying a fixed income and, in particular, to the paid soldiers of the sultan. Inflation was indeed a powerful force driving them to indiscipline and to a reiterated demand for new emoluments and donatives—a demand which had behind it the ultimate sanction of revolt. So frequent and excessive did their claims become that Sir Thomas Roe felt justified in writing that 'the Turkish emperor is now but the Janizaries treasurer'[2]

Of the personnel—officials and soldiers—belonging to the imperial household no small proportion had come to be located in Asia Minor. The process began on a considerable scale as a response to the dangerous

---

[1] Cf. above, pp. 108, 112–13, 116–17, 121–2.

[2] Cf. Zinkeisen, *Geschichte* ... , Vol. III, p. 745, note 1.

tensions visible there during the conflict over the succession to the throne between Selim and Bayezid, the sons of Sultan Süleyman, in the years 1559–61. It was intensified thereafter when the paid forces of the central régime grew more numerous as a result of the great wars against Persia and Austria. The government at Istanbul, finding it difficult to meet the new and burdensome demands on its revenue, assigned to the janissaries and to the sipahis of the Porte offices and emoluments in the administration of the provinces. These troops, in the course of time, bade fair to dominate the provincial scene and to divert a large measure of its local resources to their own advantage. Their penetration into the world of the provinces was to call forth, however, a long and violent reaction.

The sultan had at his command a numerous and influential class of 'feudal' horsemen, known in general as sipahis and established in most, though not in all the regions of the empire. The sipahi held a fief of small [*timar*] or of large [*zi'amet*] yield per annum. No title to the land itself was vested in him—he received no more than the usufruct of the land constituting his fief, that is, the right to take from the population living on it certain dues in cash and in kind. Good service would raise him from a fief of lower to one of higher yield. Out of the revenues thus granted to him the sipahi maintained himself as an efficient soldier. He came to war, moreover, with a retinue which increased in size with the importance of his fief—and this retinue he had to furnish in arms and equipment from the resources made available to him.[1]

To the 'feudal' horsemen—above all in Asia Minor, where the number of small fiefs was large—the changing circumstances of warfare had been unwelcome. The profit to be won in war against Persia and Austria was diminishing, the risk of serious loss much heightened for the individual sipahi in respect of supplies, arms and beasts of burden, so arduous were the long campaigns. To make good the loss was now, in view of the current inflation, more difficult and expensive than before. Warfare, in short, beyond Lake Van or on the middle Danube had become an unrewarding business for the sipahis endowed with a small fief. At the same time the retention in government hands or the lease as *muqata'a* of lands hitherto included in the fief system led to confusion, to a lessened prospect of advancement and to disaffection amongst the 'feudal' horsemen.

A further cause of unrest in Asia Minor was the growth of the population—a growth more rapid than the bringing of new land into cultivation. This imbalance and the resultant pressure on the means of subsistence led to the rise of a surplus element, largely of peasant origin, landless and unemployed. Their number was swollen with the accession of men whom various factors had driven from the soil, for example, the effect of inflation, the fiscal demands of a government straitened in its

[1] Cf. above, pp. 104–6.

resources, the exploitation of the tax-farmers and also the exactions of sipahis reduced to narrow circumstances.

Of this unattached and vagrant class—known as *levendat*—a large proportion became soldiers in the service of the state. The central régime, under the altered conditions of warfare, was obliged to expand its armed forces, hitherto, in general, of non-Muslim and non-Turkish provenance. Now it had to allow recruitment from amongst the Muslim-born subjects of the sultan. It was the human material of the *levendat* which made this expansion possible. Soldiers drawn from this source fought on the frontier as volunteers [*gönüllü*], acted as fortress guards [*mustahfîz*] or served as troops bearing the designation of *sarîja* or *sekban*—troops sometimes assimilated in status to the regiments of the imperial house-hold or else hired as mercenaries for one or more campaigns.

The *levendat* also found employment in the provinces of the empire. With the fief system falling into disorder under the harsh stresses of a warfare expensive to sustain, ill-suited to the capacities of horsemen and demanding above all the use of firearms, the authorities at Istanbul countenanced yet another departure from the old modes of action. The provincial governors began to recruit large retinues, infantry as well as cavalry, composed of *sarîja* and *sekban* levies from the *levendat* of Asia Minor. To maintain these troops the pashas raised in the towns and villages a tax called the *sekban aqçesi*. This recruitment was to be carried so far that the *sarîja* and the *sekban* became the most numerous element in the armed strength of the provinces and, indeed, a main element also in the imperial armies assembled for the great campaigns.

The use of the *levendat* as soldiers was of grave consequence for Asia Minor. Warfare, whether in Armenia and Adharbayjan or on the Danube and the Tisza, was laborious and hard. At times, regiments of the *sarîja* and the *sekban* might abandon a campaign rather than endure the severities of war. There were intervals also when some of the *levendat* soldiers would be out of service. The end of hostilities in 1590 against Persia and in 1606 against Austria saw a reflux, to Asia Minor, of *sarîja* and *sekban* troops bereft of employment. Of serious effect, too, was the fact that Ottoman control over the lands won from the shah in 1578–90 collapsed before the Persian counter-offensive of 1603–7. This collapse meant the return westward of thousands of *levendat* now without an assured occupation.

Of this numerous *soldatesca* no small proportion took to brigandage and revolt as a means of livelihood, acting at times in co-operation with discontented members of the sipahi class and with nomads of Turkish and Kurdish descent. These rebel elements, known in their new guise as *jelali*, exacted from the villages and towns a contribution called *qurban aqçesi* [i.e. protection tax]. The *jelalis* plundered much of Asia Minor between 1596 and 1610. It was in fact a time of hydra-headed rebellion, and of a kind unusually dangerous, the *jelali* bands consisting, for the most part, of *sarija* and *sekban* trained in the great wars, expert in the use of firearms and strengthened with a measure of assistance from another class adept in the arts of war—the 'feudal' sipahis.

The Grand Vizier Kuyuju Murad Pasha crushed this wave of revolt in Asia Minor during the years 1607–10, but armed repression was no more than a brief palliative and the basic causes of the unrest continued to operate as before. The government at Istanbul sought to overcome the internal difficulties confronting it. Under Ahmed I (1603–17) a new *qanun-name* or code of regulations was issued, together with several edicts relating to specific matters of reform. The main objectives in view were to reduce in number the troops and officials belonging to the imperial household, to end the intervention of the janissaries and the sipahis of the Porte in the conduct of affairs and to protect the provinces from the ills afflicting them in recent years.

To the advocates of reform some prospect of amelioration seemed to lie in the divergence of interest visible between the personnel of the central régime and the forces gathered around the provincial governors. The 'men of the Sultan' demanded for themselves assignments of revenue and offices of profit and privilege in the local administrations. This development was inimical to the aims of the *sarija* and *sekban* levies enrolled in the service of the pashas—levies which saw in the resources of the provincial world the means to their own well-being and advantage. It is against a perspective of this order that the death of 'Osman II should be set. The more responsible dignitaries at Istanbul, aware of the need to restore efficient rule, proposed that the sultan should move to the provinces and create there, out of the *sarija* and the *sekban* experienced in war, a powerful counterpoise to the janissaries and the sipahis of the Porte. This scheme, in 1622, brought death to the Grand Vizier Dilawar Pasha and to 'Osman II himself.[1] It also brought to the fore the antagonism separating the *levendat* of the provincial régimes from the troops and officials of the imperial household.

Amongst the *sarija* and the *sekban* in Asia Minor the events of 1622 gave rise to a bitter reaction, soon to be expressed in the great revolt (1622–8) of Abaza Mehemmed, the beglerbeg of Erzurum. Abaza Mehemmed, in 1622, drove out the janissaries stationed at Erzurum and then, with large numbers of the *levendat*, the 'feudal' sipahis and the nomadic tribesmen gathering around his banners, reduced to his own control much of eastern and central Asia Minor, killing off the 'men of the Sultan' wherever he encountered them. Although defeated in 1624 not far from Kayseri, Abaza Mehemmed was still able, in 1627, to repulse the forces which the then grand vizier, Khalil Pasha, directed against him at Erzurum. It was not until the following year that he surrendered at

---

[1] See above, pp. 136–7.

last to the Grand Vizier Khusrew Pasha. Too powerful still amongst the *sarīja* and the *sekban* to be punished with death, Abaza Mehemmed was sent to an appointment far from the region where his influence was so strong—he became now the beglerbeg of Bosnia on the north-western frontier of the empire. His removal to Europe did not mean that the 'time of troubles' in Asia Minor was over. The old grounds of disaffection and tumult remained active. Their stubborn and enduring vigour would be demonstrated on a number of occasions in the future—for instance, the revolt, in 1647, of Varvar 'Ali Pasha; the career of Ibşir Mustafa Pasha, a nephew of Abaza Mehemmed and, for a short interval, grand vizier in 1654–5; and the insurrection of Abaza Hasan Pasha in 1658.

Of the difficulties facing the Ottoman government after 1617 not the least onerous was a new war against Persia. Shah 'Abbas I (1587–1629), in the years 1603–7, had recovered the territories ceded to the Ottomans in 1590. A peace made in 1612 gave formal recognition to the success of the Persians. Further hostilities in 1615–18 led to the confirmation of the settlement reached in 1612. Conflict was to break out once more in 1623, the main theatre of operations being now Iraq.

The northern and central regions of Iraq had been conquered from Persia and incorporated into the Ottoman Empire during the years 1534–5; the southern areas, and in particular Basra, came under Ottoman control in 1546–7. The population of Iraq was of mixed racial origin, embracing elements of Arab, Persian, Turkish and Kurdish descent. It was, moreover, a population divided in its religious allegiance. Kurdistan and the northern territories followed, in large degree, the Sunni or orthodox Muslim faith; central and southern Iraq contained numerous adherents of the most notable of the Muslim heterodoxies, Shi'i Islam, which was the official creed of Persia. Over some areas Ottoman rule was precarious and uncertain—over Basra, vulnerable to attack from Persia or from the marsh Arabs located in the Shatt al-'Arab; over the desert lands, known as al-Ahsa, along the north-western shore of the Persian Gulf; and over various border zones often in dispute with Persia— in the regions of Khuzistan, Luristan and Shahrizur. The Ottomans had also to deal with the Arab tribes inhabiting the deserts to the west of Iraq —tribes able to threaten the caravan routes leading from Basra to Aleppo and ever prone to encroach on the settled areas, whenever the administration at Baghdad was involved in difficulties or rested in the hands of men not equal to the circumstances of the moment. Iraq was, in short, a frontier province complex in character and troublesome to rule.

Ottoman control in Iraq began to weaken in the time of Mehemmed III (1595–1603) and Ahmed I (1603–17). A little before or a little after 1600— the exact date is not clear—Basra fell under the domination of local dynasts known as the House of Afrasiyab. At Baghdad the Ottoman

garrison troops stationed there in the reign of Sultan Süleyman had evolved into an entrenched social class composed mostly of local recruits and
responsive, above all, to the aspirations of its own dignitaries. One of
the regimental officers, a certain Muhammad ibn Ahmad al-Tawil, was
able to assert an effective control over Baghdad during the years 1604–7.
A situation much more dangerous for the Ottomans arose, however, in
1621–3.

An officer of the janissaries, by name Bakr Subashi [i.e. Bakr, the
chief of police] created for himself a faction so strong amongst the troops
of Baghdad that from about 1619 onwards he was the most important
figure in the town—far more influential, in fact, than the pasha. Opposed
to Bakr Subashi was the faction of Muhammad Qanbar, the officer
in charge of the soldiers called 'Azeban. In 1621 the strife between the
two factions broke out into violent conflict as a result of which Bakr
Subashi became the master of Baghdad, his rival Muhammad Qanbar
being now done to death. Bakr sought to obtain from Istanbul a formal
recognition of himself as pasha of Baghdad—but without success. The
Porte ordered Hafîz Ahmed, the governor of Diyar Bakr, to reduce
Baghdad to obedience. At this juncture of affairs Bakr Subashi turned
for aid to Shah 'Abbas of Persia. The shah at once sent a force to relieve
Baghdad. Hafîz Ahmed, with a Persian intervention imminent, acceded
to the demands of Bakr and withdrew his troops, while Bakr, having
secured recognition from the Ottoman authorities, renounced his now
unwelcome allies from Persia. The Persians, however, besieged Baghdad
and took it with the assistance of Muhammad, the son of Bakr, who
wanted to govern the town himself. Bakr Subashi was executed and the
Sunni Muslims of Baghdad subjected to a fierce persecution at the
hands of the Shi'i forces of the shah.

These events marked the beginning, in 1623, of a war which was to
last until 1639. Hafîz Ahmed Pasha, as grand vizier, made a determined
attempt to wrest Baghdad from the Persians in 1625–6. A lack of sufficient
artillery contributed much to the failure of his siege operations. Moreover,
an army of relief under the command of Shah 'Abbas beleaguered the
Ottomans in their own lines and entrenchments. Hafîz Ahmed, with his
situation precarious and with discontent rife amongst his men, was obliged
at last to raise the siege and withdraw to Mosul. Not until 1629 did the
Ottomans concentrate their forces for another major campaign in Iraq.
The winter of 1629–30 was, however, exceptionally long and severe.
Snow, rain and floods made operations in central Iraq almost impossible.
The Ottoman grand vizier, Khusrew Pasha, decided therefore to under-
take a campaign in the march-lands of Shahrizur. After routing the
Persians at the Battle of Mihriban, Khusrew Pasha took and sacked
Hamadan in the summer of 1630 and then, in the autumn of that year,
led his troops to a new siege of Baghdad—a siege abandoned in Novem-

ber 1630 after a fruitless assault, the Ottomans retiring once again to Mosul.

The years following the campaign of 1630 witnessed a further out-break of factional violence at Istanbul and, in 1632, the emergence of Murad IV as sultan in fact as well as in name. Sultan Murad, before the renewal of operations against Persia, resolved to eliminate a possible source of danger in Syria. The Ottomans had never sought to exert a direct and immediate control over the Lebanon—a region which afforded a sure refuge in its mountain fastnesses to the ethnic and religious minorities established there in earlier times—the Druzes and the Maronites. The tribesmen of the Lebanon, after the Ottoman conquest of Syria in 1516, remained free to pursue, high in the mountains, their own purposes and feuds, provided that the Ottoman hold on the routes and cities of Syria was not called into question.

One Druze chieftain, Fakhr al-Din II, of the House of Ma'n, began in 1590 to consolidate and extend his influence—an endeavour so successful that it was to make him the master of the Lebanon. His efforts to win control over the northern reaches of the land, Kisrawan and the adjacent littoral, brought him into conflict with the Ottoman administration at Tripoli, while his attempts to move southward into the areas of Hawran, 'Ajlun and Nabulus threatened the pilgrimage route leading to the Hijaz and alarmed the Ottoman authorities at Damascus. A number of factors worked, however, in favour of Fakhr al-Din. At Istanbul his agents used bribes to forestall measures hostile to him. Moreover, the Ottoman officials in Syria had, in general, only a brief tenure of appointment—a fact which made it difficult for them to set in motion a long-term resistance to the Druze amir.

In 1613 the local opponents of Fakhr al-Din aligned themselves with Hafiz Ahmed Pasha, the beglerbeg of Damascus. Hafiz Ahmed, strengthened by reinforcements and by the co-operation of a naval squadron sailing off the coast of the Lebanon, now moved against the Ma'nid chieftain. Fakhr al-Din fled to Europe, where he remained for five years under the protection of Cosimo II, the grand duke of Tuscany, and later of Philip III, the king of Spain. He was able, in 1618, to secure from the Ottomans permission to return to the Lebanon. Once more Fakhr al-Din began to extend his influence both northward into Kisrawan and southward to 'Ajlun, Nabulus and Safad, all of which the government at Istanbul, in 1622, entrusted to his nominees. At 'Anjarr in 1625 the Druze amir defeated his local enemies and the beglerbeg of Damascus, who had made common cause against him. Fakhr al-Din was to dominate the Lebanon thereafter for some ten years. His power rested on his Druze adherents—but even more on a strong force of mercenaries. To support these troops, to maintain the forts guarding his territories and to provide the funds dispensed in his name at Istanbul Fakhr al-Din needed a large revenue. He obtained it through the increase of the lands under his control, but also through the efficient exploitation of the economic resources available to him. His efforts to promote a new growth of trade at Beirut and Sidon met with considerable success. An agreement that he made with Cosimo II in 1608 brought into his service Italian merchants, engineers and agricultural experts. At the same time he favoured the cause of religious toleration, extending a welcome to Christian missionaries from Europe, to Kurdish elements from the region of Aleppo and to the Maronites, some of whom settled in the southern Lebanon and helped to improve the condition of agriculture there.

The power of Fakhr al-Din rested, however, as much on the confusion rife at Istanbul as on his own abilities. In 1632 Sultan Murad assumed control of the imperial government. Murad IV was eager to launch a new offensive against Persia and reluctant, therefore, to allow the continued existence of a strong régime in the Lebanon—a régime which was of doubtful allegiance and which might seek to turn to its further advantage in Syria a renewed and major involvement of the Ottomans in the eastern war. Küçük Ahmed Pasha, the beglerbeg of Damascus, strengthened with large reinforcements, moved against Fakhr al-Din in 1634. The Ma'nid amir, beaten in the field, was captured in 1635 and sent to Istanbul where, in April of that year, he was executed on the suspicion that his influence stood behind the still active unrest in the Lebanon.

The war with Persia now entered into its last phase. Sultan Murad took the Persian fortress of Erivan after a short siege (July-August 1635) and then advanced towards Tabriz, which fell to him in September 1635. As on earlier campaigns into Adharbayjan, the Ottomans found that the Persians had adhered to their usual tactics of retreat—harassing the columns of the enemy, lengthening his lines of communication and sweeping the land clean of supplies. The sultan, with no prospect of a decisive result before him, abandoned Tabriz and retired westward into Asia Minor. By December 1635 he was once more at Istanbul. It was at the moment of his arrival there that the Persians appeared before the walls of Erivan. After a stubborn resistance the Ottoman garrison surrendered the fortress in April 1636. The events at Erivan in 1635–6 demonstrated a truth long since manifest—that, in war against Persia, there would be no enduring success for the Ottomans save through the permanent occupation of wide territories beyond their eastern frontier, a solution which was difficult to achieve and expensive to maintain, as the great conflict of 1578–90 had made clear.

Sultan Murad now turned his attention to Iraq. The years 1636–8 saw elaborate preparations in progress for a new campaign, this time with Baghdad as the main objective. On 8 May 1638 the sultan left Üsküdar and, on 15 November, began the siege of Baghdad. A fierce assault on 24 December was decisive. The Persian commander yielded the town on the following day. Some of the garrison continued to resist, however, despite the capitulation. A conflict of extreme violence ensued, in the course of which most of the Persians lost their lives. Murad IV set out on the return march to Istanbul in January 1639, leaving the Grand Vizier, Kemankeş Qara Mustafa Pasha, to conduct negotiations with the representatives of Shah Safi. A settlement was reached at Zuhab, near Qasr-i Şirin, in May 1639. This peace brought to an end the long contention between the Ottomans and the Persians begun in the time of Sultan Selim I (d. 1520) and Shah Ismaʿil (d.1524). Erivan and the adjacent territories would remain under Persian control, while Iraq was to be Ottoman. The peace terms also included measures for a demarcation of the frontier separating the Ottoman Empire from Persia— and, in fact, along a line which, at least in relation to the modern states of Iraq and Iran, has endured without serious modification until the present day. Sultan Murad did not long survive his triumphant return to Istanbul in June 1639. He died on 9 February 1640.

Amid the intrigue and violence surrounding the throne in the years after 1617 there were men able and willing to exercise power in a responsible manner, 'strong men' like Dilawar Pasha (d.1622) or Gurji Mehemmed Pasha (d.1626). Influential, too, were those officials—for instance, Koçu Beg, the author of the famous *Risale* [i.e. *Treatise*]—who analysed the reasons and explained the remedies for the troubles which beset the Ottoman state.[1] It is here among the dignitaries and soldiers intent on the restoration of efficient rule that Murad IV must be numbered, above all during the years (1632–40) of his personal control over the conduct of affairs.

To the extirpation of disobedience and revolt within the empire Sultan Murad brought a shrewd intelligence, an indefatigable resolution—and a pitiless severity. The intrigue and violence encompassing his youth did much to fashion the man that he was to become. All went down before him in a ferocious and unending sequence of executions. Vengeance, he is reputed to have said, never grows old, it only grows grey![2] In the judgement of the Venetian bailo at Istanbul, Alvise Contarini, no sultan ever attained a more absolute domination of the empire. The great physical strength of Murad, his skill in the use of arms and his vivid, though sombre character made a deep—and, for his purposes, a valuable —impression on the soldiers of the imperial household. These same qualities won for him also much favour amongst the *sarija* and *sekban* levies and, in addition, amongst the populace of Istanbul, that is, with forces which might act as a counterpoise to the indiscipline hitherto so frequent in the janissaries and the sipahis of the Porte. Contarini observed

---

[1] Cf. above, pp. 106–8.
[2] Cf. J. von Hammer, *Histoire de l'Empire Ottoman*, trans. J.-J. Hellert, Vol. IX (Paris, 1837), p. 389, note 3: 'Solea dire che non invecchiano mai le vendette benche incanutissero'.

of the sultan that he was unwearied in his application to business and eager to be well informed on all matters.[1] An elaborate 'espionage system' gave him news about events and opinions both in the provinces and amongst the people of Istanbul. It also enabled him to maintain a close surveillance over the troops of the central régime. Of relevance here are the measures that he took to restrict the use of tobacco, coffee and wine—at the establishments selling these commodities the soldiers often met and, in talk amongst themselves, magnified discontent into sedition. Sultan Murad, through means of this kind and through the fear that his implacable temper called forth, was able to restore discipline and order in the regiments belonging to the imperial household —able to reduce the troops in number, to eject the least welcome elements among them and to eradicate some of the worst abuses. A similar pro-gramme was carried out in the provinces, where much was done to reorganize the 'feudal' system and to recover fiefs which had fallen into illegal or incompetent hands. At the same time Murad IV set in train the preparation of an 'Adalet-name, a 'Book of Justice' containing measures for the protection of the peasants.

The labour of reform was long, complicated—and also expensive. Moreover, the war against Persia demanded a large expenditure of revenue. It was not accidental that the sultan had, amongst his con-temporaries, a reputation for excessive avarice—'avarizia per ecesso' in the words of Alvise Contarini.[2] Of Murad IV it was said that what he did not do for cash he would do neither for prayer nor intercession, neither for justice nor law.[3] A verdict of this kind reflects the determination of the sultan to fill the coffers of the state. An abundant treasure was one of the surest means to the achievement of his aims. It was also a safeguard for his own person, since he was able, with the ample funds at his com-mand, to ensure the regular payment—and thus the allegiance—of his armed forces. An efficient collection of revenue, measures to guide the resulting yield into the hands of the government and out of the hands of officials and tax-farmers, the use of confiscation as a further and rich source of income—such methods led to a success so great that one Venetian of this time, Pietro Foscarini, described Murad IV as the richest of all the Ottoman Sultans.[4] The years of his effective rule, with their remarkable combination of sober policy and wise management, of fierce energy and also of signal cruelty, stemmed for a while the disorders

[1] Cf. N. Barozzi and G. Berchet, *Le Relazioni degli Stati Europei lette al Senato nel secolo decimosettimo*, Fifth Series: *Turkey*, Pt I (Venice, 1871), p. 368: 'applicatissimo al governo, vago di saper tutto'.

[2] Cf. Barozzi and Berchet, *ibid.* p. 367.

[3] Cf. Hammer, *Histoire . . .*, Vol. IX, p. 421: 'quello che per il denaro non fa, non lo fa per preghiere, non per intercessione, non per giustizia, non lo fa per legge'.

[4] Cf. N. Jorga, *Geschichte des osmanischen Reiches*, Vol. III (Gotha, 1910), p. 463, note 2: 'È il più ricco di tutti i principi che sono stati della Casa ottomana.'

within the empire. But their duration was all too brief and it was not long before the work had to be done again.

The Ottomans, since the death of Ahmed I in 1617, had been involved in no major conflict with the states of Christendom. There was, however, a short war against Poland in 1620–1. Along the march-lands dividing the Polish and the Ottoman territories the raiding of Cossacks from the Ukraine and of Tatars from the Crimea was a source of continuing friction. The Cossacks also sailed down the rivers, the Dnieper and the Dniester for instance, and ventured out into the Black Sea, plundering Sinope in 1614 and Anchialos in 1621.[1] A further cause of unrest was the intervention of Poland, from time to time, in the affairs of Moldavia, seeking to establish on the throne of this small Christian state dependent on the sultan a vaivoda favourable to Polish interests. There had been in 1616 a brief outburst of hostilities, in the course of which the Ottoman frontier begs of the Danube line inflicted a severe defeat on a Polish-Cossack force operating in Moldavia. These hostilities ended in 1617 with the Peace of Buzsa, which laid it down that Poland was not to interfere in matters relating to the government of Moldavia and that measures should be taken, on the one side as on the other, to hinder the incursions of the Cossacks and the Tatars.

The peace was soon to be broken. Gratiani, the vaivoda of Moldavia, being deposed from office in 1620 on the order of 'Osman II, sought and secured aid from Poland. At Ţuţora, near Iaşi, the Danube begs, reinforced by a numerous contingent of Tatars, routed the Polish–Moldavian forces in September 1620. It was now that Sultan 'Osman resolved to undertake a major offensive against Poland—and this in opposition to the advice of the more moderate amongst the high dignitaries of the Porte and in spite of the fact that a Polish ambassador was bringing proposals for the renewal of the peace. The march northward to the Danube in the late spring of 1621 was slow and difficult because of the bad weather. After crossing the Danube at Isaqça, the Ottomans moved towards Chocim, which was not reached, however, until August 1621. The Poles held a fortified encampment on the banks of the Dniester. A first Ottoman attack met with some success, but the subsequent assaults, five in number, ended in failure. The cold and the rain presaging the onset of winter and the growing lack of supplies now brought the campaign to a close. Sultan 'Osman was obliged to make peace with Poland in October 1621, and on terms which constituted in fact a reaffirmation of the agreement made in 1617.

As for relations between Vienna and Istanbul—the involvement of Austria in the Thirty Years War (1618–48) and of the Ottoman Empire

---

[1] The Cossacks even penetrated into the Bosphorus and, in 1625, plundered Yeniköy, a suburb of Istanbul. In 1637 Azov, at the mouth of the River Don, fell to them and remained in their hands until 1642, when the Ottomans sent a strong force to drive them out of the town.

in the long conflict with Persia (1623–39) meant that neither side could envisage a serious confrontation on the Danube. The *Kleinkrieg* between Christian marcher lord and Ottoman ghazi along the frontier continued unabated as heretofore. None the less, the Peace of Zsitva-Torok, negotiated in 1606, was confirmed, with some modification of detail, at Neuhäusel in 1608, at Vienna in 1615, at Gyarmath in 1625, at Szön in 1627 and again at Szön in 1642—confirmed after long discussion to achieve the dismantling, in Hungary, of the small forts [*palanka*] sometimes erected in contravention of the articles of peace and to ascertain the dependence—on the Christian or the Muslim state—and also the taxation status of the villages adjacent to the great fortresses like Erlau, Kanizsa or Stuhlweissenburg, which were now under Ottoman rule.

The old idea of the Crusade, though shorn of compulsive force, was still not without effect in Europe. To the realization once more of this idea the men of the Counter-Reformation gave much time and effort. These years saw the unfolding of numerous designs for the invasion of the Ottoman Empire—designs centred on such 'claimants' to the Ottoman territories as the duc de Nevers (descended from one of the last Palaeologi) or the '*gran principe ottomano*', Yahya, reputed to be a son of Sultan Mehemmed III (1595–1603). Numerous, too, were the schemes for exploiting the possibilities of local resistance to Ottoman rule within the Balkans, above all in regions which had never come under the full and direct control of the Porte, for instance, the district of Maina in the Morea and also Albania and Montenegro. A good example of such schemes can be found in a project submitted to the Diet of Ratisbon in 1640, envisaging an advance into Albania and the capture of important fortresses like Kroja and Skutari, a mass rising of the Christians and the occupation of the strategic routes through Serbia in order to hinder the arrival of Ottoman relief forces from Bosnia and the lands along the middle Danube, and then, to crown these efforts, a 'break-out' eastwards and a rapid march on Istanbul. There was in fact small prospect of success for an enterprise of this kind. The states of western and central Europe, dedicated to the pursuit of their own ambitions and involved, most of them, in the Thirty Years War, had neither the will nor the means to embark on a design so grandiose and so dubious. As to the 'resistance' in the Balkans against Ottoman rule—the stress laid, in these projects of invasion, on areas like Maina and Albania is sufficient to underline the character and limitations of that 'resistance'. It reflected far more a readiness to defend local traditions and modes of life than a zeal for general insurrection in the name of a 'crusade'.

A more practical approach was available, however, to the forces of the Counter-Reformation. The Peace of Vienna (1615) contained a clause permitting the Jesuits to maintain their own establishments and churches within the Ottoman Empire. A little later, in 1622, the foundation at

Rome of the Congregatio de Propaganda Fide strengthened the activities of the Catholic church in the eastern lands. Moreover, the interest which Father Joseph, the agent of Cardinal Richelieu, showed in the work of the Congregatio led him to organize a Capuchin mission to Istanbul. The Jesuits and the Capuchins had the support of the Catholic ambassadors at the Porte—a fact which caused the Ottomans to view the two orders with some suspicion and to see in their religious endeavours a cloak for political ambitions emanating from Rome, Paris and Vienna. To the dignitaries of the Greek Orthodox church the arrival of the Catholic orders was unwelcome and resistance to them soon became concentrated around the person of Lukaris, the patriarch of Constantinople, a known and respected champion of the Greek religion, language and culture. On the side of the patriarch and his adherents stood the ambassadors of Protestant England and Holland, in opposition to the representatives of Catholicism.

The Jesuits and the Capuchins, in pursuit of their religious calling, devoted much time and effort to education. It was now that under the guidance of the two orders young Greeks, usually of good birth, went in considerable numbers to be educated at Catholic centres of learning in Rome, Padua and Venice—now, too, that with the approval of the anti-Catholic forces mustered around the patriarch young Greeks studied at Protestant centres of learning in Germany and in England. The year 1627 saw the arrival in Istanbul, from London, of a printing press for the publication of religious literature written in Greek and intended for distribution amongst the adherents of the Orthodox faith. The Jesuits induced the Ottomans to seize the press, whereupon the printer, Niko-demos Metaxas, took refuge at the house of the English ambassador, Sir Thomas Roe. A vigorous protest from Sir Thomas, who had much influence at the Porte, led now to the banishment of the Jesuits from the empire. After Roe's departure for England in 1628 the Jesuits returned to Istanbul, careful henceforth to act with greater circumspection than before and in directions less apt to awaken the distrust of the Ottoman authorities.

The Peace of Zuhab in 1639[1] left the Porte free to turn its attention elsewhere. Soon it became involved in a new and formidable war, this time against Venice and for possession of the island of Crete. Along the eastern shore of the Adriatic, on the borders of the enclaves still under Venetian rule, there was often friction between the Ottoman frontier warriors and the mercenaries—Albanian, Greek and Cretan—in the service of the Signoria. At sea the situation was still more uncertain. Here the maritime forces of Venice came into conflict with the corsairs of Algiers, Tunis and Tripoli.

A moment of crisis had occurred in the summer of 1638, when a

---

[1] See above, p. 147.

squadron from Tunis, commanded by a well-known renegade, 'Ali Piccenino, sailed into the Straits of Otranto, raided the coast of Apulia and then captured a Venetian ship off Cattaro. The Signoria ordered Marino Capello, cruising at that time in the waters of Crete, to deal with the corsairs. Piccenino found refuge under the guns of the Ottoman fortress at Valona. Capello, after a blockade of Valona lasting about a month, entered the harbour, bombarded the town and made off with the corsair vessels. Murad IV, with the Persian war still in progress, restrained his anger and agreed to negotiate. The affair ended peacefully when, in 1639, Venice paid 250,000 *sequins* as compensation for the ships taken by Capello.

A further source of tension was to be found in the militant religious Orders of Christendom—the Knights of Saint Stephen and the Knights of Saint John at Malta. Around the orders there hung, in pious Christian eyes, an aura of splendour deriving from long-maintained conflict with the Muslim infidel. To the Muslims the Knights of Saint Stephen and Saint John—not less than the corsairs of North Africa to the Christians—were pirates greatly to be feared because of their raids at sea and along the shores of the Levant. The activities of Malta, to an especial degree, envenomed the relations existing between the Ottoman Empire and the Christian states. Even in Europe itself, as a report from France written in 1627 made clear, the view was gaining ground that the orders had outlived their usefulness. Venice, in general, regarded with disfavour the depredations of the knights, which were sometimes indiscriminate at the expense of friend and foe alike, and discouraged her subjects from serving with the orders. The Signoria found it impossible, however, to close to the knights the harbours in Crete and in the other islands and mainland territories under her control.

A Maltese squadron in September 1644, near Rhodes, encountered a number of Ottoman vessels laden with a rich cargo. The knights captured these ships after a stiff fight and then sailed with their plunder to Crete. This episode sufficed to bring to the fore the faction hostile to Venice amongst the dignitaries at the Porte. The winter of 1644–5 saw the Ottomans engaged in elaborate preparations for war—preparations which included the building of ships, the casting of guns and the gathering of munitions and supplies in the harbours of the Morea and along the western coast of Asia Minor. On 30 April 1645 the Ottoman fleet sailed for Crete, moving first to Chios and then to Navarino. Ottoman troops, transported from Navarino, landed in Crete on 23–4 June 1645, some distance to the west of Canea.

The Porte had now committed itself to an arduous war—and against no mean foe. Crete would not become Ottoman until 1669. The fact that Venice was able to bear the expense of so long a conflict underlines the richness of the resources still at her command. The decline of Venice is not to be dated from the conquests of the Portuguese around the shores of the Indian Ocean after 1498. Those conquests disrupted for a time, but did not end the flow of spices and other eastern commodities from India through the lands of Islam to the Mediterranean world. The transit trade across Egypt and Syria soon recovered its former amplitude. Not till the arrival in the Indian Ocean—and also in the Mediterranean—of powers stronger than the Portuguese, i.e. the English and the Dutch, was the balance altered decisively in favour of the sea route to Europe via the Cape of Good Hope. By the second quarter of the seventeenth century the two Protestant states had won a preponderance in the spice trade from the East and a large share, too, in the local traffic of the Mediterranean itself. Venice was able, none the less, to offset in no small degree the consequences of this change in her situation. She strove, and with success, to retain some of her commerce to and from the Levant and to extend her trading activities in the regions behind the eastern shore of the Adriatic. The readiness of the Signoria to grant concessions in respect of tolls, customs and labour dues brought numerous Dutch and English ships to Venice and thus enriched the finances of the state. Moreover, the government and the citizens of Venice began now to exploit more than ever before the abundant resources, agricultural and industrial, of the *Terra Firma*, that is, of the north Italian lands under their control. It was from measures of this order, much more than from the expedients usual in a time of crisis (donations, the sale of titles, new taxes and the like) that Venice drew the means to defend Crete so well against the Ottomans.

The balance of success, during the first campaigns of the war, inclined towards the armies of the sultan. The rule of the Signoria in Crete amounted to little more than the domination, often harsh and intolerant, of a small class of soldiers, officials and administrators, Italian and Roman Catholic in culture and religion, over a population Greek Orthodox in faith and Greek in speech and tradition. There was no prospect that the people of Crete would rise *en masse* in defence of Venetian rule over the island. Canea fell to the Ottomans in August 1645. Retimo surrendered to them in November 1646. The able soldier Hüseyn Pasha, in command of the Ottoman forces since September 1646, blockaded Candia in the summer of 1647 and began a formal siege of the fortress in April 1648. Of the naval operations in progress at this time it will suffice to mention that the Venetians, in 1645, sailed from Zante to Patras, bombarding and plundering the town; also that their fleet, in 1646-8, penetrated deep into the Aegean Sea, but failed to achieve a major success. There was fighting, too, in Dalmatia, where the Ottomans took Novigrad in 1646. An Ottoman attempt, in 1647, to capture Sebenico ended in defeat and the Venetians thereafter occupied a number of important fortresses, including Dernis, Knin and Klis, in 1647-8.

By 1648 the main lines of the war had become clear. Some areas of conflict would have only a local significance. On the Dalmatian front Venice used her command of the sea to reinforce a stubborn defence against Ottoman incursions into the Adriatic littoral. Moreover, the attempts of the Signoria to awaken resistance to the Ottomans, for instance amongst the Mainotes of the Morea in 1653 and in 1659, achieved only a limited result.

The Ottomans had to overcome Venetian naval pressure in the waters of the Aegean Sea. Of no less importance was their need to maintain as an effective force the army fighting in Crete—a task which involved the large-scale movement of men and supplies from southern Greece and from Asia Minor. To meet this continuing need the Ottomans organized 'convoy campaigns' at sea, employed also numerous small vessels which slipped out of the harbours in the Morea and on the coast of Asia Minor and, in addition, hired or impressed into their service foreign ships, notably of English and Dutch origin.

Venice was to centre her defensive effort in Crete on the maintenance of one great fortified base, Candia—a course of action which enabled her to concentrate her troops on the island in a manner at once economical and effective and, through her fleet, to reinforce them at will. As long as Candia remained unconquered, Crete was not yet Ottoman. The offensive operations of Venice would be carried out at sea. To cut off the flow of men and munitions to Hüseyn Pasha was to reduce the Ottoman army in Crete to desperation. The Venetians directed the most massive of their naval campaigns to the fulfilment of this aim, that is, sought to crush the Ottoman battle fleet in a major action or else to blockade the mouth of the Dardanelles and even penetrate, if possible, through the straits into the Sea of Marmara—a threat so dangerous that the Ottomans, during the earlier years of the war, fortified the Dardanelles anew. Although well and resolutely led by captains like Lazaro Mocenigo and Francesco Morosini, the Venetian fleet was not able to realize this programme. One reason for its failure to win a decisive success was the fact that the Ottomans had an alternative concentration area at their command—the 'canal of Chios', between that island and the coast of Asia Minor, where ships, reinforcements and supplies could be brought together for transport to Crete. The naval resources of the Signoria did not suffice for a firm blockade both of the Dardanelles and of the waters around Chios.

It was in 1654–6 that Venice made her supreme challenge at sea. A great battle off the Dardanelles in June 1656 shattered the Ottoman fleet and enabled the Venetians to seize the islands of Lemnos and Tenedos close to the mouth of the straits. The Ottomans, with a rapid and astonishing deployment of their rich resources, now built a new fleet and, in 1657, used it to regain Tenedos in September and Lemnos in November of that year. The war would in fact continue, with intervals of relative calm, until at last the Porte, under the guidance of the Grand Vizier Ahmed Köprülü, made a vast effort to bring the conflict to an end. Candia, in the course of a long defence begun in 1648, had been transformed into an almost impregnable fortress. Ahmed Köprülü, after a siege which lasted more than two and a quarter years and was perhaps the greatest feat of arms of the age, took Candia in 1669. Venice now accepted the peace terms offered to her. The war was over and Crete, henceforth, a province of the Otto-man Empire.

The firm rule which Murad IV had achieved remained in force for a little while after his death in 1640—that is, during the administration of the last of his grand viziers, Kemankeş Qara Mustafa Pasha, who was to hold the office from 1638 to 1644. Qara Mustafa was faithful to the precepts and practice of Sultan Murad. He sought to reduce in number the janissaries and the sipahis of the Porte. At the same time he was careful to ensure that the troops were paid well and regularly. He set himself, therefore, to reform the coinage, to introduce a more effective and just assessment of taxation and, by these means, to have at his command a full treasury. Qara Mustafa, however, was a grand vizier and not a sultan. Under the eccentric Ibrahim (1640–8) intrigue and faction grew once again to formidable proportions. The rigorous control of Qara Mustafa and his promptitude to punish wrong-doing awakened resentments against him—of the Walide Sultan Kösem, the mother of Ibrahim; of the vizier Sultanzade Mehemmed Pasha; also of the Silahdar Yusuf, who was the favourite, and of Hüseyn Efendi, who was the khoja of Sultan Ibrahim. These powerful figures conspired successfully to bring about the fall of the grand vizier. In 1644 the sultan gave the order for the execution of Qara Mustafa.

The rule of courtiers and officials, faction around the throne, the mis-management of the state revenues, renewed turbulence amongst the troops of the central régime—all the evils so strong before 1632 now, after 1644, dominated the scene once again and with undiminished force. There was also a marked revival of *jelali* dissidence in Asia Minor under such men as Varvar 'Ali Pasha, Ibşir Mustafa Pasha and Abaza Hasan Pasha during the years 1644–58.[1] A revolt of the janissaries and the sipahis of the Porte in August 1648 led to the deposition and death of Sultan Ibrahim, whose ineptitudes and extravagance had earned for him the distrust of the soldiers and dignitaries belonging to the imperial house-hold. The rivalries between the old Walide Kösem, the mother of Ibrahim, and the new Walide Turkhan, the mother of the young Mehemmed IV (1648–87) and their respective adherents called forth, in 1651, a new outburst of violence, in the course of which Kösem, a potent influence behind the throne during the reign of her sons, Murad IV and Ibrahim,

[1] See above, p. 143.

was done to death. An end had to be made to the sequence of intrigue, rebellion and murder. The Venetians, now at the summit of their naval offensive, were threatening in earnest a 'breakthrough' from the Aegean Sea into the Sea of Marmara. With the destruction of the Ottoman fleet in June 1656 a return to order was imperative. It was at this time of crisis that Mehemmed Köprülü came to the grand vizierate. The restoration of efficient rule was swift and sure. His tenure of office (1656–61) and still more the tenure (1661–76) of his son Ahmed Köprülü gave to the Ottoman Empire a further, though brief interval of glittering, but illusive splendour.

6

THE REIGN OF MEHMED IV, 1648–87

SULTAN MEHMED IV who ascended the throne in 1648 inherited a vast empire which had been conquered by the sword of his ancestors and stretched over three continents. In Europe the frontier of the Ottoman Empire was a mere eighty miles from Vienna; in North Africa only Morocco did not belong to it; it included Upper Egypt and extended to Aden; the Black Sea and the Red Sea were Turkish lakes; in the east it stretched to the shores of the Caspian and of the Persian Gulf. It is impossible to give the exact figure of its population, but in the seventeenth century it amounted to approximately 25 or 30 millions. The Turks, although the dominant race, were only a minority. Probably the Muslims —Turks, Arabs, Kurds, Bosnians, Albanians, Circassians, Crimean Tatars and Turkic peoples of the Caucasus—were stronger than the Christians—Greeks, Serbs, Hungarians, Bulgars, Wallachians and Moldavians. Outstanding among the Turks of this period were the famous historian, geographer and bibliographer Kâtib Tchelebi (1609–57) and the renowned traveller Evliya Tchelebi (1611–78), who described the cities, customs and peoples of the Ottoman Empire in his huge ten volumes. Its heart was the city of Constantinople (Istanbul), the seat of the military and administrative institutions of the empire, the centre of commerce and culture as well as amusement and pleasures. It was inhabited by more than half a million people, Muslims, Christians and Jews, all living side by side for centuries, observing their own customs. The city contained the palace of the sultans, the Serail, the splendid mosques of Sultan Ahmed, Suleymaniye, Bayezid, Selimiye and Sultan Mehmed the Conqueror, many *Medrese*'s (colleges), libraries, public baths, hospitals, inns and food distribution centres, maintained by pious endowments. The 'second capital' of the empire was the city of Adrianople, where the sultans spent many of their leisure hours, and which served the army as a base at the beginning of a campaign against the Christian powers. The holy cities of Mecca and Medina stood under the sultan's special care, for as the caliph it was his duty to protect these places, which were visited every year by hundreds of thousands of pilgrims from every corner of the Muslim world, and to give large donations to them.

Basically the empire was an agricultural country with many fertile areas, and taxes on land and farming were the principal source of revenue. The methods of agriculture, however, were very primitive and the tools used were rudimentary. The status of the peasants was that of serfs; the Muslim peasants gave the tithes from corn and were subject to many other obligations, while the Christian peasants in addition had to pay the *Djizye* or poll-tax which exempted them from military service, its amount varying according to the peasants' status and incomes. As the empire dominated the main trade routes from the Mediterranean to the East, trade, although hampered by many obstacles, played an important part. Constantinople and Smyrna were the main centres of trade with foreign countries, while Adrianople, Brussa and Thessalonica were famous internal trading centres. The customs duties were another source of large revenues. There were many Jewish, Greek and Armenian merchants, for the Turks as a rule considered trade derogatory to their honour and preferred military and administrative appointments. Foreign merchants too were extremely active and enjoyed a privileged position, for example with regard to the payment of customs for imported goods. The leading position was held by the English Levant Company which had succeeded in ousting the Venetians and the French. Venetian cloth, however, was imported side by side with English cloth for the use of the upper classes, as were precious furs from Russia. Coffee came from the Yemen, and tobacco was imported by English and Dutch merchants: although severe penalties were imposed for smoking it spread rapidly, and tobacco cultivation began at this time.

The stability and security of the empire rested on its army, an ancient institution going back to the fourteenth century. It consisted of the standing army known as the Janissaries and provincial feudal levies raised by the tenants of fiefs held on a military tenure. Each tenant according to the amount of his revenue was obliged to equip and mount a certain number of horsemen and to participate with them in the campaigns. This system provided the army with something like 100,000 horsemen, but it had become corrupt and inefficient. Fiefs were often distributed illegally, and the obligations to render military services were ignored although legally such a refusal should have ended the period of tenure. The corps of the Janissaries (*Yenitcheri* or new troops) had been founded in the fourteenth century and was based on the system of *Devshirme*, the conscription of Christian children from the Balkans. They were converted to Islam, educated and trained under special regulations and a severe discipline: this highly superior force had enabled the Turks to make their great conquests. The corps was divided into more than 150 *orta*'s of varying size, known by their numbers and with their special standards and ensigns. The soldiers wore uniforms, lived in barracks, and received wages according to the length of their service as well as a special *bakhshish* on the occasion of the accession of a new sultan. The total strength of the corps amounted to about 50,000 men, but its discipline and power as a fighting force had declined. The problem of controlling the mutinous

Janissaries was of vital importance, for their outrages shook the foundations of the empire. Furthermore, during the reign of Mehmed IV the system of *Devshirme* was abolished, and only Muslims, especially the sons of Janissaries, were conscripted for the corps, another factor contributing to its decline. Apart from the Janissaries, the standing army had smaller numbers of gunners, bombardiers, sappers, drivers and armourers.

The navy too was of great importance, the admiralty occupying a large area at the Golden Horn where new ships were built and damaged ones repaired. The sailors were mainly recruited from the Greek population and known as *Levend*'s (a corruption of the Italian word *Levantino*). But the Ottoman navy had equally decayed, so that the Venetians could establish their mastery not only in the Mediterranean but even in the Aegean Sea, with fatal consequences for the Ottomans. In other fields too their innate conservatism prevented them from making the necessary changes and adjustments. No attention was paid to the rapidly changing economic conditions and the technical advances made in Europe. Many important posts were given to unqualified people and administrative appointments often went to the highest bidders.

The Ottoman Empire had reached its zenith during the reign of Suleiman the Magnificent (1520–66); it then possessed well-developed and efficient institutions which matched its political greatness. But Suleiman's successors, with only two exceptions, lacked the gifts and the enthusiasm of their predecessors and no longer played a conspicuous part in public life, preferring to stay behind the walls of the Serail. As early as the later sixteenth century, the reign of Murad III, there were signs of decline. The government was subject to intrigues by the sultan's favourite wives or to the influence of the queen mother. The chief of the harem, a black eunuch, often played a part in the most important affairs of State, while the sultan ceased to be an active ruler. According to the established tradition the government rested in the hands of the Grand Vizier, who exercised far-reaching powers. Yet, until the accession of the Köprülüs in 1656, the intrigues of the Serail and the interference of the sultan's favourites caused a decline of the Grand Vizier's authority and of the whole system of government. The *Divan* (Council) which was presided over by the Grand Vizier and was attended by certain other Viziers and high dignitaries, such as the Kadis of Rumelia and Anatolia, was only a consultative organ.

As the empire was a Muslim State the Mufti (Sheikh-ul-Islam) played an important part in the government. He was the head of all Muslim legal and spiritual institutions and enjoyed a privileged status. His approval was required for many important decisions, such as the declaration of war, the conclusion of peace, or the deposition of a sultan. In contrast with the Grand Vizier, the Mufti was never executed if found guilty, but only exiled. Less important than the Mufti were the Kadis (judges) who also had many other duties. In their districts they had to carry out the instructions of the central government and to supervise the municipalities and the supply of food. The highest among the Kadis was the Kadi of Rumelia, and after him the Kadi of Anatolia; they were the judges of the army and judicial matters concerning the army came under their jurisdiction. The legal system was based on Islamic law, the *Sheriat*, a knowledge of which was essential in the judicial and administrative spheres.

The empire was divided into thirty-two provinces, the most important of which were Rumelia, Anatolia, and the territories along the coasts of the Aegean and the Mediterranean. The latter stood under the jurisdiction of Kapudan Pasha, the Grand Admiral, while the other important provinces were administered by *Beylerbeyi*'s, appointed by the central government, who received high salaries and large lands as fiefs. They exercised legislative and executive powers, had to supervise the fulfilment of certain military duties connected with the levy of troops and to participate in campaigns as the commanders of the troops of their provinces. Among the military obligations which they supervised was the institution of *Timar* which obliged their holders to render feudal services. The smaller provinces were governed by *Vali*'s, also appointed from Constantinople. The provinces were subdivided into *Sandjak*'s (standard of an army unit) which corresponded to the districts from which a certain number of troops was recruited. The *Sandjak* was in the charge of a *Sandjakbeyi*, the political and military representative of the central government, who also held a large fief, was responsible for recruiting in his district and commanded its troops during a campaign. The system thus combined military and administrative functions to an extraordinary degree; it appeared to be highly centralised, but in reality it proved impossible to maintain order in the remote provinces and to control the powerful governors. Incompetent men were frequently appointed governors of provinces and districts, who then extorted illegal impositions from the population.

Certain provinces, such as Damascus, Yemen, Abyssinia and Egypt, enjoyed a special status and separate privileges. The system of taxes and obligations which were imposed on the Turkish provinces, for example the institution of *Timar*, was not applied in Egypt and the Arab provinces. Egypt was not only one of the principal sources of revenue, but also an important centre of commerce and the granary of the empire. Almost the entire burden of maintaining the government and the armed forces fell on the Turkish provinces proper; but only Muslims had to render military services, while non-Muslims paid instead the *Djizye* or poll-tax. The Christian principalities of Moldavia and Wallachia possessed autonomous status. Their princes were appointed by the Porte, but their subjects were not obliged to military services, nor were the principalities garrisoned by Turkish forces. They had to provide corn and sheep for the Ottoman army and owed tribute to the Porte, otherwise they were administered according to local customs. The same applied to the Khanate of the Crimea, which was an autonomous Muslim state whose Khans were installed and deposed by the Porte. They were watched by the Ottoman governors of Kaffa and Özü, who intervened when necessary. The Tatar Khans paid no tribute, but were obliged to participate in Turkish campaigns with some 20,000 to 30,000 horsemen, who served as the advance guard of the army, and had to defend the Ottoman territories against the raids of the Dnieper and Don Cossacks. In their turn, the Tatars nearly every year raided Poland and Russia and took many prisoners whom they shipped from Kaffa or Azak to sell them as slaves in Constantinople or Egypt. Looser still were the links of the Barbary States—Tripolis, Tunis and Algiers—with the Ottoman Empire. They were more or less independent, had their own military and administrative organisation, and their obligations towards the Porte did not exceed certain presents which they sent to the sultan.

While in Europe new ideas were developing in many fields, the institutions and society of the Ottoman Empire lost their dynamic character and began to stagnate and to decline. The gap between Orient and Occident became wider, especially in the field of technology, but the Ottomans were not aware of this fact. They continued to regard their empire as the strongest in the world, and their Islamic way of life as the best. Nor did the European powers notice the weakness of the Ottoman Empire—until the catastrophe before Vienna opened the eyes of contemporaries and the real situation began to be appreciated.

As the empire was governed in the form of a medieval despotism with the corresponding institutions, the ability and the competence of the sultan and of the Grand Vizier were vitally important. When, in the person of Murad IV (1623–40), an energetic and competent sultan ascended the throne the Ottomans' financial and military power revived. The anarchy and corruption of the preceding reigns were brought to an end, and the lands which had been lost to Persia were reconquered at the cost of much bloodshed. During the reign of Murad's brother Ibrahim (1640–8), however, the signs of decline became more marked. The sultan spent his days and nights in the pursuit of his passions and his mental health deteriorated quickly. The misgovernment and abuses spread to the provinces where local rebellions broke out. In addition to these mutinies the Venetians and the Cossacks invaded the Ottoman Empire. The Venetians soon succeeded in occupying the islands of Lemnos and Tenedos, and thus in blockading the Dardanelles and threatening Constantinople itself. In these circumstances, which threatened the spread of anarchy and the outbreak of revolution, some influential persons persuaded the Grand Mufti and Kösem sultan (the sultan's mother) that Ibrahim must be deposed.

This was accomplished in August 1648, and Ibrahim's son Mehmed, then seven years old, ascended the throne. Eleven days later Ibrahim, to prevent him from regaining power and challenging the succession of Mehmed, was murdered. As Murad IV had killed three of his brothers, Ibrahim being the only exception, Mehmed and his younger brother were indeed the only surviving male members of the Ottoman dynasty, so that the news of Mehmed's birth had been greatly welcomed throughout the empire, in spite of certain bad omens.

Mehmed was much too young to assume the government himself, and it remained in the hands of successive Grand Viziers as well as Mehmed's grandmother and his mother Turhan who was of Russian descent. Therefore the instability of government continued and intrigues were rife at the palace; this was soon reflected in the spread of robberies and rebellions in the provinces. In the war with the Venetians the fortress of Canea on the island of Crete had been conquered by the Turks during the reign of Ibrahim; but it was now necessary to send reinforcements to Crete and to lift the blockade of the Dardanelles which the Venetians had imposed in return. Thus in 1649 the Turkish fleet set sail from Chanak, only to suffer another defeat at the hands of the Venetians. Thereupon the Grand Vizier Sofu Mehmed Pasha was dismissed and executed. But the struggle for power between Kösem, Mehmed's grandmother, and Turhan, his mother, continued. In this struggle Kösem relied on the support of the Janissaries and planned the elimination of the other party through the accession of Mehmed's younger brother, Suleiman. When her plans were nearing completion and an agreement had been reached with the leaders of the Janissaries, she was murdered in September 1651 by the partisans of Turhan. This was followed by the execution of her accomplices, so that the Janissaries lost their influence for the time being and that of Turhan, supported by the palace eunuchs, became supreme. The Grand Viziers and government officials were appointed according to their wishes, while the education and training of the young sultan were completely neglected. He spent most of his time with toys and games and soon developed an interest in the hunt which became the great passion of his life. This tendency was encouraged by his mother who thus achieved complete mastery in the State. Therefore Mehmed IV was called 'the Hunter' by the Ottoman chroniclers: a passion he was unable to give up even when his army was marching on Vienna and when it had been annihilated before its walls—a passion which became the cause of his deposition and imprisonment. He never showed much interest in literature or the art of government.

In the person of Tarhondju Ahmed Pasha a Grand Vizier of great honesty was appointed by Turhan in June 1652. At this time the revenue for the following two years had been anticipated and the coinage debased. The new Grand Vizier attempted to restore the shattered economy of the

Empire and put forward a budget, according to which the revenue was estimated at 14,503 purses of silver and the expenditure at 16,400, leaving a small deficit of 1900 purses;[1] but the real difficulty arose from the fact that the taxes of the two following years had already been levied so that very little revenue could be expected for the time being. The bulk of the expenditure—about 10,000 purses—was allocated to the army and the navy; of this sum, 3866 purses went to the corps of Janissaries which then numbered 51,647 registered soldiers, and only 988 purses to the navy which comprised fifty galleons and thirteen galleys. 966 purses were allocated to the Imperial kitchen and 255 to the Imperial stables. In view of the financial situation a veritable hunt for money set in, for the soldiers had to be paid regularly. New arbitrary duties were introduced and even the estates of rich people were confiscated. Drastic measures were employed to curtail favouritism and the illegal levies made by followers of the Grand Mufti. But these proceedings antagonised many influential people: their intrigues were eventually successful in bringing about the downfall of Tarhondju Ahmed Pasha, and with him fell his policy of reform. He was dismissed from office after only nine months and immediately executed.

His successors were equally unable to solve the administrative and financial difficulties of the empire. The Grand Vizier Ibshir Pasha was executed in August 1655. Revolts broke out in Asia Minor; taxation continued at a very high level; the provincial governors showed an entirely irresponsible attitude. The threat from the Venetians did not diminish and their admiral, Lazzaro Mocenigo, gained a great victory over the Turkish navy, while the struggle for the possession of Crete continued unabated. On account of the Venetian blockade of the Dardanelles the transport of food and supplies to Constantinople nearly came to a standstill and prices rose steeply. Among the citizens there was grave anxiety and dissatisfaction because the government failed to take any security measures to protect the capital against an attack through the Straits. Many complaints were made to the palace and the officials concerned; but the Grand Vizier Mehmed Pasha was unable to decide what measures should be taken, and the sultan was busy hunting at Scutari, on the opposite side of the Bosporus. The *Divan* met, but with no result. It became clear that the government was incapable of dealing with the internal and external dangers, that an able man must be appointed Grand Vizier, and that drastic measures had to be taken to cope with the situation. Those who realised its gravity approached the sultan's mother, Turhan, because no important decisions could be taken without her assent. The chief architect of the palace suggested to her that the appointment of Köprülü Mehmed Pasha, an Albanian like himself, to the post of Grand Vizier would solve the difficulties. This was accepted by Turhan,

[1] The 'purse' (*kese*) of silver was worth 500 piastres.

and the seal of the office was offered to Köprülü who was then seventy-one years old. Previously he had served in various official posts, in the palace and in the Treasury, on the staff of a former Grand Vizier and as the governor of several provinces, but he had been out of office since 1655. He lacked the education required for the post of Grand Vizier, but he was shrewd, very experienced and had a sound knowledge of the government machine and its defects. Accordingly he put forward several conditions on which he would be prepared to accept the office: no criticisms of the Grand Vizier should be permitted or taken into account; no vizier should be entitled to oppose the proceedings of the Grand Vizier; there should be no interference with the appointment of officials, regardless of rank; and all the reports presented to the court should go through the hands of the Grand Vizier. Turhan, on behalf of her son, agreed to these terms and Köprülü was installed in office in September 1656: the eleventh Grand Vizier of the reign which until then had lasted only eight years. He remained in office until his death in 1661, and during that time he was in an extremely strong position.

On his appointment Köprülü carried through a purge of the government offices. Those notorious for their irregularities were dismissed, among them great dignitaries such as the Chief Treasurer and the Grand Mufti, as was also the commander-in-chief of the navy. The Chief Eunuch, the principal engineer of intrigues in the Serail, was exiled to Egypt. Many new Kadis and magistrates were appointed. Köprülü, however, not satisfied with the removal of those whom he distrusted, had many of his opponents and potential rivals exterminated. The admiral, who was considered responsible for the fall of Lemnos, and the commander of the Janissaries, who was found guilty of lack of discipline, were executed. So were a tax-collector accused of cruelty towards the people and the governor of Silistria indicted for his ill-treatment of the Tatars. The Orthodox Patriarch, Parthenios III, was hanged, being accused of having provoked the Hospodars of Moldavia and Wallachia to revolt against the Turks. Many pashas, viziers, agas and senior provincial officials who had incurred the Grand Vizier's enmity suffered the same fate. Altogether the number of the victims is said to have reached 50,000 to 60,000. All unnecessary expenditure was curtailed, and a campaign against corruption was launched. According to the budget of 1660 the revenue was estimated at 14,531½ purses (hardly more than in 1652), and the expenditure at 14,840 purses, leaving an insignificant deficit. In contrast with 1652, however, the revenue had not been anticipated so that the financial situation had greatly improved. In general, Köprülü was no innovator but was satisfied with making the existing machinery of government work well and with the strict enforcement of the existing laws.

Rebellions against the government were put down with great severity. Among these the revolt of Abaza Hasan Pasha in Asia Minor constituted a real danger to the government in the years 1657–8. Its centre was at Broussa from where it spread into the neighbouring provinces. Many viziers, pashas, agas and other government officials participated in the movement which found support among the people and was not just another rebellion of outlaws. Abaza Hasan aimed at establishing his power in Asia Minor, and a rebel government was formed there. Köprülü had to be recalled from Transylvania where he was engaged in the suppression of another, equally dangerous uprising. A large force was dispatched against Abaza Hasan and succeeded in crushing the revolt after heavy fighting. Many rebels were killed or executed. Thirty-one heads were sent to Constantinople—among them those of Abaza Hasan, four pashas and two viziers—to be publicly displayed.

Köprülü was equally successful in the field of foreign policy. He dispatched the navy against the Venetians, who were still threatening the Dardanelles, and after some initial failures they were forced to lift the blockade which they had imposed. Then Köprülü without delay undertook to recapture the islands which had fallen into Venetian hands. He himself directed the embarkation of the force sent to reconquer the island of Tenedos which fell in August 1657; Lemnos followed in November. Thus a great victory was gained: not only were the Dardanelles freed from the Venetian threat, but the Ottoman navy regained its superiority in the Aegean Sea so that it became possible to send reinforcements to Crete. At the entrance to the Dardanelles two great castles, Seddülbahr and Kumkale, were built to protect the Straits against future attacks.

Even more important from Köprülü's point of view was the struggle over Hungary and Transylvania—the key to central Europe and a bone of contention between Ottoman and Habsburg since the days of Suleiman the Magnificent. More than half of Hungary was under Turkish rule, and the princes of Transylvania often sought the sultan's consent and sanction for the exercise of their government. For the maintenance of Ottoman rule in Hungary and the securing of Turkish influence in Poland Transylvania was of supreme importance. The result of the decline of the Ottoman Empire in the early seventeenth century was that its hold on Transylvania became very loose. During the years of crisis at the beginning of the reign of Mehmed IV Prince György Rákóczi II attempted to liberate his country from Turkish rule.[1] During the War of the North (1655–60), when large parts of Poland were occupied by Sweden, Rákóczi aimed at seizing the Polish throne,[2] and equally at intervening in Moldavia and Wallachia. As these projects were prejudicial to the interests of Turkey, Köprülü decided on intervention. He demanded the deposition of Rákóczi and the election of another prince. In November 1657 Ferenc Rédei was duly elected, but two months later he was expelled from Transylvania by Rákóczi; Köprülü then decided to lead an expedition

[1] See *NCMH*, vol. v, pp. 487–8.   [2] See *ibid.* p. 486.

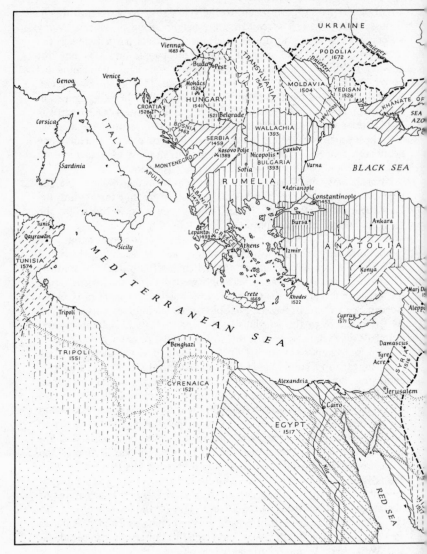

мар 3. The expansion of the Ottoman Empire to 1683.

Legend:

- Ottoman Lands 1359
- Ottoman Lands 1451
- Conquests of Mehmet II 1451–81
- Conquests of Selim the Grim 1512–20
- Conquests of Sulayman the Magnificent 1520–66
- Conquests 1566–1683
- 1521 Year of acquisition
- ✕ Battle
- Boundary of the Ottoman Empire in 1683
- Approximate extent of desert

M. Verity

into the principality. Before he left Constantinople he succeeded in imposing firm discipline upon the Janissaries and many whom he distrusted were executed. The Crimean Tatars and the Cossacks, who had recently accepted Ottoman protection, joined the expedition, and a great force was assembled. In spite of Rákóczi's resistance the Turks were soon in complete control of Transylvania. An agreement was concluded with the new prince, Ákos Barcsay, according to which the annual tribute was to be increased from 15,000 to 40,000 florins and several fortresses were to be occupied by Turkish garrisons. Rákóczi had to seek refuge in Habsburg territory and appealed to Leopold I as king of Hungary for support; but he had to continue his struggle alone, was wounded in an engagement in May 1660 and died a fortnight later. Yet his supporters in Transylvania did not give up the fight. Early in 1661 they elected János Kemény as Rákóczi's successor and succeeded in kidnapping and killing Barcsay, his pro-Turkish rival. As Köprülü in 1658 had had to return to Constantinople to deal with the revolt in Asia Minor, Transylvania could not be brought under control for many years. The Porte in its turn proclaimed Mihály Apafi prince of Transylvania; he disputed control of the country with Kemény. In 1662 the latter was killed in an encounter with Apafi who then succeeded in bringing Transylvania under his control, and thus Turkish suzerainty was restored.[1]

Köprülü did not live to see the consummation of his policy in Transylvania; in October 1661 he died, more than seventy-five years old. His achievements indicate that the Ottoman Empire was capable of surmounting great difficulties if competent men were employed in the offices of State; but a régime of terror had to be established to obtain that end. In the eyes of the contemporaries he was an 'atrocious and ruthless man' and not a great statesman, as later historians have argued. He was particularly criticised for the killing of many innocent people and the confiscation of the estates of the executed, not for the sake of reform of the empire, but for that of enriching the Treasury. Yet it cannot be denied that he halted the decline and that the power of the empire revived rapidly. The sultan and his mother, Turhan, were especially pleased with Köprülü's conduct of affairs which relieved them from the burdens of government. Thus Mehmed IV could devote himself entirely to hunting at Scutari or at Adrianople; or hunting parties were arranged for him in the Balkans where more than 10,000 of his Christian subjects had to leave their occupations and serve the royal pleasure as beaters or in some other capacity. Vast numbers of pedigree hounds and falcons, often brought from Russia, were provided for him. In accordance with Köprülü's advice, his son, Köprülü Fazil Ahmed Pasha, was appointed his successor at the age of twenty-six; he remained in office from 1661 to 1676.

Fazil Ahmed was entirely different from his father. As a provincial

[1] For further details, see *ibid.* pp. 488–9.

governor he had acquired administrative experience. He was intelligent and wise as well as a distinguished commander and clearly was one of the great statesmen of the time. As Grand Vizier he did not adopt a policy of terror and soon became popular on account of his fair methods of administration and his humane conduct; his modesty and politeness earned him general respect. He refused to take bribes and through his good example succeeded in curtailing corruption. He was opposed to religious fanaticism; Christians and Jews were well treated and protected from injustice. In spite of many military expeditions the treasury was not short of money. Owing to his administrative skill and his patronage of the arts the Ottoman Empire experienced one of its golden eras: he was perhaps the most successful Grand Vizier after Sokollu Mehmed Pasha who was in office under three different sultans between 1565 and 1579.

In the field of foreign policy Fazil Ahmed's greatest achievement was the conquest of Candia which had been besieged by the Turks since 1647. After a struggle lasting for more than twenty years the Venetians found it impossible to withstand the large forces brought to Crete and surrendered the fortress in 1669.[1] The conquest of Crete transformed the eastern Mediterranean into a Turkish lake and considerably strengthened the Ottoman Empire.

On land the Turkish forces were almost equally successful. The Habsburg intervention in Transylvania caused considerable tension between the two empires. In order to maintain Turkish influence there Fazil Ahmed with an army moved from Constantinople to Belgrade in the spring of 1661. Thereupon the Austrians sent an envoy to Belgrade to open negotiations. Fazil Ahmed demanded that the Austrians should evacuate Transylvania, demolish their castles facing the fortress of Kanisza, release all their Muslim prisoners and terminate all military operations. When the Turkish forces reached the river Drava he in addition demanded the payment of the annual tribute of 30,000 florins which the Habsburgs had paid in the time of Suleiman the Magnificent. When they refused to comply the advance was resumed. In the summer of 1663 at the head of an army of 100,000 men the Grand Vizier marched through Buda and laid siege to the fortress of Nové Zámky (Neuhäusel) in northwestern Hungary, which was under Habsburg rule. There was little resistance. The Austrians were satisfied with a show of force—Montecuccoli assembled 6000 men near Pressburg—and no succour was sent to Neuhäusel. The garrison defended the fortress with determination, but when further resistance became impossible an agreement was reached in September 1663 by which it was permitted to evacuate the fortress. After this victory Fazil Ahmed returned to Belgrade to spend the winter there.

The revival of Turkish military strength and the threat this entailed for Europe had important repercussions. The Imperial Diet at Ratisbon voted

[1] For further details, see *ibid.* pp. 462–3.

unanimously in favour of granting the Habsburgs financial and military aid.[1] Not only Spain, but even Louis XIV, contrary to his pro-Turkish reputation, promised to send help, in spite of his recent quarrels with the Habsburgs; and a French contingent of 6000 men was dispatched to Hungary, as were those of many German princes. Under the auspices of Pope Alexander VII a Holy League was formed against the Infidel. Thanks to this aid the Austrians were able to take the offensive in the spring of 1664. Montecuccoli reinforced the fortress of Raab (Győr), an important frontier post, to protect the Habsburg lands against a Turkish advance. Fazil Ahmed crossed the Mur, occupied Zerinvár, and arrived before the fortress of Komárom on the Danube, intending to occupy all the castles which barred his advance on Vienna. This enterprise was known to the Turks as *Kyzyl Elma*, the 'Red Apple', and became a symbol of their political aspirations. In view of this threat the Austrians decided to reach a peaceful settlement. Negotiations began at Vasvár at the end of July: according to the terms agreed upon the Austrians were to acquiesce in the Turkish occupation of Neuhäusel and Nagyvárad (Grosswardein), to recognise Apafi as prince of Transylvania, which was to be evacuated by both sides, to terminate all military activities, and to present the sultan with a gift of 200,000 florins, while the latter would also make a suitable gift to the Emperor. This treaty was to be valid for twenty years (beginning in 1662), but until its ratification by both sides the Turks retained their freedom of action, in order to force Leopold to agree without delay. While the text was on its way to him for ratification Fazil Ahmed crossed the Raab and advanced westwards up its left bank where he encountered Montecuccoli's army; if this force had been destroyed the advance on Vienna could have been resumed and the capital might have fallen. On 1 August 1664 the Turks attacked Montecuccoli's army at St Gotthard with superior forces, but made the mistake of not bringing all their troops across the Raab. They were at first successful against the Imperialists' centre, but were finally repulsed and forced back to the river. They lost about 5000 men and fifteen guns, but their enemies also suffered heavy losses and Montecuccoli did not dare to follow the Turks across the Raab; they then retreated to the Danube. The battle of St Gotthard indicated the Austrian superiority in arms and tactics; it became obvious that Turkish military strength was not as formidable as had been feared. With the battle of St Gotthard hostilities came to an end, for in spite of the victory Leopold ten days later confirmed the terms of the Treaty of Vasvár which gave Neuhäusel and Nagyvárad to Turkey and guaranteed Turkish influence in Transylvania.[2] Only western and northern Hungary was retained by the Habsburgs: there was as yet no indication of the eastward spread of Habsburg power, and Fazil Ahmed was received in Constantinople as a victorious general.

[1] See *ibid.* p. 446. [2] See *ibid.* p. 490.

At this time Turkish influence also extended into the Ukraine. The Cossack hetman Petr Dorošenko sought the protection of Mehmed IV who undertook to defend it against both Poles and Russians and to protect it against the raids of the Crimean Tatars. After the armistice of Andrusovo, by which Poland and Russia temporarily settled their differences,[1] Dorošenko entered into even closer relations with Turkey, hoping to conquer the Russian Ukraine with Turkish help, but the aid promised proved insufficient. In 1672, however, a large Turkish army, supported by the Khan of the Crimea and 15,000 Cossacks, marched into Poland, conquered the fortress of Kamenec and advanced as far as Lwów. Yet a treaty, by the terms of which Poland would have had to pay an annual tribute to the Porte, was not ratified by the Polish diet; neither was the independence of Dorošenko recognised by Poland, nor did Podolia—between the rivers Dnieper and Dniester—become a Turkish province. In 1673 Sobieski's victory of Chotin[2]—like that of St Gotthard nine years before—revealed the military weakness of Turkey. Yet the Turks succeeded in reoccupying Chotin and in capturing other castles in Podolia. By the terms of the peace of 1676 they retained the fortresses of Chotin and Kamenec as well as Podolia, so that they were able to put pressure on Poland and to oppose the seizure of the Ukraine by Russia. Ottoman power was established to the north-west of the Black Sea, but a few months later Fazil Ahmed died: Turkish domination between the Dnieper and the Dniester only lasted for a few years.

Fazil Ahmed's successor was Kara Mustafa Pasha, then forty-three years old, who had been educated with his predecessor and had married his sister, thus entering the Köprülü family. He had held various posts under both Köprülüs and during Fazil Ahmed's campaigns he was appointed deputy Grand Vizier. He was very ambitious and spiteful and at times mean, making many enemies for himself, among whom were the Chief Eunuch and the Marshal of the Imperial Stable. Continuing the methods of his predecessor Kara Mustafa succeeded in maintaining internal order and peace as well as the economy through his great authority. But his real desire was the achievement of fame through victory and conquest. The Turkish claims to the Ukraine were not maintained, although in 1678 he led an expedition thither which captured the fortress of Chihirin, the capital of the Dorošenko Cossacks: the Turks left it in ruins and withdrew. In 1681 a treaty was signed with Russia; the Turks renounced their claim to the Ukraine, which they considered of little value, and the campaigns for which had brought them little satisfaction. Kiev and the left bank of the Dnieper remained Russian, and Podolia and the right bank (with the exception of Kiev) soon became Polish, while the Turks withdrew from this contested area. The problem which began to

[1] See *ibid.* pp. 568–9, 575–6.
[2] See *ibid.* p. 569.

attract all the attention of Kara Mustafa was the advance westwards, the 'Red Apple', the conquest of Vienna.

The Treaty of Vasvár of 1664 was valid until 1682, but the struggle for influence in Hungary and Transylvania was continuing. The Magyars of Hungary were reluctant to submit to Austrian rule, and the Protestants of the area feared the Catholicism of the Habsburgs—factors which played into Turkish hands. As the Hungarians under Turkish rule were allowed religious toleration, the Protestant Hungarians were hoping for Turkish support in their fight against the Catholic Habsburgs. The Hungarian leader, Imre Thököly, sent an envoy to Constantinople who was to seek Ottoman protection, but this request was at first refused by Kara Mustafa. Yet in 1682 he recognised Thököly as king of western Hungary and promised him help in case of need, and a small Turkish force actually went to his aid. With its support Thököly attacked and captured two Austrian fortresses. To avert this new threat to their territory the Austrians sent an envoy, Count Albert de Caprara, to Constantinople to renew the Treaty of Vasvár which was due to expire in August 1682. His proposals, however, were rejected by Kara Mustafa who was bent on war: he was only willing to abide by its stipulations if the Austrians surrendered the fortress of Győr and refunded the expenses the Porte had made in preparation for war. In order to reinforce his threats he persuaded Mehmed IV to spend the winter with the Janissaries at Adrianople, whither the Austrian representatives repaired to continue the negotiations. But the Turkish attitude remained uncompromising. The commander of the Janissaries once more demanded the surrender of Győr, whereupon the Austrian envoy replied: 'a castle may be taken by force of arms, but not by force of words'. Thus war became inevitable. The sultan himself led his army as far as Belgrade whence Kara Mustafa led it into Hungary. The most important campaign in Turkish history had begun.

The number of Kara Mustafa's army is not exactly known. Together with a maintenance force of 150,000 it has been estimated at about 500,000, but some chroniclers give the figure of 200,000. According to Silâhdar Mehmed Aga, the Ottoman historian, the engineer and artillery units alone had 60,000 men. The Crimean Tatars mustered 40,000 to 50,000 horsemen. But all these figures have to be treated with caution and the real numbers were probably much smaller. The fighting units were accompanied by many artisans and tradesmen and a great number of pack-animals, so that the army appeared larger than it actually was. According to the Turkish sources the plan was to conquer the fortresses of Győr and Komárom and not to march on Vienna, and some Ottoman historians have asserted that Mehmed IV was not aware of the intention to extend the campaign as far as Vienna. It has also been asserted that it was the Foreign Secretary, Mustafa Effendi, who was aware of Kara Mustafa's thirst for glory and fame and urged him to undertake the expedition. Yet it seems very unlikely that the capture of the two fortresses would have satisfied the Grand Vizier while such a large army was available, and it seems much more likely that he intended from the outset to march on Vienna. Probably the intervention of the Foreign Secretary was adduced later as proof that Kara Mustafa was not alone responsible for the failure. What he did was simply to make use of the might of Turkey which had re-emerged as a great military power under the two Köprülüs. But in order to keep his strategic plan secret the name of Vienna was not mentioned and the targets announced were the fortresses of Győr and Komárom. It was indeed of the greatest importance to reduce all enemy garrisons barring the way to Vienna before attempting an assault on the capital. Muradgerey, the Khan of the Crimea, criticised Kara Mustafa for advancing on Vienna before Győr and Komárom were taken, but thus made himself the Grand Vizier's enemy. Ibrahim Pasha, the aged commander of Buda, suggested that the two fortresses should be reduced now and that in the following spring the moment would have come to attack Vienna. Kara Mustafa, however, was irritated by these suggestions and—arguing that after the fall of Vienna 'all the Christians would obey the Ottomans'—gave the orders for an attack on the capital.

Before the declaration of war by the Porte the Austrians did not consider a siege of their capital likely, but believed that Kara Mustafa would engage in military activities in Hungary. Only when war was imminent did the Habsburgs call on the other European powers for help. Yet the situation in Europe was not propitious for this purpose. Louis XIV, in particular, did not conceal his hostility to the Habsburgs; if the Austrian armies were defeated by the Turks this would enable him to become the champion of Christendom and after an overwhelming success to win the Imperial Crown. The attitude of Frederick William, the Elector of Brandenburg, who was the close ally of Louis XIV, was equally doubtful. But Max Emanuel, the Elector of Bavaria, and John George III, the Elector of Saxony, promised to send help. Pope Innocent XI, as the head of the Catholic Church, made strenuous efforts to provide aid for the Habsburgs. He appealed to the sovereigns of many Christian countries and sent large sums of money to Leopold I. Following his appeal many Italian cities contributed, as did Portugal. The most effective aid, however, came from John Sobieski of Poland, who had fought the Turks successfully in the past.[1] On 31 March 1683 Austria and Poland signed a defensive and offensive alliance; if Austria were attacked Sobieski promised to come to her aid with 40,000 men. Austria's own military strength was insufficient to withstand the Turkish invasion, for after the Peace of Nymegen (1679) she kept only 30,000 men under arms; General Montecuccoli, the victor of St Gotthard, died in 1681, and his successor, Duke Charles of Lorraine, the brother-in-law of Leopold I, was not of the same calibre.

[1] See *ibid.* p. 569.

The Ottoman army advanced up the right bank of the Danube, reached Stuhlweissenburg (Székesfehérvár) and crossed the Raab on ten bridges, which were constructed on the spot, without encountering any resistance. Only a small force was left behind as a pretence of laying siege to Győr. When the Turks crossed the Raab Leopold I left Vienna with his family and court and fled to Passau, while Charles of Lorraine retreated with his forces from the vicinity of Nové Zámky, which he had intended to besiege, to Linz higher up the Danube. After a week's march the Turkish army approached Vienna and began to surround it. Its walls enclosed the *Burg*, and, by the standards of the seventeenth century, the fortress was easy to defend and difficult to conquer. But when the Turks appeared the defence measures were far from complete and there were only 12,000 to 13,000 soldiers within the walls of Vienna. Its defence was entrusted to Count Rüdiger von Starhemberg, the governor, who, together with the mayor, Andreas Limberg, played a prominent part in the operations. It may be that the Turks, if they had advanced quickly from Győr, could have taken Vienna by storm; but the army moved very slowly and only arrived before Vienna on 14 July; three days later the town was completely surrounded. The Turkish camp was pitched to the west of Vienna, between Grinzing and Schönbrunn: with its 25,000 tents it looked like a large town. The tents, the 50,000 carts and the pack-animals—mules, camels and buffaloes—made it appear extremely crowded.

The Turkish batteries were placed in position on the evening of 14 July in preparation for an attack on the following day. Before it began, according to custom, a message in Turkish and Latin was shot by arrow into the town demanding its surrender and the conversion of the citizens to Islam. If they refused but consented to abandon Vienna, a safe-conduct was guaranteed to every inhabitant. Count Starhemberg, however, sent no reply to this proposal. Therefore the Turkish artillery opened fire— 154 years after the first siege of Vienna by Suleiman the Magnificent. Then the Turks had possessed no heavy guns, and this mistake was repeated in 1683. According to Silâhdar Mehmed Aga, who took part in the campaign, the Turks had only nineteen small guns, some howitzers and 120 guns of medium calibre. But the heaviest Turkish gun, the *Balyemez*, was not used. This lack of heavy guns may be attributed to the fact that the avowed target of the campaign was only the capture of the fortresses of Győr and Komárom. The Viennese, on the other hand, were superior in artillery, both in quality and quantity, and this fact was to play a decisive part in the defence. The Turks intended to make up for this deficiency by mining the walls and bastions and thus opening breaches for an assault. This they had done successfully at Chihirin five years before; but the walls of Vienna were much more solid and its defenders much more courageous, determined, and better·disciplined than those of the Cossack capital. The garrison did not adopt merely static defensive tactics but

made sorties which caused heavy losses among the Turks. The long duration of the siege caused dissatisfaction among them; since many had
already collected enough booty they wished to return home as soon as
possible. During the siege the Crimean Tatars penetrated westwards to
the vicinity of Krems and Stein and as far as the frontiers of Bavaria, their
raids causing panic among the people. If Kara Mustafa had attacked
with all his strength Vienna might have been taken; but he feared that, if
the city fell as the result of attack, there would be no booty left on account
of the soldiers' plundering. His greatest mistake, however, was his
disregard of the forces sent to relieve Vienna.

Since the beginning of the siege the allies of the Habsburgs doubled
their efforts to send help, and Charles of Lorraine awaited reinforcements
from Poland and Bavaria. He was in continuous contact with the
beleaguered city and was successful in opposing the Tatar raids towards
the west and in preventing the capture of Pressburg by Thököly. Thus
John Sobieski succeeded in joining the Austrian forces without encountering any resistance. The two commanders met at Hollabrunn to the
north of Vienna, where the Bavarian and Saxon contingents also joined
them. Although Sobieski led only 20,000 men into the allied camp, the
command of the army which numbered some 70,000 in all was left to him
because of his royal rank. But the strategical planning was in the hands of
Charles of Lorraine and his soldiers had to bear the brunt of the fighting.
News of the advance of the allied army reached the Turkish camp on
4 September. It would have been possible to try to prevent it from
crossing the Danube, and allegedly Kara Mustafa ordered the Khan of the
Crimea to do so, but the latter, out of animosity towards the Grand Vizier,
permitted the enemy to cross safely to the right bank. In fact, however,
the Khan could not achieve much against an army which possessed
artillery, and Kara Mustafa committed a grave mistake in not himself
commanding this operation and in not using more troops and artillery
for it. After the catastrophe the Turkish chroniclers used the Khan as a
scapegoat. Before the arrival of the allied army Vienna was living through
its most critical days, for early in September the Turks succeeded in the
mining of some bastions, in opening several breaches in the walls and in
forcing their way to the inner precincts of the *Burg*, so that the fall of the
city seemed imminent. Count Starhemberg urgently demanded aid, but
would hardly have been able to withstand a major assault. Yet before any
materialised the desperate Viennese were informed of the arrival of the
allied army by bonfires lit on the slopes of the Kahlenberg. From there
the allies launched their attack on 12 September. Kara Mustafa thought
that cavalry would be sufficient to repulse it—in contrast with the Khan
of the Crimea who advised him to use the Janissaries for a counter-attack
on the allies. These proved far superior in every respect: they chose an
eminently suitable terrain for their attack, their artillery and manœuvres

were perfect, and their fighting morale was very high, since the deliverance of Vienna was deemed a holy duty. By the evening the Turkish forces were defeated and the Polish cavalry entered the Ottoman camp. Then the Turks began to flee towards Győr, but the allies did not pursue them because they believed that this speedy retreat was a ruse. The Turks suffered more than 10,000 casualties—against about 5000 or fewer of the Christians—and lost their whole camp with its treasure and provisions.

The result of this Turkish catastrophe was the occupation of Hungary by the Habsburgs. As early as mid-October the Austrians captured Gran (Esztergom), the first of many Turkish fortresses that were to fall into their hands. Kara Mustafa eventually reorganised his panic-stricken forces, but was unable to stop the Austrian advance into Hungary. He therefore returned to Belgrade, intending to spend the winter there and to start a new offensive in the following spring; but his harsh measures had created many enemies. The Chief Eunuch and the Marshal of the Sultan's Stables persuaded Mehmed IV to sanction the execution of the Grand Vizier, who was strangled in Belgrade on 25 December 1683. Yet his execution was a loss to Turkey, for he alone would have been capable of taking revenge on the enemy, as was admitted by many of the pashas in spite of their intense dislike of Kara Mustafa. Mehmed IV, however, had no longer the peace of mind to go hunting. He asserted that Kara Mustafa had failed to ask his permission for laying siege to Vienna and made him personally responsible for the defeat; but none of the later Grand Viziers possessed his ability.

The situation of the Ottoman Empire was indeed alarming. The Austrians drove the Turks out of Hungary, and the Venetians occupied the coast of Dalmatia and even the Morea.[1] But Mehmed IV did not change his mode of life. The people were saying that the country was lost but that he never sacrificed his hunting: if he took no account of the people, did he not fear God? Meanwhile Mehmed, while hunting at Davud Pasha near Constantinople, invited a certain Sheikh to deliver a sermon at the local mosque, but the latter declined, for in his opinion he could only preach on the necessity of the sultan's giving up hunting and occupying himself with the affairs of the State. The clergy then took up the case, the Grand Mufti, Ali Effendi, putting himself at the head of the movement. Thereupon Mehmed IV dismissed him and appointed Mehmed Effendi as his successor; but the new Grand Mufti warned the sultan that there would be an uprising if he did not give up hunting. This Mehmed did for one month, but felt so desperate and had so many sleepless nights that he announced his intention of hunting again within the neighbourhood of Davud Pasha. Then the army, blaming him for all the setbacks which the empire had suffered, joined the opposition. When the sultan was faced with this critical situation he promised that he would

[1] For these events see below, chapter 7.

never hunt again, dissolved all the hunting establishments, distributed his hounds, sold his horses, and undertook to observe the maximum economy in all his expenditure in future. Several hundred women were released from the harem. But it was too late. The mutinous army marched on Constantinople and deposed the sultan on 9 November 1687. He spent the rest of his life as a prisoner in the 'cage', to die five years later. He was succeeded by his younger brother, Suleiman II, who had been imprisoned since September 1651 when his grandmother had wanted to put him on the throne in place of Mehmed.

With the close of Mehmed's reign Turkey ceased to be a threat to Europe, and the Christian powers assumed the offensive.[1] The military reforms in the European armies and the battle of St Gotthard indicated the changes which had taken place. It was indeed fortunate for Turkey that the European powers did not realise their superiority until the catastrophe before Vienna, a superiority caused by the scientific and technological advances of western Europe. The two Köprülüs, for all their successful administration, only put the out-of-date institutions of the Ottoman Empire into working order. They deserve credit for transforming a declining empire into a great power reminiscent of the days of Suleiman the Magnificent. But with the mistakes of Kara Mustafa the tide of decline returned: the main objective of his campaigns was the gaining of booty and prestige, and not the annihilation of the forces that threatened the security of the Ottoman Empire, but in doing this he merely revived its classical policy. The exit from the Ukraine and the failure of the ambitious siege of Vienna made the decline of Turkey obvious; but much more so did the great victories of Prince Eugene at the beginning of the eighteenth century.

[1] See below, chapter 7.

7

THE RETREAT OF THE TURKS, 1683–1730[1]

THE Ottoman empire attained its largest dimensions in Europe with the conquest in 1672 of the fortress of Kamenets in Podolia (Kamieniec Podolski), which extended the Domain of Islam as far as the middle course of the Dniester. To the south-west, between this river and the Danube, lay the two tributary principalities of Moldavia and Wallachia, rich lowlands under palatine rulers chosen by the sultan. Divided from these by the Carpathian mountains, the prince of Transylvania stood in a similar relation to the Porte. The greater part of Hungary, only about a fifth of which lay under Habsburg rule, was divided into directly governed vilayets: Temesvár in the east; Nové Zamky (Neuhäusel), Kaniza, and Varasdin in the far west; Eger (Erlau) and above all Buda in the north. In the empire as a whole there were nearly forty vilayets, subdivided into departments (*sanjaks*), more or less on a uniform administrative plan but very variable in size, in which the sultan was normally represented by a resident pasha, the *vali* and *sanjak-bey* respectively. South of the Danube and the Drava, the grand vilayet (*beylerbeylik*) of Rumelia included all of what is now European Turkey, Bulgaria, Thessaly, most of Yugoslavia, and Albania; but Bosnia and the Morea had been formed into separate governments, while most of Croatia was ruled by Vienna and portions of the Dalmatian coast by Venice; the republic of Ragusa (Dubrovnik), like Salonica an important gateway to Balkan trade, merely paid tribute to the sultan. The Greek Archipelago, together with certain coastal districts of the Aegean (such as Gallipoli) and the *sanjak* of the Morea and Lepanto, was directly administered by the Kaptan Pasha of the imperial navy; Crete had been annexed to this vilayet, from Venice, as recently as 1670. On the far side of the Mediterranean the 'regencies' of Barbary, where rule by Turkish garrisons did not extend into the mountains or desert, acknowledged the sultan's suzerainty;[2] they paid no tribute, but received presents of gunpowder and took active part in his wars at sea.

In Asia the empire had contracted since 1612. The Peace of Zuhab (1639) had consecrated the loss of six Persian provinces and of Georgia. In Iraq the efficacy of Ottoman rule depended on the fluctuating success of the pasha of Baghdad in repressing the desert Arabs, an increasingly

---

[1] Mr V. J. Parry, Mrs Nermin Streeter and the Rev. H. S. Deighton very kindly gave advice on certain points in this chapter.
[2] On Turkish methods of keeping the local population divided, cf. M. Emerit, 'Les tribus privilégiées en Algérie dans la première moitié du XIXe siècle', *Annales* (*E.S.C.*), 21e année (1966), pp. 44–58.

disturbing factor throughout the region of the Red Sea and even in Syria; in 1694, in alliance with the marsh Arabs, they captured Basra, which was only restored to the sultan after Persian intervention. Nomadic Arab or Turcoman pastoralists, as also the semi-nomadic Kurds, often threatened the caravan routes between Aleppo and Baghdad, so that trade was diverted northwards via Trebizond and Erzurum into Persia. Ottoman influence was stronger in Syria, but gravely compromised by annual changes in the person of the governor, who had to contend with strongly entrenched local factions without being able to rely on the garrison troops: only the emergence of dynastic pashaliks from these struggles was to offer some hope of stability in the eighteenth century. The turbulent region of Mount Lebanon was left largely to its own devices, though the governors of Sidon and Damascus were expected to ensure a flow of taxes and thus drawn into the quarrels of its complex tribal and religious divisions; from 1711 it was to be more or less dominated by the Shihab clan, which allowed Christian influences to increase.[1]

None of the Arab provinces was so thoroughly under control as were Anatolia and Rumelia, which bore a far larger share of the imperial burden. Despite reforms in 1695–6, Egypt remitted at most two-thirds of its estimated surplus, and often less, to the Ottoman treasury.[2] Since 1586 the viceroys in Cairo had had to handle many military revolts, but their situation was further complicated by the institutional survival of the Mamluk beylicate, a small order of grandees mainly Circassian in origin but now including emirs (beys) from Bosnia and elsewhere.[3] This aristocracy had been known to depose the sultan's representative and to intrigue at Constantinople against him, but it was deeply divided within itself. After the 'great insurrection' of 1711, when seventy days of bloodshed attended the attack on the janissaries by the six other military corps in Cairo, the struggle for power in Egypt was again, as in 1631–60, centred on the deadly rivalry between two great households, the Kasimiyye and the Fikariyye. Each created a following among artisans, peasants and even nomads, absorbing older lines of division as far as Upper Egypt, where the Fikariyye were often powerful. The viceroy could only govern by relying on one or other of these extensive clans—effectively the Kasimiyye from 1714 to 1730—in spite of their inherent tendency to split into sub-factions. Between 1692 and 1711, however, the frequent rioting in Cairo owed most to indiscipline among the janissaries and to the resentments they aroused: and to this restlessness, here as elsewhere, high food

---

[1] The ancient regional distribution of the Druze and Maronite communities also began to break up: see P. M. Holt, *Egypt and the Fertile Crescent, 1516–1922* (1966), p. 122.

[2] S. J. Shaw, *The Financial and Administrative Organization and Development of Ottoman Egypt, 1517–1798* (Princeton, 1962), pp. 6, 297, 304–5, 316, 400. Much of the Egyptian tribute took the form of gold from Abyssinia: R. Mantran, *Istanbul dans la seconde moitié du XVII siècle* (1962), pp. 234–5.

[3] Holt, pp. 73 ff.

prices (coupled with privileges and extortions) made a contribution which has yet to be investigated.

By 1700 the *sherif* of Mecca, ruler of the Hejaz, already defied the sultan, though the Red Sea ports, as far as Massawa and Kunfidha, still had Turkish governors and garrisons. Already, too, the arm of the central government had relaxed towards some of the hereditary Kurdish chieftains in the mountainous country between the Persian frontier and the Black Sea.[1] North of the Black Sea, however, the Porte exercised a strong suzerainty over the khanate of the Crimea, which in turn held sway over Circassia and Bessarabia. With that much justification was the Black Sea, even more than the Red, regarded as an Ottoman 'lake': yet the Turks had not forgotten how recently, while their navy was occupied in the Cretan war, the Cossack 'seagulls' had raided its coasts, nor how the Don Cossacks had captured Azak in 1637 and offered it to the tsar. The political instability of the southern steppes, like that of the Caucasus, was a prime factor in causing friction between the Ottomans and their neighbours—divided less by known frontiers than by the fluctuating homelands of the warlike and semi-nomadic tribes whom each in turn protected or sought to use. The Tatars were the chief suppliers of the Ottoman slave-markets.

The frontiers were defended, often in depth, by numerous fortresses and permanent garrisons of some size, especially in Hungary and along the Danube, whose lower course was commanded by Vidin, its upper by Buda and by Belgrade, the most remarkable specimen of Turkish mastery in the art of fortress-building, having a powerful citadel surrounded by three walls at the point where the Sava enters the Danube. This Holy House of War was linked with the capital by a military road running through Nish, Philippopolis and Adrianople, but the Danube itself was much used for the movement of supplies in the European campaigns, for which Bulgaria was the broad supply base, especially in horses. The heart of the empire was protected by the impregnable fortifications with which the first Köprülü had provided the Dardanelles, and by a system of fortresses north of the Black Sea: Kamenets and Chotin (Chocim) near and on the middle Dniester respectively, Bender (Tighina) on the lower Dniester, Ozü (Ochakov) near the mouth of the Bug, and Kilburun across the Dnieper estuary to the south. Further east, the keys of the Sea of Azov, whose integrity was considered vital to the empire, were held by Azak and Kerch.

Communication between the far from homogeneous regions of the empire depended principally on boats and baggage-animals. Where

[1] Sir W. Foster (ed.), *The Red Sea and Adjacent Countries at the Close of the Seventeenth Century*...(1949), p. xviii. On the confused situation in Ottoman Armenia, Kurdistan and Georgia, see H. A. R. Gibb and H. Bowen, *Islamic Society and the West*, vol. I (*Islamic Society in the Eighteenth Century*), pt. i (1950), pp. 162-5.

roads existed—chiefly in the Balkans—they were often, like the rivers and caravan-tracks, exposed to brigands or badly maintained by the villages or charities responsible for them. The movement of men—of couriers, soldiers, pilgrims, nomads and migrant peasants—was more in evidence than that of goods, and external commerce more than internal. Elaborate bureaucratic controls on the distributive trades (often geared to the supply of armies and the larger centres of population), with the piling up of indirect taxes, fettered the enterprise of commercially-minded minorities like the Greeks and Jews, who owed most to the stimulus of external trade with the West. Within the empire the major routes converged by land and water on the capital, but such historic ports as Trebizond, Smyrna and Alexandria still sustained a considerable traffic between the Mediterranean, Persia, the Red Sea and Indian Ocean, while there was a vast amount of petty commerce along the many Muslim routes to Mecca. Much of the great variety of foreign coin[1] which flooded the Levant from the West found its way to Persia and India—not without adding to the monetary disequilibrium of the empire in its passage.

Since 1584 budgetary deficits, foreign speculation and American silver had contributed to successive devaluations of the Ottoman aspre[2] —a fate swiftly shared by the copper coinage and more slowly by the Turkish piastre, both introduced in 1687–8. Since most salaries were fixed, this huge inflation must be held to blame for much of the rapacity of officials and soldiers, some of whom expected a present with every message. Contrary to the experience of some other countries, the price revolution does not seem to have fostered the emergence of any significant new capitalist class in Turkey, where political and fiscal opportunities did more to found great fortunes than did the generally stagnant condition of trade.[3] In the eyes of an improving Westerner like Defoe, the Turks themselves were 'Enemies to Trade...distressedly poor!'[4] To the extent that it was not managed by Europeans—increasingly by French and English—external trade was largely in the hands of Jews, Armenians, Greeks and Lebanese. In the chief ports, Jewish intermediaries were indispensable to European merchants, but much of the overland trade from Persia and the East, in Turkey as in Russia, was Armenian; there were Armenian as well as Jewish colonies in Leghorn and Marseilles. Greek shipowners, with a brilliant career still to come, already dominated the Black Sea and grain trades; in the Mediterranean their freedom of movement received further impetus when the papal Curia espoused their

[1] See *NCMH*, vol. VI, p. 552.
[2] This small silver piece (*akche*), weighing only a quarter of the finer coin of *ca.* 1570, survived only as a money of account; the silver Turkish piastre of 1687 was then worth 160 aspres. For the Ottoman currency see Mantran, pp. 233 ff.
[3] B. Lewis, 'Some Reflections on the Decline of the Ottoman Empire', *Studia Islamica*, vol. IX (1958), pp. 111–27.
[4] *A Plan of the English Commerce* (1728: repr. Oxford, 1928), pp. 10–11.

interests against the Maltese prize courts in 1702; and Greek business houses, often based on the rising Macedonian port of Salonica, were developing a commercial network in Italy as well as throughout the Ottoman empire by 1700.[1] Banking, such as it was, seems to have been very largely the preserve of the Jews but also, increasingly, of the ubiquitous Armenians: both, as short-term lenders, could strongly influence the local pashas. In the maze of Constantinople's alleys, the Jewish community was the largest in Europe. It included craftsmen, besides middlemen.

On the other hand, there was a most impressive range of traditional Turkish industrial crafts, subject to a high degree of marketing police and to a comprehensive gild system which maintained quality at the expense of competition. In the chief towns, large numbers of the Muslim gildsmen were also enrolled in the privileged military corps of the janissaries, who had thus a double organization for the expression of grievances: indeed, they had yet a third, for most of them belonged to the affiliated lodges of the Bektashi order of dervishes, the most influential of the many heterodox religious bodies which flourished among lower-class Muslims. This triple association served as a link between the great cities and provides a main clue to the domestic politics of the period, when the sultans had more to fear from a riot in the capital than from the rebellion of a whole province.

Town and country were even more sharply contrasted in the Ottoman empire than in Christendom. Besides containing in their numerous gilds and densely populated quarters (often characterized by common faith or racial origin)[2] ready-to-hand organizations for communal action, the towns were the active centres of religious teaching and of private and public spending. Only in their vicinity, where freeholds were commonest, does the cultivator seem to have produced a surplus not wholly absorbed by forced sales or payments in commutation thereof, taxes, dues and gratuities—the burden of these last deriving not only from the venality of officials but also from the frequency of administrative cross-postings. The surplus of the countryside at large was appropriated more and more by the extension of tax-farms in substitution for the old military service fiefs, *ziamet* and *timar*,[3] which tended increasingly to fall legally or illegally into the hands of courtiers and other speculators, who sometimes consolidated them into larger units. Some of these leaseholders, develop-

---

[1] R. E. Cavaliero, 'The Decline of the Maltese Corso in the XVIIIth Century', *Melita Historica*, vol. II (1959), pp. 224–38; Mantran, p. 56; N. G. Svoronos, *Le Commerce de Salonique au XVIIIe siècle* (1956), pp. 193 ff.

[2] For the population of some Ottoman towns see above, p. 542; Mantran, pp. 37 ff. analyses that of Constantinople (with maps).

[3] The yearly income of a *ziamet* was 20,000–100,000 aspres, the more numerous *timar* anything below 20,000; a fief worth more than 100,000 was called a *hass*. Both *ziamet* and *timar* are enumerated for each *sanjak* as at *ca.* 1668 by Sir Paul Rycaut, *The History of the Present State of the Ottoman Empire* (5th edn, 1682), pp. 332 ff., with estimates of their military levies.

ing hereditary claims on their tax-farms, were beginning to form a new aristocracy of country notables, but there were many absentees; their bailiffs, as in other times and places, could be harsher and less far-sighted than the old resident sipahi class. The tax-farmers naturally strove to recoup their outlay—itself the result of competitive bidding, like the price of most public offices—without regard to the resilience of the cultivator. Although the introduction of life-contracts in 1692 supplied some corrective, there could be no more eloquent illustration of the weakness into which the central government had fallen, as well as of its growing cost.

The administrators and collectors of pious foundations (*evkaf*)—the economic basis of the Muslim religious institution and of many public services—notoriously exploited their peasants. The non-Muslims had also to pay a poll-tax and, if Orthodox Christians, to suffer the extortions of some of the Greek clergy. In any case, stagnancy, if not contraction, was the prevailing condition of an agriculture upon whose methods the weight of village custom and of the family pressed heavily, which aimed chiefly at local self-sufficiency, and in which animal-raising and barter exchange figured prominently. Few of the Balkan towns were anything more than centres for these purposes; those of the Hungarian Lowland had long since shrunk into small refuges for man and beast in a waste of forest, marsh and steppe country. More generally, Kochu Bey in 1630 had already noted the number of deserted villages, and an early eighteenth-century Turkish critic[1] was to emphasize the evil of peasant migration, which it was the sultan's traditional policy to prohibit.

These conditions told adversely on military manpower. In the first place, the burden of war-service and taxation fell mainly on Rumelia and Anatolia. The 'feudal' organization was principally characteristic of European Turkey and Asia Minor, and from this source came the largest single element in the army, including cavalry levies from the fiefs held by the provincial pasha himself and his subordinates—the nucleus of the private mercenary armies of the later eighteenth century. But the sipahi tenants-in-chief were both reduced in number and often unable to bear the strain of a long war, since ultimately their financial capacity came to reflect the fall in income from their peasants. Moreover, those who could best afford to honour their feudal obligation were precisely those who could bribe themselves out of it, while others feared that absence on campaign would allow rival claimants to their fiefs to collect the income

---

[1] Mehmed Pasha the *defterdar* (chief treasurer), whose work is translated by W. L. Wright in *Ottoman Statecraft: The Book of Counsel for Vezirs and Governors* (Princeton, 1935): see esp. p. 119. According to M. Pécsi and B. Sárfalvi, *The Geography of Hungary* (1964), p. 167, the number of Hungarian villages fell by over half during the Turkish occupation. Cf. H. Antoniadis-Bibicou, 'Villages désertés en Grèce', in R. Romano and P. Courbin (eds.), *Villages désertés et histoire économique, XI–XVIIIe siècle* (1965), pp. 379 ff.

from them.[1] Hence the pashas were increasingly driven to raising territorial troops out of the proceeds of tax-farms. On the other hand, a huge increase in the paid professional soldiery had long since reflected sixteenth-century changes in the art of war. Of this regular army, it is true, the standing sipahi cavalry, tainted by sedition, had been much thinned out[2] by the first Köprülü; and the efficiency of the janissary infantry, despite the hereditary character of its main cadres, had been diluted by the sale of exemptions from service and the admission of too many raw men. 'They never had so many Soldiers, nor such small Armies,' remarks Pitton de Tournefort, the sharp-eyed naturalist who travelled through Anatolia in 1701: 'the Officers...pass their own Domesticks for Soldiers, and put the Pay of those who ought to bear Arms...into their own Pockets. The Corruption which is introduc'd into this great Empire seems to threaten it with some strange Revolution.'[3] Many janissaries practised civilian trades, so that the Corps came to resemble a militia; and civilians might pay to be enrolled in it for the privilege of not being bullied by janissary neighbours in out-of-the-way places like Erzurum.[4] Rivalry between these locally enrolled auxiliaries and professional troops could be an important factor in the complex web of town-politics, as was jealousy between the leaders of the Corps and between its companies or 'hearths'. Although their religion and love of booty could make them brave in action—so that it needed a long period of peace to ruin their fighting efficiency altogether—the janissaries no longer compared favourably as soldiers with the garrison troops of European Turkey, which (despite absenteeism) were stiffened by some of the toughest elements in Ottoman service, Albanians and Bosniaks. It can almost be said that the janissaries were terrible only to their own sultan; even the grand vizier, who commanded the army in war, when his powers reached their fullest extent, had no power to punish offenders without their officers' concurrence. Some of the more subversive among them belonged strictly to the corps of armourers, transportmen and gunners. These last, provided with well-stocked arsenals, were still formidable in battering walls, but their field guns differed only in calibre from their huge siege guns.[5] Long before the reforms of Bonneval, however, Turkish military engineers had profited from other converts to

[1] Gibb and Bowen, vol. I, pt. i, p. 190. The terms 'feudal' and 'fief' are approximates only.
[2] Ibid. p. 185 n. for varying estimates, suggesting a figure between 15,000 and 26,000 in 1687–1703. Cf. A. N. Kurat (ed.), The Despatches of Sir Robert Sutton, Ambassador in Constantinople (1710–1714), Camden Soc. 3rd ser., vol. LXXVIII (1953), p. 32. On the composition of the Ottoman forces generally, see NCMH, vol. VI, p. 743.
[3] A Voyage into the Levant (tr. J. Ozell, London, 2 vols. 1718), vol. II, p. 35.
[4] Ibid. p. 195. For the large numbers of civilian artisans still levied by the gilds to accompany military expeditions, see O. L. Barkan, 'L'organisation du travail dans le chantier d'une grande mosquée à Istanbul au XVIe siècle', Annales (E.S.C.), 17e année (1962), pp. 1097–8.
[5] See C. M. Cipolla, Guns and Sails...1400–1700 (1965), p. 93 n. Turkish gunners and gun-founders were still valued in India (ibid. p. 128 n).

Islam; English and Dutch sappers had aided in the siege of Candia, and in 1705 the fortifications of Kerch and Bender were committed to a Modenese.[1]

The most striking application of imported skills was the adoption of sailing-ships by the navy, first during the Cretan war but above all under the impulse of a great Kaptan Pasha, Mezzomorto, in the 1690s, when European influences gained ground as fear of Europe took root. Mezzomorto's reforms were the most radical experienced by the Ottoman navy since the sixteenth century. Nevertheless, while enviably independent of foreign supplies and capable of impressing its enemies, the navy had serious weaknesses. Kara Mustafa had given it a reformed admiralty in 1681–2, and it had excellent arsenals at Antalya, Gallipoli, Sinop and Suez, above all at Constantinople; but the resources of the Kaptan Pasha's own vilayet, mainly the poll-tax on Christians there, no longer met the navy's needs in money or kind. One consequence was the sale of commissions, often to renegade Italian, English, French and Dutch captains, such as usually commanded the Barbary frigates—themselves often a powerful accession of strength to the sultan's fleet. Officers, from the Kaptan Pasha downwards, sought to recover their outlay by traffic in public stores and provisions. Like other Mediterranean powers, too, the Ottomans had difficulty in finding enough slaves for their galleys, which still had many uses. In the 1690s they could at times assemble a single force of a hundred galleys; but those of the Archipelago, theoretically in readiness all the year round, were seldom up to strength and their captains, less favourably placed financially than those of the summer squadron based on Constantinople, had a strong interest in avoiding loss by battle. The use of sailing-ships, including large armed merchantmen ('caravellas'), called for many more seamen and gunners. Of these there was no regular establishment, but only a summer strength largely recruited from the Greek coasts and islands, as refractory to discipline as the galley-soldiers known as 'levends'.[2] The Turks, though good oarsmen, were poor sailors and the Greeks anything but scientific pilots, while the only competent gunners seem to have been renegade Europeans.

The entire Ottoman State, as became its origins in a frontier organization, was primarily built for war against the infidel; even its domestic critics still urged preachers to proclaim 'the benefits of the Holy War'. The army was usually commanded by the grand vizier in person, with the provincial pashas at the head of the feudal levies. Occasionally the sultan still accompanied it, but the extreme seclusion in which heirs to the throne were now brought up engendered neither military nor political capacity in them. The main burdens of state were carried by the grand

---

[1] B. H. Sumner, *Peter the Great and the Ottoman Empire* (Oxford, 1949), p. 24.
[2] 'The Plague and the *Leventis*, next to Fire, are the two Scourges of Constantinople' (Tournefort, vol. I, p. 352). A western-style fire brigade was introduced in 1720.

vizier and the large personal secretariat of his chancery at the Porte. It was this able and loyal group of efendis or 'Men of the Pen', some of them trained in the palace-schools instead of in the college-mosques, that now held the empire together. The path of administrative promotion increasingly ran through this bureaucracy, rather than that of the treasury, and its chief writer (*Reis Efendi*) stood a good chance of appointment to a provincial government or even, as in the case of Mehmed Rami in 1703, to the grand vizierate itself.[1]

So long as he enjoyed the sultan's confidence, the powers of the grand vizier were limited only by the world of intrigue in which all business had to be conducted, by the necessity of humouring the janissaries, and by such interference as the Muslim Institution—the judicial as well as ecclesiastical organization—might bring to bear on all levels of civil and military administration. The higher ranks of the ulema, ultra-conservative custodians of law and education, still exercised a power of veto on all important policy decisions, and not simply because they were represented in the imperial Divan—a merely consultative body—and in the councils of the local pashas: the janissaries might overthrow a sultan now and then, but the ulema could bring daily pressure on him by dominance of Muslim opinion. Their chief spokesman, the Mufti of Istanbul, though formally subject to dismissal by the sultan, was either the grand vizier's necessary friend or his fatal enemy. Both, however, had most to fear from the chief of the black eunuchs. For the *Kizlar Agasi* not only disposed of an immense patronage as superintendent of the royal mosques:[2] from being master of the Harem he had become the tyrant of the whole Imperial Household (Seraglio), in which the sinister alliance of women and eunuchs formed the hub of all the wheels of court intrigue. These revolved without cease round every public position and source of profit, for which there was also a well-established tariff of presents. Fortunately, many efendis remained immune to victimization, if not to bribery. The higher officers, including the provincial pashas, were all vulnerable, and none more so than the grand vizier himself. Only a master of intrigue was likely to attain his position. Few held on to it for long. Between 1683 and 1702 there were no less than twelve grand viziers. All but the strongest had to manoeuvre between the largesse they must distribute and the extortions they could safely demand. Many of their adherents, knowing they might last no longer than their chief, naturally did their best to make hay while

[1] A. Hourani, 'The Changing Face of the Fertile Crescent in the XVIIIth Century', *Studia Islamica*, vol. VIII (1957), pp. 89–122; N. Itzkowitz, 'Eighteenth Century Ottoman Realities', *ibid.* vol. XVI (1962), pp. 73–94. Rycaut, who estimated the Grand Vizier's 'Court' at 'about 2,000 Officers and Servants', comments on the 'incredible' daily output of orders, etc. (*Present State*, 5th edn. pp. 81, 103).
[2] According to Tournefort (vol. I, pp. 363–4), these, with the educational and charitable organization dependent on them, consumed a third of the land tax; a surplus was available for the defence of religion, and hence for war.

the sun shone, not least if they had had to pay more for an office or a tax-farm than it or they were worth. It is arguable that the worst consequence of the abandonment of *devshirme*—the system of slave-enrolment from the sons of Christian subjects—was less the decadence of the freeborn, married Muslim janissary than the opening of the civil offices of state to those who could intrigue most successfully for them, and very often to the highest bidder. In this special sense, however, the Ottoman polity did offer a *carrière ouverte aux talents*.

The Köprülü, father and son, had saved the empire from near-collapse in the third quarter of the seventeenth century, but they had not contemplated any structural reform of its institutions. Critics of proved abuses—more numerous and perceptive than is generally realized—looked for remedy, unless they were Muslim converts with knowledge of the West, to a rejuvenation of morality and the drastic punishment of offenders, under the guidance of a Sacred Law which was supposed to have foreseen all requirements. Confident of the superiority of Islam and wilfully ignorant of the world outside its Domain, the Ottomans appreciated only the war techniques of the West; not until the French Revolution did western ideas make any deep impression on Islam.[1] What long remained lacking was the regenerative power of inductive reasoning. The ulema, with their virtual monopoly of higher education and learning, were profoundly hostile to what they understood of the infidel's 'rational' sciences and used their immense influence to forbid knowledge of Christian languages to the faithful. Even in the comparatively advanced study of medicine, though there were skilled Jewish and even Frankish physicians in Turkey, Muslim writers in the eighteenth century were only beginning to take account of European discoveries of the sixteenth.[2] Nepotism and venality also gave the religious hierarchy a large material stake in the established order, particularly as their property, unlike that of the sultan's secular servants (still technically 'slaves'), was both inheritable and safe from confiscation. This 'Learned Profession' was increasing in size.

Some of its failings, however, might also be imputed to many of the very numerous Greek Orthodox clergy. The Oecumenical Patriarchate, whose influence was recovering at Constantinople, was itself an incubus on fresh ideas, as well as on the purses of its following; bishops who failed to satisfy its fiscal demands might find their dioceses 'adjudg'd to the highest bidder'.[3] In general, its tributaries were on better terms with the contemptuously tolerant Muslims than with the Catholic minorities who lived uneasily beside them here and there, as in Turkish Croatia and some of the Greek islands, where the French Capuchins had established missions. Orthodox, not Muslim, persecution was to force the emigration of Abbot

[1] See B. Lewis, *The Emergence of Modern Turkey* (1961), pp. 53 ff.
[2] Something was known of western geographical science and the Turks were able to chart their own coasts (*ibid.* p. 44).
[3] Tournefort, vol. I, p. 79.

Mekhitar, whose foundation of a Catholic community in 1700 was the principal influence on the revival of Armenian culture.

It was at least as much the spirit of mountain tribesmen as of religious revolt, no doubt, that resisted the assimilation of some Slav, Georgian, and Armenian Christians to Ottoman rule. But this was a spirit working ultimately for anarchy, scarcely for improvements: the improvements conceivable to them were simple and not peculiarly the needs of Christians—less extortion and better justice. Such a ferment as Slav race-consciousness, too, in spite of the unsettling effect of alternating régimes in parts of the Balkans, was still far in the future. If the mass exodus of 'Rascian' Serbs to the southern marches of Hungary in 1690 was organized by Orthodox clergy, it also owed much to population pressure and the drive for larger pastures; it was a novel phenomenon only in its scale and speed. Muslim and Christian alike, the villages lived largely to themselves. Even the rebel Montenegrins, who did not lack leaders, never rose as one man at the call of Peter the Great.[1] Economic hardship had more to do in these years than ideological separatism with disturbances among the Christians, although the Turks were quick to suspect them of sympathy with hostile Christian States—an occasion of massacre in the long run, as in the 1730s. As for the Jews, it is enough to say that foreign ambassadors found their physicians an easier channel to the ears of the higher ranks of the ulema, and sometimes of the sultan himself, than were the Greek dragomans (interpreters) who were fast becoming normal intermediaries with the central bureaucracy at the Porte.

Only members of this last, the skilled 'Men of the Pen', could compete in education with the men of religion, Christian or Muslim. Their influence was growing, but the ulema in particular possessed an incomparable hold over the mentality of the mass of subjects. Hence, even if the limits of fatalism were sooner reached than is supposed, any constructive or even durable uprising from below was hardly to be expected. The repeated janissary risings, though they might champion the poor as well as express the grievances of one among many conservative gilds, were more properly mutinies, or strikes with violence, than real social revolutions. It remained to be seen whether the Ottoman polity would be changed by conquest from without.

Between 1683 and 1730 the Ottomans enjoyed less than twenty years of peace. The war which began with the siege of Vienna[2] was alone to last nearly as long—and severely to test that over-confidence which was responsible for the undertaking and for its failure alike. The rout of Kara Mustafa's vast army in September 1683 was followed by further serious losses during its crossing of the Danube at Párkány and by the abandonment of Gran (Esztergom) and other fortresses in Upper Hungary. On

[1] Below, p. 204.　　　　[2] See above, pp. 172–6.

25 December the grand vizier was strangled in Belgrade. The formation of the Holy League at Linz on 5 March 1684 meant that the Emperor Leopold, yielding to his generals and clergy, had turned aside from action against Louis XIV to rally German opinion behind Innocent XI's crusade. It is true that Leopold, suspecting John Sobieski of designs on Hungary, had cold-shouldered the saviour of Vienna and declined an all-out pursuit of the Turks in 1683. In succeeding years, moreover, his own domestic difficulties prevented the Polish king from mobilizing forces sufficient to recover Podolia or to realize his ambition of annexing the Rumanian principalities, although he attempted to do both.[1] On the other hand, the adherence to the Holy League of the sea power of Venice and Malta, together with the privateers of Greek islands under Venetian control, could seriously harass Ottoman commerce and divert forces from the Danube. The Venetians could stir up trouble among the Christians in Bosnia and Greece. In 1684, therefore, the Turks found themselves fighting on three fronts—in Hungary, the Polish Ukraine, and the Adriatic— besides having to defend vital routes across the Aegean. In October, the fierce Tatar horsemen of the Crimea broke a fresh Polish assault on Chotin, the scene of Sobieski's triumph in 1673; but the Venetians seized the Ionian island of Santa Maura (Leukas) and the Imperial commander, Duke Charles V of Lorraine, swept up more fortresses in northern Hungary.

It was in Hungary, which they had held since 1526, that the Turks resisted most bitterly, in support of their vassal king Imre Thököly, leader of the Hungarian insurrection since 1678. In 1685 Charles of Lorraine mastered the great stronghold of Nové Zamky, only 200 surviving out of a garrison of 3,000. This blow was so sharply felt that the commander of the main Ottoman army, Ibrahim Pasha, opened parleys for a general peace. He was executed for acting without authority from the new grand vizier, himself dismissed soon afterwards. Such frequent changes of viziers and seraskers (commanders-in-chief) added to the confusion at the Porte and in the army. Strange indeed was the behaviour of the sultan himself, for Mehmed IV, in face of so many disasters, was obstinately absorbed in personal pleasures, notably hunting. Already murmurs could be heard about his blatant indifference to the developing crisis. This deepened in 1686 with the fall of Buda, the chief centre of Ottoman Hungary, 'the shield of Islam'. Abdi Pasha of Buda is still remembered in Turkey for his heroic 78-day defence against an army of 40,000; when the place was taken by storm on 2 September, nearly all the Turks perished, Abdi Pasha at their head. The whole Hungarian resistance broke down in consequence, and Thököly had to abandon his remaining towns to the judicial terror supervised by General Caraffa at Eperjes.[2]

[1] See *NCMH*, vol. vi, pp. 683-4.
[2] Cf. *NCMH*, vol. v, pp. 498-9 for the Habsburg advance down to 1691, and vol. vi, pp. 576 ff. Hungarian historians admit that the liberation of Hungarian soil by foreign forces

While the main Turkish forces were thus engaged on the Danube, Francesco Morosini was able to use his command of the sea, not only to threaten important convoys from Egypt, upon which the Ottoman treasury greatly depended, but also to seize strongpoints on the coast of the Morea in 1685. Morosini's army of 11,000 was half composed of Hanoverian and Saxon troops, under Count Königsmark, which suffered badly from fever and complained of Morosini's firm discipline. His only significant success in 1686 was the capture of Nauplia (Napoli di Romania), which became his forward naval base. Next year, however, having lost control of the entrance to the Gulf of Corinth, the Turks were driven out of the Morea (though Malvasia held out till 1690), and then Athens itself[1] came under Venetian occupation; a Venetian bomb largely destroyed the Parthenon, then in use as a powder magazine.

These were not the only military misfortunes of 1687, a year also of drought and soaring food prices. Sobieski led his troops deep into Turkish territory as far as Jassy, capital of Moldavia, though once again his strength was unequal to the abstemious and mobile horsemen of the able Selim-Girei, four times khan of the Crimea.[2] The Turks themselves took the initiative on the Danube, where the grand vizier, Süleyman Pasha, hoped to recover Buda. Against all expectations he suffered a defeat costing some 20,000 men, while Imperial losses were trifling. This was on 12 August, at Nagyharsány (Berg Hasan), near Mohács. The news was carried to Vienna by a young and rather reserved cavalry officer, Eugene of Savoy, who received his military formation in these campaigns. On 9 December the Archduke Joseph received the Crown of St Stephen at Buda.

After these reverses the main Ottoman army revolted. It elected Siyavush Pasha general and asked the sultan to name him grand vizier; retiring from Belgrade to Adrianople, the troops called for the execution of Süleyman Pasha. Mehmed IV offered no resistance, but his acceptance of Siyavush as grand vizier was not enough to save him. His neglect of affairs had pushed resentment so far that on 8–9 November 1687 the ulema combined with the army to dethrone him.[3] So Mehmed 'the Hunter' was at last replaced by his half-brother Süleyman II, who was to show better qualities as a ruler (1687–91). He was at first hampered by the janissaries, now temporarily masters of the capital: in fact, their arbitrary government continued for four months, during which they appointed their

aroused no enthusiasm in the local populations: cf. O. Jászi, *The Dissolution of the Habsburg Monarchy* (Chicago reprint, 1961), p. 41, and H. Marczali, *Hungary in the Eighteenth Century* (tr. H. Temperley, Cambridge, 1910), p. 2.

[1] Its population had shrunk since 1580, when it has been estimated at 17,000: O. L. Barkan, 'Essai sur les données statistiques des registres de recensement de l'empire ottoman aux XVe et XVIe siècles', *Journal of Econ. and Soc. Hist. of the Orient*, vol. I (1957), p. 27.
[2] 1671–8, 1684–91, 1692–9 and 1702–4.
[3] Cf. above, p. 177.

nominees to high posts, pillaged the Seraglio and behaved as in a conquered country. There were disturbances also in Anatolia, Crete and Belgrade. As was characteristic of the dramatic revolutions of Turkish politics, however, such excesses produced their own cure, at least for a time. With the help of an outraged civilian population, the new sultan's government contrived to put down the disorders, punish the janissaries, and execute some of their agas (officers).

During these troubles the main Habsburg army could advance without much opposition. Eger, to the north, was taken in December 1687. Southwards, under Elector Max Emmanuel of Bavaria, the Imperialists captured the key fortress of Peterwardein in the spring of 1688. The road to Belgrade thus lay open. It was expected that Belgrade itself would long hold out: it surrendered after only three weeks, on 6 September, probably after treason. As its fall threatened Serbia, Bulgaria and the Principalities —in all of which there were elements making contact with Vienna[1]—the Porte now attempted peace negotiations in earnest. Zulfikar, a senior official, and Alexander Mavrocordato, the highly influential First Dragoman of the Porte, were sent to Vienna, ostensibly to announce the accession of Süleyman II, in fact to probe the possibilities of agreement. The emperor's terms, which extended to the absorption of Transylvania as well as Hungary, were wholly unacceptable. To force the Habsburg to a more reasonable peace, therefore, the Turks mounted a new campaign in the late summer of 1689. It was hoped that the sultan's presence would fire the zeal of his troops to recover Belgrade. Instead, they lost the important city of Nish (150 miles further south) to Margrave Lewis of Baden on 24 September, and soon afterwards Vidin. This brought the enemy close to Adrianople, the summer residence of the sultans. Although the arrival of Selim-Girei Khan, with a great body of Tatars, saved Bulgaria and Thrace, some of Baden's troops penetrated Wallachia as far as Bucharest during the winter.[2]

With the whole military situation now so critical, public opinion in Constantinople, supported by the ulema, was calling for a strong personality (normally so unwelcome to court parasites) in the post of grand vizier—exactly as in 1656, when Köprülü Mehmed Pasha was given unlimited power. On 25 October 1689 the sultan nominated Fazil Mustafa Pasha, the youngest son of Köprülü Mehmed. Mustafa Pasha, entitled Fazil (the Virtuous) and one of the ablest grand viziers ever known, was to be killed in battle less than two years later, but meanwhile he succeeded in putting some order into public business and the army's shaken discipline; offices were suppressed and salaries reduced, even in the Seraglio, and the aspre devalued by a third. There was also reason to expect that he might succeed in driving the enemy out of the Balkans. For the emperor's position was now complicated by the outbreak of the

[1] See *NCMH*, vol. VI, pp. 577-8.   [2] *Ibid.* pp. 579-80.

Nine Years War. As Louis XIV intended, the French movement in 1688 to the Rhineland held down important Austrian forces which could otherwise have been employed in the east, where another ten years of Balkan fighting, in the event, were to bring them no further permanent gains. The Hungarians, moreover, were restless under Habsburg rule: the prince of Transylvania, Michael Apafi, formerly appointed by the Turks, had submitted to the emperor, but Thököly maintained the struggle for Hungary's independence. The fortunes of war in Greece had turned already, in 1688, when the Venetians evacuated Attica and failed against Negroponte; and control of northern Greece was more or less recovered in 1690 from the bandits who terrorized it—often Albanian and Dalmatian deserters from the Venetian army. In 1690, also, Fazil Mustafa scored notable successes in the Balkans, recapturing Nish on 9 September and Belgrade itself a month later. Serbia and part of Bosnia were again under Turkish rule. It was then that occurred one of the most celebrated episodes in Serbian history. Led by the patriarch of Peć, the holy place of Serb Orthodoxy, many thousands—some say as many as 200,000—moved into the depopulated lands of south Hungary, hoping to find better treatment from new overlords.[1] Nevertheless, Fazil Mustafa forbade punishment for their disloyalty, allowed the building of new Orthodox churches and the repair of old ones, stopped arbitrary oppression, and took what other steps he could to improve the lot of people who had inevitably suffered much by the passage of armies and the destruction of all normal life.

Süleyman II died in 1691 and was succeeded by his half-brother Ahmed II (1691–5). Of the five sultans who reigned between 1648 and 1730, these were the only two to escape deposition. Fazil Mustafa survived the change of sultan and personally led the army into Transylvania, but met a hero's death in the slaughter near Zalánkemén on 19 August 1691.[2] The Turks withdrew into the Banat, and there followed a standstill in operations of about a year, both sides weary of war. Before a new campaign opened, the British and Dutch representatives at Constantinople, Lord Paget and Jacobus Colijer,[3] offered their mediation. Britain and the United Provinces were naturally anxious to extricate their Imperial ally from what to William III was a diversion of sorely needed troops from the more important struggle against France. The Turkish demands were pitched too high, however, for mediation to succeed. The effort was repeated in 1693, but this time, as in 1688–9, it was again the Austrian demands which were

[1] V. L. Tapié, *Les Relations entre la France et l'Europe Centrale de 1661 à 1715* ('Cours de Sorbonne', 2 vols. 1958), vol. II, p. 187, calls attention also to the later migration from the Principalities into Transylvania; there had been a movement in the reverse direction after the Habsburg persecution of Hungarian Protestants in 1670. Cf. *NCMH*, vol. VI, p. 580.

[2] See *ibid.* p. 580, and vol. V, p. 499, for the effects of this battle on Transylvania.

[3] Having gained experience under his father, Colijer had succeeded him as resident envoy in 1684 and remained at Constantinople till 1725. For much of this time he also acted as an unofficial Russian agent.

too stiff. So hostilities dragged on in face of the desire of both powers for peace. The Austrians made an unsuccessful attempt to retake Belgrade in September 1693; equally, the Turks failed against Peterwardein in 1694. The rivers and marshes between these places virtually imposed stalemate.

Presuming on the weakness of Ottoman sea power, however, in September 1694 the Venetian fleet crossed the Aegean to land some 8,000 troops in Chios (Scio), which was rapidly overcome. Such an occupation threatened a blockade of the Dardanelles (several times undertaken during the Cretan war), besides the loss of a rich island with a useful dockyard, regularly used as a way-station by the Alexandria-Constantinople convoys. For the sultan this might mean deposition or worse. As so often in the past, the Turks were able to concentrate a large fleet at the point and at the moment of extreme danger; in addition to their galleys, they now had a score of fast and powerful sailing-ships, supplemented by 16 Barbary privateers.[1] On the other hand, Antonio Zeno, who had succeeded to the Venetian command on Morosini's death in 1693, was short of men and money. Plunder embarrassed his relations with the Chiotes. His own commanders were not on good terms. His Maltese auxiliaries withdrew. There were rumours of a Turkish counter-attack on Argos, in the Morea. In fact, Zeno found himself in the predicament which the dying Morosini had advised his countryman at all costs to avoid: too far from his sources of supply, he had dispersed his limited manpower, thus endangering the Venetian hold on the Morea instead of seeking to protect it by clearing the Turks out of Negroponte. He had wasted the republic's carefully husbanded fighting resources on an easy conquest which could be retained only at Turkish discretion.[2] In February 1695 the Venetians evacuated Chios.

Under a new and energetic sultan, Mustafa II (1695–1703), the Turkish military offensive briefly flared up again. He insisted on taking personal part in it in June 1695; some small places were taken from the Austrians and Mustafa was hailed at home as 'Gazi', victor over unbelievers.

In view of their many crushing defeats and the loss of such extensive territories, it is remarkable indeed that the Turks still preserved so much of their old fighting spirit. After every forlorn battle the Porte succeeded each spring in furnishing a new army, guns, warships. But this was accomplished at the cost of much economic dislocation and the intensification of many social evils. Expenditure was met, or partly met, by higher taxes—notably on coffee, tobacco, official salaries—and by confiscating the fortunes of fallen officials. A courageous attempt was made in 1696–7

[1] The sailing-ships, unlike the galleys, remained in the Mediterranean when the Russians invaded the Sea of Azov. In each year after 1696 there were indecisive fleet-actions, in which the Venetians were slightly outnumbered. See R. C. Anderson, *Naval Wars in the Levant* (Liverpool, 1952), pp. 223 ff., and *NCMH*, vol. VI, pp. 565–6.

[2] P. Argenti (ed.), *The Occupation of Chios by the Venetians, 1694* (1953), pp. xli ff.

to restore the currency by striking a new piastre and a new gold coin worth 300 aspres. In these years the treasury had more difficulty in making ends meet than at any time during the seventeenth or eighteenth centuries; in 1691, expenditure (about three-quarters military) had outstripped receipts by more than a quarter.[1] It is true that under Turkish practice the maintenance of many military services as well as virtually all public works was the responsibility of charitable trusts (*evkaf*): Ottoman piety endowed not only mosques, hospitals and almshouses, but roads, ships, and fortresses on 'the ever-victorious frontier'. But the administration of *evkaf* was an object of lively competition among the influential and much of the income was diverted, the property sometimes being converted into private ownership.[2] Similarly, a border garrison might find itself defrauded of its pay by the malversations of the agent who managed a government property alienated expressly to support it. Such properties often went out of cultivation, for lack of capital to maintain them or because the cultivators had fled, while unpaid garrison troops deserted.

As a chief treasurer (*defterdar*) later pointed out, the treasury was also the ultimate loser by maltreatment of the peasants, for 'the state exists through them and the treasure produced by them';[3] and since the treasury depended on 'abundance of subject people', it was not compassion alone that condemned the janissaries in these blistering lines:

Saying 'We are on campaign', they commit all sorts of shameful acts...Practising brigandage, they are not satisfied with free and gratuitous fodder for their horses and food for their own bellies from the villages they meet. They covet the horse-cloths and rags of the rayas, and if they can get their hands on the granaries they become joyful.[4]

Many normally quiet areas were now afflicted with bands of deserted soldiers, while in others (such as Thessaly) there was an increase of endemic brigandage. Many peasants found it best to join the brigands and even made their way into the *corps d'élite* itself, like those 'pretence janissaries' who drew their pay without going a day's journey from Constantinople.[5] The intrusion of these adventurers, sometimes as officers brought in over the heads of veterans, undoubtedly contributed to the decline of janissary discipline; and no item of expenditure strained the treasury so much as the quarterly sums—amounting to half the military budget—due to this swollen standing army, which could extort increases as well as arrears of pay under threat of mutiny. Since, also, the strength of the 'feudal' force

[1] Mantran, pp. 236, 240, 257-9.
[2] Many families converted their property (especially in and near a town) into *evkaf* to secure it from confiscation. It was a main aim of the great reforming sultan Mahmud II, after his destruction of the janissaries in 1826, to centralize administration of these pious foundations as well as to divert their revenues to himself (Lewis, *Modern Turkey*, pp. 91-4).
[3] Wright, p. 118.
[4] *Ibid.* p. 126.
[5] *Ibid.* p. 111.

could hardly fail to reflect the growing impoverishment, the empire had to fight for life with the aid of less disciplined volunteer levies.

At this difficult time a quite unexpected danger appeared from the north. The Turks habitually regarded Muscovite Russia with a certain disdain. In general, it was not the sultan but the khan of the Crimea who had direct dealings with the Muscovites; they indeed suffered mounting losses—in men, stock, and ransom-money—from the raids of Tatar horsemen, especially in the recently settled and ill-defended Slobodskaya Ukraine, centred on Kharkov. The insignificance of Russian military power appeared to be confirmed by the failure of V. V. Golitsyn's expeditions to the Isthmus of Perekop in 1687 and 1689. Although Sobieski had persuaded Muscovy to join the Holy League in 1686 (in return for the permanent cession of Kiev by Poland),[1] no serious danger arose from that quarter until 1695. Then the Russians, instead of another direct move on the Crimea, attacked Azak (Azov). The young tsar, Peter, opened a new era in Russo-Turkish relations as well as in Russian history. Besides Polish and Austrian appeals for aid, Peter had every reason to put a stop to Tatar raiding. He was also encouraged by spokesmen of the Balkan Orthodox, Serb and Rumanian as well as Greek, now thoroughly alarmed lest liberation from their Muslim masters should come from the Latin 'Swabians': as a Wallachian envoy in Moscow was to write in 1698, 'The secular war may finish some time, but the Jesuit war never.'[2] Beyond question, however, the tsar's leading motive was a thirst for 'warm seas'.

After the failure of his first attempt on Azak, which was reinforced by sea, Peter ordered warships to be built at Voronezh on the upper Don in the winter of 1695-6. The flotilla, which was commanded by the Swiss François Lefort, consisted of 17 galleys and 6 light sailing-ships in addition to fireships and some 40 Cossack small craft.[3] The Turks, taken by surprise, had neglected to repair the damage of the previous year. Azak fell in July. This was the first Russian victory over the Turks and it had far-reaching consequences. It was of immense importance as a demonstration of superiority over a power which the Muscovites had hitherto treated with all possible caution. At last they did reach the coasts of a sea, though not yet those of the Black Sea. At Taganrog, only 20 miles across the water to the north-west of Azov, Peter established a naval yard capable of building 14 ships-of-the-line by 1699. His troops were not very successful in other directions, however. In 1695 Boris Sheremeteyev had taken four small strongholds on the lower Dnieper and threatened Tatar communications with the west, but an advance on the Straits of Kerch, which give entry to the Black Sea itself, was frustrated. This is why Peter objected

---

[1] Cf. *NCMH*, vol. vi, p. 683.   [2] Quoted Sumner, p. 34.
[3] For operations down the Dnieper and along the Black Sea Coast (as far as Akkerman), the Russians built a large number of small craft at Bryansk, on the river Desna, still further from the sea than Voronezh: Anderson, *Naval Wars*, pp. 239-40.

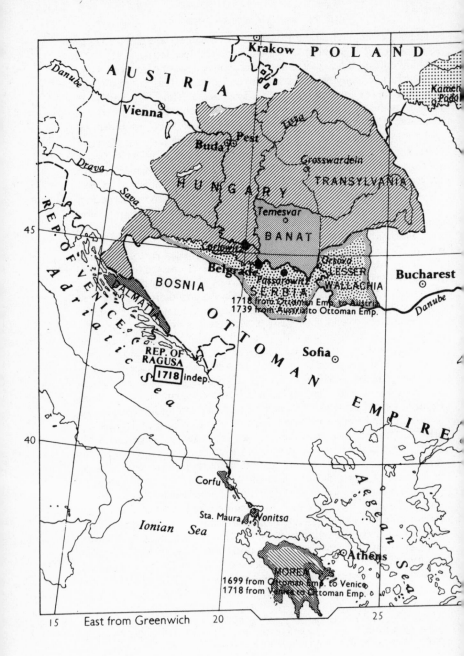

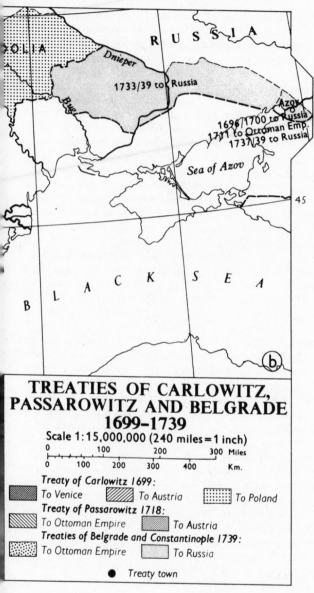

RUSSIA

OLIA

Dnieper

1733/39 to Russia

Bug

Azov

1699/1700 to Russia
1711 to Ottoman Emp.
1737/39 to Russia

Sea of Azov

45

B L A C K   S E A   A

B

TREATIES OF CARLOWITZ, PASSAROWITZ AND BELGRADE
1699–1739

Scale 1:15,000,000 (240 miles = 1 inch)

```
0        100        200        300  Miles
0    100    200    300    400       Km.
```

Treaty of Carlowitz 1699:
To Venice   To Austria   To Poland

Treaty of Passarowitz 1718:
To Ottoman Empire   To Austria

Treaties of Belgrade and Constantinople 1739:
To Ottoman Empire   To Russia

● Treaty town

Map 4.

bitterly to the peace negotiations which Prince Eugene's first sensational victory against the Turk was to bring about, in unexpectedly decisive fashion, once Eugene had been released from the emperor's war in Italy by the Convention of Vigevano.[1]

Insisting that he again lead the army in person, Mustafa II took the military initiative for the recovery of Hungary in the summer of 1697. Yet the Turkish command acted without any definite plan and there were serious discords within it: while the grand vizier, now Elmas Mehmed Pasha, preferred to march north across the Banat, others wanted to go west in the direction of Peterwardein. The grand vizier prevailed and the army proceeded across the difficult swampy country of the lower Tisza, neglecting to watch the enemy's movements. Eugene, who had expected an attack on Peterwardein, made a remarkable forced march and caught the Turks just when most of their cavalry had crossed the Tisza eastwards and the infantry were still on the right bank. This was on 11 September, towards nightfall, near Zenta. Surprised by Eugene's appearance and immediate decision to attack, the Turks lost about 20,000 killed and perhaps 10,000 drowned, while the Imperialist losses were trifling. Mustafa II, who witnessed the slaughter across the river, fled. This 'frightful blood bath' (as Eugene himself called it) was accentuated by a mutiny of the janissaries, who in desperation killed the grand vizier and many high-ranking officers. By the end of October Eugene was deep in Bosnia, burning and plundering the important trading town of Sarajevo.

The sultan appointed Hüseyn Pasha, the fourth Köprülü, as grand vizier, hoping he would find means to halt the run of calamities. This was an appropriate juncture for the English and Dutch mediators to intervene again, especially as the imminent death of Carlos II threatened new complications for the Austrian Habsburg in the West. Both sides agreed to negotiate on the basis of *uti possidetis*, the territories actually occupied by each side to be left in its possession. This ruled out any Russian hope of winning the Straits of Kerch by diplomacy: the tsar's visit to Vienna in 1698 failed to renew the first Austro-Russian alliance against Turkey made only a year earlier. Eventually, at the small town of Carlowitz near Peterwardein, after 72 days' negotiation, with Mehmed Rami Efendi (afterwards grand vizier) and the experienced Alexander Mavrocordato as the Turkish plenipotentiaries, agreements were reached on 26 January 1699 with all but the Russians. With Russia an armistice of two years was concluded, to be followed by a peace for ten years in 1700, when the outbreak of the Great Northern War made it an urgent matter for Peter. But he never forgave the Habsburgs for their desertion at Carlowitz.

The Peace of Carlowitz is significant as the first agreement between the

---

[1] *NCMH*, vol. VI, p. 250. Nevertheless, money and supplies were too short for much to be hoped at Vienna from the 1697 campaign, which in fact began late and was regarded even by Eugene as defensive in purpose: M. Braubach, *Prinz Eugen von Savoyen*, vol. I (1963), pp. 248 ff.

Turks and a coalition of European powers, as the first occasion when the Turks accepted the mediation of neutrals, and as the first formal acknowledgement by the Ottoman empire of a defeat. It lost vast territories: Hungary and Transylvania (though not the heavily depopulated Banat of Temesvár) to the emperor;[1] Dalmatia and the magnificent Montenegrin harbour of Cattaro (Kotor), Santa Maura, the Morea and Aegina to Venice; Podolia, with Kamenets, to Poland. Further, by the Treaty of Constantinople in 1700, the Turks ceded the Azak area and accepted a regular Russian diplomatic mission for the first time—a right (lost in 1711 but regained in 1720) which gave Russia the same opportunity of studying and exploiting the inner convolutions of Turkish politics as was enjoyed by France, Britain, the Empire, the Netherlands and Venice. In addition, the Turks repudiated the Crimean khan's claim to an annual tribute, so much resented by the tsars: it had not been paid since 1683 and by 1700 the arrears amounted to perhaps a twelfth of Peter's revenue in that year.[2] Peter in turn agreed to destroy the four forts below the Dnieper cataracts which he had hitherto insisted on retaining, but the Turks did not recover them. The Russians also obtained recognition of an old demand for unhindered pilgrimage to the Holy Land. Together these treaties mark the beginning of Turkish retreat from European soil. Occasionally thereafter the Turks did recover some of their losses, as in the case of Azov (1711), the Morea and island of Aegina (1715). For a time, too, they were able to stabilize their Russian frontiers and even to extend their holdings in the Caucasus. It was only in 1774 that Russia obtained the freedom of the Black Sea for her navigation and recognition of a right to protect her Orthodox co-religionists in the Turkish Balkans, though Peter had staked out both claims at Carlowitz; and it was not until 1783 that Russia absorbed the Crimea. And yet, small as were the sacrifices of 1699–1700 by comparison with the vast area still under Ottoman rule, they were strategically and economically important. Above all, these losses gravely diminished Ottoman prestige as a great military power. It was evident that 'the Turkish menace' was a thing of the past.

In some ways the very survival of the empire was imperilled. The western approach to the Aegean was in Venetian hands and the Venetian fleet might again threaten the Dardanelles. In the north, the Sea of Azov had ceased to be a Turkish 'lake'; east of it the district of the lower Kuban river and parts of the northern Caucasus were coming under Russian influence, while the new fort of Kamenny Zaton on the left-bank Dnieper to the west was a reminder of the recent threat to the Tatar grazing and hunting grounds. The Crimea, the Dnieper mouth, the Black Sea itself were now shadowed by the tsar. Entry to the Black Sea, hitherto barred to the western nations that traded with Constantinople, might

[1] Cf. *NCMH*, vol. VI, pp. 581 ff.
[2] Sumner, p. 77n. The Ottoman treasury also lost certain tributes.

soon be open to the Russians, who made no secret of their ambitions in this direction; it was seen as a portent when Ukraintsev, who came for the peace negotiations in 1700, arrived at the Bosporus in a 52-gun warship equipped at Taganrog. The Great Northern War by no means halted Peter's work of fortification and naval construction there and at Azov, for which a labour force of over 18,000[1] was demanded as late as 1709. The great uneasiness felt at Constantinople was occasioned, however, as much by the implications of the loss of a major frontier fortress as by any effective increase in the power of Muscovy. In the Russian south, this was slight enough when compared with Peter's acquisitions in the north; but what he accomplished in the south was of less significance than that he did it at all. The loss of Azak and the Dnieper forts had come as a violent shock to every good Osmanli. Henceforward the Turks were hypersensitive to every rumour of Russian moves.

In addition, the social and economic dislocation of war took years to put right. Many desperate peasants in Anatolia and other provinces had left their homes to become wanderers or brigands, or to pick up a living in the capital. In some areas corn reached famine prices, and in some the government was unequal to the maintenance of public order. The Grand Vizier Hüseyn Pasha worked hard from 1697 to redress both economy and administration. After the war he abolished many of the compulsory payments necessitated by it; in particular, by cancelling arrears of war contribution and otherwise, he sought to alleviate the deplorable condition of the Christian peasantry, who had suffered not only by the wide breakdown of local administration but above all by the campaigning in the Balkans.[2] Hüseyn even dared to attack the abuse of *timar*, for the long years of war had multiplied openings for the misuse of fiefs by persons who did not in practice perform military service; yet it was impossible in a short time to get rid of the thousands of illegal holders of these estates. He also tried to curb the janissaries by cutting down their numbers, with considerable savings to the treasury. Barracks were rebuilt, fortresses reconditioned. These were the years when naval efficiency made its greatest strides, notably by Mezzomorto's clarification of the chain of command and the increased building of square-rigged sailing-ships; Tournefort, who was favourably impressed by the organization of the dockyard at Constantinople, counted 28 fine ships there (from 100 to 60 guns) in 1701.[3] The combined strength of the standing army and navy was

[1] Already lower than this when the Cossack rebellion of 1706–8 (see *NCMH*, vol. VI, p. 732) had reduced it to a few hundreds. Construction continued in the yards up the Don and its tributaries.

[2] Ankara, Turkish National Archives, Mühimme Defteri, no. 145, p. 485. Gibb and Bowen vol. I, pt. ii (1957), p. 237 mention especially Bulgaria, which had always to endure the passage of armies leaving the capital for the Danube. Cf. Svoronos, p. 122, on the disruption of Salonica's Balkan trade.

[3] *A Voyage into the Levant*, vol. I, p. 374. A Venetian list of 1716 estimates Ottoman strength in sail at one ship of 112 guns, two of 88, one of 72, twenty-five of 64–50, and six of

estimated at 196,227 men, costing nearly 7 m. piastres a year. Writing in 1703–4, the *defterdar* Sari Mehmed Pasha placed the size of the standing army alone at 96,727, excluding another 70,000 in frontier garrisons or on pension and 23,500 'who have the duty of saying prayers'.[1]

More might have been achieved had not Hüseyn Pasha encountered a formidable obstacle in the wealthy and ambitious Mufti Feyzullah, a former tutor of Mustafa II who possessed great influence, placed his many sons in lucrative posts, and interfered constantly in public business. The position of the Mufti of Constantinople, the highest religious and therefore legal authority, whose rulings on points of sacred law included decisions of peace and war, commanded greater esteem than that of the grand vizier himself: disharmony between the two was fatal to the working of the higher administration. Feyzullah was a learned legist and did much to raise standards of religious discipline and teaching,[2] but he embodied the fierce opposition of the ulema to change. The grand vizier's health broke down and he resigned on 5 September 1702, shortly before his death. His successor, Daltaban Mustafa Pasha, a coarse and tyrannical creature of Feyzullah's, was neither able nor willing to continue his work, despite an improved administration of such *evkaf* as he controlled.[3]

Sultan Mustafa II, a man of culture and humanity but fond of his pleasures, now stayed permanently at Adrianople, so causing rumour to spread that he would make it his capital. Away from Constantinople, he could more easily escape the pressures of opinion in the college-mosques, coffee-houses and workshops, as well as in the palace itself. It was also a sinister fact that the chief janissary aga was mainly responsible for the police[4] of the capital. In 'the Adrianople affair' of August 1703, the armourers, angry about long arrears of pay, headed a military rising to compel the sultan's return. The army forced him to abdicate in favour of his brother, Ahmed III (1703–30), and it suborned the ulema into sanctioning this. As was doubtless foreseen, the confiscated estates of the fallen administration went far to provide the largest sum ever paid to the troops on such an occasion.[5] With less authority from precedent, the rapacious Feyzullah was abandoned to the fury of the mob, on the orders of his successor. Mavrocordato, who had been in his confidence, temporarily effaced himself.

48–28, exclusive of a Barbary squadron (Anderson, 248n.). The construction of three-decker galleons, first attempted in 1682, made rapid progress in these years.
[1] Wright, pp. 104–5.
[2] J. von Hammer, *Hist. de l'empire ottoman* (tr. J. J. Hellert, 18 vols. 1835–46), vol. XIII, p. 68.
[3] *Ibid.* vol. XIII, p. 83.
[4] Fully discussed by Mantran, pp. 148 ff.
[5] 3,688 purses or 1,537,666 piastres. The rest of the money was found by sales of offices and tax-farms. Another 1,000 purses went to the frontier garrisons in the shape of drafts on government properties. See Wright, p. 6.

The new sultan, then aged thirty, had spent his life in seclusion but with some freedom. Although fond of women and of verse, a distinguished calligrapher and flower-painter, he did not devote himself exclusively to the pleasures of the Seraglio. During the first part of his reign at least, from 1703 to 1714, Ahmed showed intelligent interest in public business, as was seen in a number of reforms in the judiciary and in the coinage. Unhappily, his morose, unsteady and ambitious character laid him open to the influence of favourites, although his early resolve was to trust no one too far and he concentrated on securing himself against conspirators. By causing or acquiescing in the deaths of thousands of suspected persons, he certainly filled the treasury but also deprived the empire of some of its ablest soldiers. While he shared the profound desire of many of his subjects to see the greatness of the empire restored, he understood well enough that its condition precluded any aggressive foreign policy. The first needs were to increase revenue and the efficiency of the armed forces. In pursuit of these objectives, Ahmed frequently changed his viziers until he found in Ali Pasha of Chorlu a man fitted for the task. Chorlulu Ali Pasha, grand vizier 1706–10, was a strong and intelligent statesman who had already done much to restore public order in Syria. His hand was soon felt by the provincial rulers. He removed restless elements from the Corps of Janissaries. He strengthened vital coast defences, notably on the Straits of Kerch, while the continued expansion of the fleet was such as to alarm other Mediterranean states. Desiring only peace, however, he made no attempt to exploit the Spanish Succession or Great Northern Wars, resisting persistent pressure from the French ambassador, Ferriol, to bring about a breach in Ottoman relations with the emperor and (from 1707) with the tsar. It is hardly too much to say that Chorlulu Ali's obstinate neutrality saved Russia from disaster in 1708–9.[1] When the turbulent Devlet-Girei II, thrice khan of the Crimea[2] and a fanatical Russophobe bitterly resentful of the drying-up of income from the tsar, wished to join the Swedes and Mazepa's Cossacks in July 1709, he received an order from the Sublime Porte to remain quiet—a good instance of the firm hand which the Turks still kept on their vassal. This restraint helped to make possible Peter's crushing victory at Poltava, whence Charles XII and Mazepa escaped to Ochakov, before being transferred soon afterwards to Bender, a Bessarabian fortress on the Dniester.

Poltava fundamentally altered the political balance of eastern Europe. Russia was now, incontestably, the strongest power there, as was quickly felt in Constantinople, where the new Russian legation under Tolstoy intrigued and bribed more extensively than ever, while preparations for

[1] For the Swedish invasion of Russia, see *NCMH*, vol. VI, pp. 664 ff.
[2] In 1699–1702, 1707–13 and 1716. He was the most remarkable of the five sons of Selim-Girei between whom the khanate revolved from 1705 to 1736. In 1707 he replaced his brother Gazi-Girei, who had failed to repel an irruption by the Noghai Tatars from beyond the Kuban river. For a list of the Khans see Sumner, p. 13 n.

war were always to be feared at Azov and Taganrog. Alarming above all was the state of Poland, which swarmed with Russian troops. These had not hesitated to violate Turkish soil in pursuit of the fugitive Swedish king, whose presence now became a matter of critical importance in Russo-Turkish relations. The sultan accorded Charles an expensive hospitality and rejected the tsar's demand for his extradition. Turkish tradition demanded that asylum be granted to any who sought it, but here was an opportunity for bringing pressure on Peter to revise the treaty of 1700. This, since he was occupied with the Baltic war, Peter agreed to adjust in favour of the Turks by demolishing the small forts on the Lower Dnieper. In return the Porte undertook to send Charles XII away as soon as possible, through Poland or Russia, but with a Turkish escort of only 500 men so as not to alarm the powers. Here Chorlulu Ali was mistaken in his calculations. The 'Iron Head' refused to leave. Instead, he intrigued against the grand vizier, rightly seen as chief obstacle to his plan of using the Ottoman forces against Peter.

In this far-reaching plan the Swedish king came near to success. He was eagerly abetted by Devlet-Girei Khan, another redoubtable intriguer who attended sittings of the Divan, and by General Stanislas Poniatowski—an adherent of Stanislas Leszczyński, the exiled Polish king. Poniatowski had accompanied Charles to Bender and was able to influence the sultan through the latter's mother and doctor, Fonseca. This group of 'northerners' was ably supported by Mazepa's successor, Philip Orlik, whose objective was nothing less than the reconstitution of an independent Ukraine—a policy which his Polish collaborators, however, could like no better than his Russian enemies. These troublemakers contrived to harden anti-Russian feeling among the Turks. Their task was eased by the extreme nervousness aroused in governing circles by signs of war preparations at Azov and Taganrog and along the lower Dnieper, where the erection of new forts revived fears for the Crimea. It is true that Peter had no wish to try conclusions with the Ottomans at this juncture, when his troops were still engaged with the Swedes in Pomerania; but it was not difficult to represent his ultimate ambitions as immediately dangerous to Turkey, especially as the janissaries were not alone in Constantinople in thirsting to wipe out the dishonour of Azov. Though the mood of the capital generally did not favour another Russian campaign, the leaders of the ulema were sensitive to the propaganda of Devlet-Girei and it is symptomatic of their growing political influence that, against so much caution and faint-heartedness, they were to get their way. The position of the pacific grand vizier was rapidly undermined. His neutral foreign policy was now read as pro-Russian, and he was accused of showing a too independent attitude towards his sovereign: he had, notably, made a startling attempt to rid the harem of the negro eunuchs, whose chief was the channel of communication between grand vizier and sultan. In July

1710 Chorlulu Ali fell to a palace intrigue, his property being confiscated though his life was spared.

His successor was the cultivated Köprülü Numan Pasha, son of the hero of Zalánkemén. Like his predecessors of this family, he was a man of high principles and he tried to dispense impartial justice, especially in financial matters. But he lacked the ruthlessness of the first Köprülü and his honest methods incurred the sultan's disapproval. He held office for only 63 days. As his family still enjoyed considerable popularity, he was politely relegated to the governorship of Negroponte. By contrast, Baltaji Mehmed Pasha, 'the Woodcleaver', who attained the signet on 26 September 1710, had been brought up in the more athletic educational stream of the Seraglio known as the 'Foreign Boys'.[1] This is as much as to say that he understood obedience better than command, and yet he had recently been governor of Aleppo.

Although it had an unusually prolonged Egyptian rebellion on its hands,[2] the Porte finally made up its mind to declare war on 20 November and orders went out to the provincial pashas to join the main army in the spring of 1711. On receiving this news, Peter twice attempted to persuade the Porte to cancel its decision; as soon as it was clear that it was in earnest, he ordered an immediate march. Moreover, following the example of Leopold I,[3] he was willing to give this war a religious character. In imitation of Constantine the Great at the battle of Milvian Bridge in A.D. 311, he had the Cross inscribed on his Guards' standards with the words, 'Under this sign we conquer'. He proclaimed that his aim was to liberate the Balkan Christians from 'the yoke of the infidels'. For the first time Russia openly appealed to them to rise against their Muslim masters.

This historic pronouncement, an omen for the future, seems to have been composed by Sava Vladislavich *alias* Raguzinsky, a Serb from Ragusa who had been a Russian agent among the Serbs and Montenegrins. These tough peasants were virtually new material for tsarist policy. It is possible that Peter's chagrin over the Austrian desertion at Carlowitz was in part occasioned by the frustration of his ideas about the Balkans, and that his new-found distrust of the Habsburg made him listen more readily to Orthodox grievances against the Catholics. As early as 1687 the metropolitan of Skopje had visited Moscow to denounce the treatment of Orthodox bishops in Hungary; in 1698 the Serbian patriarch there made a similar appeal during Peter's stay at Vienna; and in 1702 Dositheus, patriarch of Jerusalem, wrote to him comparing Leopold I with Diocletian. Between 1704 and 1710 at least four Serb fighting leaders went to Moscow to offer their services 'on behalf of their Orthodox tsar', and to beg funds.[4] In the Black Mountain of Montenegro and in southern

[1] For the distinction between these and the 'Inside Boys', see Gibb and Bowen, vol. I, pt. i, pp. 56-7, and Tournefort, vol. II, pp. 8-14.   [2] Holt, pp. 88-90.
[3] *NCMH*, vol. VI, pp. 579-80.   Sumner, p. 45 and Marczali, pp. 202-3.

Herzegovina, where banditry was always difficult to suppress, a sporadic guerrilla war had already begun with a massacre of Muslims at Christmas 1702. Its leader was the prince-bishop, Daniel Petrovich. In 1711 he was joined by a *haiduk* (bandit) chieftain from Herzegovina, Michael Milo- radovich. Poorly armed as they were, they were to inflict a defeat on the Turks as far to the east as Nish, but they were isolated from the Russian forces, with whose fate their own was bound up.

In many respects Peter himself was out of sympathy with the doctrines and practices of Orthodox religion, but Moscow had of course ancient and intimate ties with the Greek ecclesiastics. The seventeenth century had seen a thickening traffic in relics, pilgrims and erudition: the Greek patriarchs collaborated with Moscow in the revision of sacred rites and were to some extent dependent on Russian financial support.[1] If their strictly theological influence on Muscovy had declined in face of the 'Latin' culture transmitted by the Academy of Kiev, now the most vital centre of Russian Orthodoxy, the final condemnation in 1691 of the 'Calvinistic' doctrine of Cyril Lukaris once again brought the two hierar- chies together. Moreover, the Austrian and Venetian conquests had sharpened the antagonism between Orthodox and Catholic, as did the diplomacy of Louis XIV in protecting the stealthy formation of new Uniate communities by Jesuit and Franciscan missionaries in many parts of the Ottoman empire. A specially bitter blow fell in 1690, when French influence purchased the keys of the Holy Sepulchre for the Latins, thus compromising the normal preference of the Muslim authorities for the Orthodox. The return of the keys was placed formally on the Russian agenda in 1692, and the outraged feelings of the patriarch of Jerusalem were invaluable to Peter's information service. With good reason, however, the Russians were too wary to place much reliance on the Greek clergy. Rather different was the attitude of some of the great Rumanian land- owners, faction-ridden though they were. For half a century contacts between Muscovy and the Principalities had been developing. After Poltava the prince of Moldavia, Demetrius Cantemir (1673–1723), agreed in the event of a Russo-Turkish war to join the Russians, in return for acknowledgement as hereditary prince of Moldavia under Russian pro- tection; he promised to have food and forage ready for the invading troops. These undertakings were sanctioned by treaties in April 1711, which ensured Cantemir's safety in Russia in case of failure. Constantine Brancovan, prince of Wallachia and an enemy of the Cantemirs, had also been moving closer to Russia for some years but prudently decided to await the verdict of battle before deserting the sultan.[2]

The Russian army, a disciplined force of 40,000 infantry and 14,000 cavalry, set off through Polish territory towards Moldavia, with the

[1] Cf. *NCMH*, vol. v, pp. 586–9.
[2] For earlier Wallachian intrigues with Vienna, see *ibid.* vol. vi, pp. 578 and 580.

confidence born of Poltava. It was accompanied by the tsar and his wife Catherine, by many of the generals' wives, and the busy Raguzinsky; the tsar's presence served only to impede the commander-in-chief, the aged Sheremeteyev. The cavalry was led by General Rönne, the infantry divisions by Ensberg, Janusch, Hallart, Bruce and Repnin—the only Russian among them. Before reaching the Dniester they began to suffer shortage of food and water as well as the surprise attacks of the Tatars, but they entered Moldavia—for the first time since the tenth century—without resistance and were in Jassy by June. Cantemir at once declared himself under Russian protection and called on his people to assist the tsar. Contrary to expectation, however, the Russians were not furnished with ample victuals and forage, for the crops had failed as a result of drought and locusts. This was the first serious setback. The second was the unexpected appearance of the whole Turkish army.

Peter had given orders to reach the Danube before the Turks crossed it. According to his intelligence, the Turks were afraid of him and reluctant to cross the river: their main force was thought to be some 60 miles away. Nobody in the Russian quarter was aware that Baltaji Mehmed Pasha was already close to the Russian army, which had had to be divided into three forces to ease provisioning. The Turks—reinforced by a large body of Tatars, with the Cossacks and Poles from Bender—advanced north along the right bank of the Pruth tributary, crossed it, and on 20 July moved against the Russians. The latter were already pulling back, but the Tatars blocked the road leading south from Jassy behind them. The Russians halted not far from Stanilesti, in a narrow plain with the river in their rear and an extensive marsh on one side. They were surrounded. Since the Turkish position was on hills that dominated theirs, so that the Turkish artillery could easily sweep them—and the river behind them—the tsar was completely at the mercy of his enemy. On 21 July 1711, Baltaji Mehmed was signing orders for a grand assault when the Russians hoisted white flags. Hungry, sick and tired, they could hardly resist an army at least twice as large; they must sue for peace or be annihilated. Peter, in his depression, scarcely knew what to do. At this critical moment Catherine was able to calm him and persuade him to ask for peace, which was supported by the Vice-chancellor Shafirov. It looked as if the calculations of Charles XII were to prove correct, for now the tsar expected to have to surrender most of his conquests from Sweden, though of course he offered much less. Lacking both confidence and foresight, however, Baltaji Mehmed was too easily content with the Russian proposals. He hurriedly granted terms: that Azov be retroceded, Taganrog, Kamenny Zaton and the new Dnieper fortresses entirely demolished; that the tsar no longer interfere in Polish affairs and no Russian reside in the quality of ambassador at the High Porte; that all Turkish prisoners be freed and the king of Sweden allowed safe passage. Baltaji Mehmed gave the Russians food

and an unofficial promise to expel Charles XII. As hostages, the tsar sent
Sheremeteyev's own grandson and Peter Shafirov, to whom he owed much.

The *dénouement* at the Pruth 'may deservedly be looked on as one of
the most surprizing and extraordinary events that ever happened', wrote
Sutton, British ambassador at the Porte (1701–16).[1] He regarded the
victory as undeserved. Yet the fate of Peter and of his new Russia had
depended within a hair's breadth upon the decision of the grand vizier,
more ruthless action on whose part might have changed the course of
East European history. Baltaji Mehmed seems to have been carried away
by his own unexpected success, but it is only fair to add that the janissaries
had little stomach for fighting in this country and that the impoverished
sipahis were reluctant to face the cost of prolonged fighting at all. Moreover, the grand vizier's deep distrust of the whole Bender circle may have
induced him to come to terms before Charles XII could appear on the
scene.[2] The peace was certainly well received in Constantinople, except by
the wavering sultan, who soon had Baltaji in prison. The victory was felt
to have wiped out the disgraces of the previous war: in fact, the mercurial
Turks were now able to convince themselves that the Russian menace
could be held off quite easily. There was some justification for this illusion
in the poor showing made by Peter's navy, said to have been carrying
35,000 soldiers and marines, when a powerful Turkish fleet appeared off
Azov; a few months later, whatever remained of value in Peter's southern
navy, including the stores at Taganrog, was sold to the Turks. Above all,
it had been amply demonstrated that Russian and Balkan Christians were
still incapable of effective combination. Though the Montenegrins held
out till 1714, the tsar could do little for them, while the Principalities had
done little enough to help the tsar.

From 1716 the government of the Principalities was regularly entrusted
to the Mavrocordatos and a few other Greek families of the well-to-do
Phanar quarter of Constantinople, where the Oecumenical Patriarch
resided. Having paid highly for posts from which they always risked
dismissal, the Phanariot governors and their numerous clients fleeced the
Rumanians ruthlessly. Here indeed is a striking example of that working
alliance between Greek and Ottoman which in some sense was to make
European Turkey 'a Greco-Turkish régime'[3] and had already made the
patriarchate itself a fiscal and police agent of the Porte. To the 'third
Rome' of the tsars many educated Greeks preferred the hope of a new
Byzantium, to be realized by improving their position in the Ottoman
administration as a whole, where the posts of First Dragoman and
Dragoman of the Fleet had become perquisites of the Phanariot commu-

---

[1] *Despatches*, p. 60: like Colijer, he was strongly pro-Russian.
[2] Thus Sumner, pp. 40–1, who doubts the charges of excessive bribery later levied against
the grand vizier. Turkish opinion, not unnaturally, explained too much in such terms.
[3] D. Dakin, *British and American Philhellenes, 1821–1833* (Salonica, 1955), p. 10.

nity. The patronage thus acquired itself fertilized wealth and political influence. Moreover, the Porte, like the embassies accredited to it, had increasing technical need of the relatively westernized Greek aristocracy, now that it was coming to depend more on diplomacy to preserve its empire—against powers so often at odds with one another. Although nearly a century was to pass before regular Ottoman embassies were established in the West, it has been said that the plenipotentiaries at Carlowitz introduced something of the western diplomatic spirit into the Porte, largely animated in those years by the adroit Alexander Mavrocordato.[1]

By the Pruth treaty Russia had given up all that had been gained in 1700, but months of wrangling passed before practical effect was given to its rather general terms. Both sides desired to improve them, while doubting the other's sincerity. The tsar's initial dilatoriness, in fact, resulted in a new rupture on 2 October 1711 and the displacement of Baltaji Mehmed by the more bellicose Yusuf Pasha. With the indispensable support of the Dutch and British representatives, Shafirov and Tolstoy worked hard for agreement against Swedish efforts, backed by the French and Venetians, to prevent it. Something was done to clarify the divided loyalties of the Cossacks and to establish responsibility for, if not to abolish, raiding and reprisals between Cossack and Tatar in the frontier zone of the Black Sea steppe and southern Ukraine. Here Peter formally withdrew to the line of the Dniester. But he was slower to recall his troops from Poland, where the continued presence of Russian garrisons caused the sultan, with French encouragement, to threaten further hostilities after a definitive agreement seemed to have been reached in April 1712. This question was linked with that of Charles XII's return across Polish or Russian territory, both sides fearing further complications were he given a Turkish escort strong enough to guarantee his safety. Reports from frontier commissions convinced the Ottomans of Peter's insincerity, and on 3 November the horse-tail was again hung in front of the Seraglio as a sign of war. Then, in March 1713, when the sultan had freed himself of any sense of obligation to his embarrassing guest, Charles was forcibly brought to Adrianople and Devlet-Girei was banished to Chios. Despite a further Turkish proclamation of war on 30 April (the fourth from 1710), encouraged by the Swedish success at Gadebusch in the previous December, these measures in fact removed the main obstacles to Russo-Turkish reconciliation. A 25-year peace was concluded with Peter at Adrianople on 5 June. Peter's southern frontier was now withdrawn—vaguely enough,

---

[1] See Von Hammer, vol. XIII, pp. 8–9. Son of a Chiote silk merchant, Mavrocordato (1636–1709) had been educated in medicine at Padua and professed it at the patriarchal college in Constantinople. His rise, which may have owed something to the protection of the Mufti Feyzullah, illustrates the special opportunities at court open to both physicians and those with a mastery of Christian languages. Wealthy Phanariots were frequently educated in Padua.

it is true—as far north as the river Orel, and he was to evacuate Poland within two months. Further, in April 1714 the sultan acknowledged Augustus II as ruler of the Polish Ukraine. In September Charles XII, Stanislas Poniatowski and Philip Orlik left Turkish soil to continue their struggles elsewhere.

A key to this decisive turn in Ottoman foreign relations is to be found in the preparations already going forward for a renewed trial of strength with Venice. With the Morea under the Venetians and a Venetian fleet in the Archipelago, no Turk could sleep quietly in Constantinople. The hardest sacrifice at Carlowitz had been the Morea; even during the vizierate of the peace-loving Chorlulu Ali there was talk of revenge. The Swedish king's refuge in Turkey, combined with Russian threats, had instead produced the war of 1711. The Morea appealed more than did war beyond the lower Danube to most Turkish politicians and to the janis-saries, who disliked wintering in desolate country far from home but whose restlessness, according to some foreign observers,[1] was such as to tempt the authorities to find occupation for them. After the Russian danger had receded and the question of Poland been somewhat settled, the Porte decided on the recovery of the Morea. The war party was led by Silahdar Ali Pasha, the sultan's son-in-law and favourite, who had personal connections with the Morea and had been an active politician for some time already. It was he who had engineered the overthrow of Chorlulu Ali and Baltaji Mehmed, with the aid of two personages always dangerous to grand viziers, the Mufti and the *Kizlar Agasi*. In April 1713 he became grand vizier himself.

His policy accorded well with the interests of the Phanar, for the Venetian senate had deprived the patriarchate of its revenues from the Morea and switched to Venice what remained of Moreote export trade. The Venetian administration, despite good features,[2] had struck no deep root in the Morea itself, which it could only govern by creating a party on the brittle foundation of privileges and places. Injustices were done in its name by the native Greek primates, merchants and magistrates as well as by Venetian nobles—enough to curtail the benefits of the Venetian commune as the unit for a restored public order, of land resettlement, and of the conversion of State leases into freeholds. Nor did an improved educational provision compensate for an influx of Italian priests. The general-proveditor (governor) described the Moreotes in 1708 as unwearied in chicanery, inexorable in revenge.[3] When the Ottomans returned, there-

---

[1] *The Present State of Europe*, vol. xxv (1714), p. 483: advices from Turkey, 8 December.
[2] Notably in the restoration of agriculture, which seems to have been reflected in a three-fold population increase to 250,000 (H. Antoniadis-Bibicou, *op. cit.* p. 391).
[3] G. Finlay, *A History of Greece* (1877 edn., 7 vols.), vol. v, p. 208. Cf. Tournefort's impression of the Greeks of the Archipelago (vol. I, p. 97): 'a Family-Quarrel cannot always be made up among them with Mony'.

fore, they were greeted as liberators, especially as they paid for food and forage. With a civilian population thus disaffected, a military establishment of some 8,000 was confronted by a Turkish army of over 70,000, supported by a much superior strength at sea. With reinforcements from Barbary and Egypt, the Kaptan Pasha, Janum Hoja (Koggia), commanded 58 sail against 19 Venetian assisted by 4 Maltese.

A pretext for war, formally declared on 11 January 1715, was found in the assistance allegedly rendered by Venetian agents to the Montenegrin rebels, and in the refusal of the Bank of Venice to surrender the fortune deposited with it by Constantine Brancovan, the prince of Wallachia who had been executed in 1714. In June the Turkish fleet easily captured the islands of Aegina and Tinos (Tine, which the Venetians had held against attack for five centuries), while the grand vizier was still encamped on the plain of Thebes. Silahdar Ali's ability to enforce discipline on the march conciliated the Greek peasants, and his movements were not obstructed by shortage of provisions. Soon, on 7 July, he mastered the fortress of Corinth, after which the Ottomans proceeded to capture the other Moreote strongpoints—Argos, Nauplia, Koron, Navarino, and Methone (Modon). This last might have been saved had the Venetian fleet given battle to the Kaptan Pasha, whose command of the coastal waters goes far to explain the weak resistance of the Venetian garrisons. There was no clash between armies. The campaign consisted entirely of sieges. It was completed in exactly a hundred days. In July 1716 the Turkish land and sea forces proceeded to attack Corfu itself, so often the rendezvous of Venetian fleets and now ably defended by Marshal Schulenberg, a Saxon who had fought with Eugene at Malplaquet. It looked as if Venice was facing collapse when Austria came to her rescue.

At the outset the emperor had tried mediation, although Louis XIV urged Vienna to war—an inversion of his earlier habit of encouraging the Porte against Vienna. Even in 1715 Charles VI was too much occupied with the legacies of the Spanish Succession War readily to resume Balkan campaigning, with Venice as his only ally; his Spanish entourage particularly favoured peace with the Ottoman, in opposition to Eugene, who threw his influence against any risk of some western enterprise diverting the concentration of Imperial strength against the Turk.[1] It was the threat to Dalmatia (and conceivably to Croatia and Styria) which led to the signature of a defensive alliance with Venice on 13 April 1716. The emperor demanded an indemnification for all the republic's losses. The interpretation of his ultimatum created difficulties at Constantinople: some of the Divan believed that it meant what it said, nothing less than restitution of the Morea, which had had nearly two and a half centuries of Turkish rule; others, that the emperor would be satisfied with the old Venetian possessions, Tine and Cerigo (Kythera). Contrary to reports

[1] Braubach, *Prinz Eugen*, vol. III (1964), pp. 309–10.

reaching Vienna,[1] it is certain that many of the viziers (ministers) were opposed to another war with the emperor. To avoid it had been a constant concern in their dealings with Charles XII; for this they had even refused asylum to Rákóczi's defeated followers; operations against Venice had been undertaken in reliance on Habsburg neutrality. Silahdar Ali, however, after his easy victory over the Venetians, flung caution to the winds. Regarding the Imperial intervention as a breach of the Peace of Carlowitz—though it was, rather, a reaction to the Ottoman disturbance of the balance of power erected by it—he persuaded the Divan to cut matters short by declaring war on Vienna. At the same time the Porte planned trouble by installing Francis II Rákóczi as king of Hungary: a messenger was sent to invite him from Paris to organize the struggle, and he came.

In the summer of 1716 a Turkish army of (at most) 120,000 began operations from Belgrade. Following Silahdar Ali's wishes, the council-of-war decided to attack the fortress of Peterwardein. Here, on 5 August, a major battle was fought. Eugene had 70,000 men, including 187 squadrons of cavalry. When Eugene ordered a cavalry charge, Silahdar Ali ignored advice to intervene at the point of danger; and when, finally, at the head of his officers he galloped into the thick of the battle, it was too late. He was struck by a bullet and died on the way to Belgrade. Others killed on this field included the governors of Anatolia and Adana, Türk Ahmed Pasha and Hüseyn Pasha. The loss of these leaders produced a rout. The whole Turkish camp, as at Vienna in 1683, fell into enemy hands—the grand vizier's magnificent ceremonial tent, 114 guns, 150 standards and 5 horse-tails.[2] The Turkish casualties have been much exaggerated but were probably double those of the Imperialists, which are estimated at nearly 5,000 dead and wounded.[3] Impressed by the stout resistance of the janissaries, Eugene did not pursue the defeated army to Belgrade. Instead, he ordered a difficult march to Temesvár, the 'Gazi' (victorious) fortress which controlled the Banat and had resisted assault for 164 years. Its garrison of 10,000–15,000 held out fiercely, but troops sent to relieve it were beaten back and it capitulated on 12 October, with the honours of war. From fear of disturbances, its fall was not at once made public in Constantinople. Eugene placed the Banat under the command of his close friend Count Mercy, who sent a small force to raid Bucharest, capital of Wallachia since 1698. The siege of Corfu had already been called off after Peterwardein, when the Turkish forces were also withdrawn from Butrinto on the mainland and Santa Maura further south.

[1] The decisive impulse to the deliberations of the Wiener Hof was imparted by Fleischmann, the Austrian Resident at the Porte, who was convinced that the Turks intended a war of revenge against the emperor: *ibid.* p. 308.
[2] A badge of high rank suspended from a pole at the top of which was a golden ball; an ordinary bey had the right to one horse-tail, a *vali* or *beylerbey* to two, an ordinary vizier to three, the grand vizier to five.
[3] Braubach, vol. III, p. 320.

The death of Silahdar Ali had further consequences. For all his ex-cessive self-confidence, he had been well fitted to restore the tarnished prestige of the empire and impose needful reforms. His successor, Halil Pasha, was ordered in July 1717 to the relief of Belgrade, to which key position Eugene and Mercy were already laying siege with a strength estimated at 80,000. The garrison of 30,000 under Mustafa Pasha pre-pared to resist while the Austrians dug trenches between the Danube and Sava, bridging both rivers. Halil Pasha, indecisive and incompetent, failed to use his initial advantage. Eugene was dangerously caught between a strong garrison in front and a field army twice the size of his own behind him. Instead of moving at once, Halil Pasha ordered his troops to entrench and open fire from high ground. Exploiting this indecision and a chance fog, Eugene surprised the Turkish lines in the early hours of 16 August. There ensued a good deal of confused fighting, during which a gap occurred in the Austrian centre; only when the fog cleared about 8 o'clock were the Austrians able to storm the Turkish artillery positions. At this point the grand vizier, who had had no clear idea of what was going on, ordered a retreat. The Turkish losses were more severe than at Peterwardein—perhaps 10,000 killed and as many wounded. The Imperialists suffered about 5,000 casualties. Besides 150 guns and 60 standards, a large supply of ammunition and food fell into their hands. On 18 August the battered citadel itself surrendered, and four days later the surviving two-thirds of the garrison marched out to freedom. After the fall of Belgrade the Turks evacuated their remaining outposts on the Sava river-line, but the garri-sons of Zvornik (on the Drina) and of Bihach and Novi (on the Una) held out against strong attacks, with the result that Bosnia was not overrun as it had been in the aftermath of Zenta. And signs had already appeared of the malaria which was to cost the Imperialists thousands of their best troops in the next two years.

Meanwhile, the Venetians had reoccupied some of their lost Adriatic positions and resumed the offensive at sea, with the support of six well-armed Portuguese vessels in addition to Maltese and papal auxiliaries. An engagement off Cape Matapan in July 1717 was less disastrous to them than a three-day running battle near Cerigo a year later, when a superior Turkish fleet inflicted nearly 2,000 casualties on a Christian fighting-line of 26 sail, whose order was imperfectly preserved with the aid of galleys. Vienna was disappointed with the performance of its ally and no longer disposed to insist on the restitution of the Morea, which Venice lacked the strength to retain.[1]

As has been seen, many of the Divan had opposed the rupture with the emperor in the first place. At that time also British and Dutch diplomacy, at Vienna as well as Constantinople, had been strongly exerted to prevent it. Late in 1717 a new (and pro-Turkish) British ambassador to the Porte,

[1] Braubach, vol. III, pp. 335, 370, 372.

Edward Wortley Montagu, together with Colijer, again tried mediation. Vienna thought it could obtain better terms by direct negotiations. These were delayed because the Porte wanted first the restoration of Temesvár and then of Belgrade, the conquest of both of which was the essential Austrian war aim; also, a foreign statesman, this time Alberoni, intrigued to keep the Turks and the Hungarian malcontents engaged in what was for him a vital diversion.[1] Spain, which had landed troops in Sardinia, now seriously threatened the Habsburg position in Italy. For this very reason the emperor, while preparing another campaign in the Balkans, was anxious to settle his account with the Turks and willing to accept the mediation of the British, themselves also alarmed for the stability of the Utrecht settlement. Early in June, at Passarowitz, a small town near Semendria (Smederevo), the arduous task of mediation was again undertaken by Sutton, with Abraham Stanyan and Colijer in the offing.[2] Once more the principle of *uti possidetis* was adopted as the basis, though the Austrians repeatedly tried to go beyond it—successfully in the case of the Venetians, with whom the Turks were unwilling to treat at all. The treaty of 21 July provided for the cession of the districts of Temesvár, Semendria and Belgrade and for a new frontier along the Sava and Drina rivers, whence it ran eastwards just above Nish and then north to Orsova. To the loss in 1699 of Hungary, therefore, the Banat, Little Wallachia (as far as the Aluta), and the most fertile portion of Serbia were now added. Francis II Rákóczi and other Hungarians whom the Porte had supported were not to reside in the vicinity of the new frontier. The Austrian government more or less successfully handled the rehabilitation of the Banat, into which many German settlers, especially veteran soldiers, were introduced on Eugene's initiative; but it did little in Serbia beyond strengthening the fortress of Belgrade, which it was to lose in 1739. A commercial treaty was also signed with the emperor, who in 1719 chartered an Eastern Company at his new 'free port' of Trieste with an ambitious programme for developing his Balkan trade,[3] in some degree at the

[1] Cf. vol. VII, p. 197.
[2] D. B. Horn (ed.), *British Diplomatic Representatives, 1689–1789* (Camden Soc. 3rd ser. vol. XLVI, 1932), p. 152. Wortley's recall had been decided upon in London in September 1717, after Stanyan (then at Vienna) had informed Sunderland that the emperor, who in any case preferred to treat without mediators, would have nothing to do with him. Sutton, who had sailed from Constantinople in March, then hastened to Vienna. He told Addison that the Hanoverian minister, St Saphorin, had encouraged Stanyan to intrigue for the Turkish embassy. Stanyan was appointed to it in October without the usual prior consultation with the Levant Company, who still paid the ambassador's salary. See R. Halsband, *The Life of Lady Mary Wortley Montagu* (Oxford, 1956), pp. 77–9; W. Michael, *England under George I*, vol. I (1936), pp. 362–8; and Braubach, vol. III, p. 371.
[3] Some of Charles's advisers had argued for the acquisition of the Principalities and a Black Sea coast, in preference to Serbia: J. W. Stoye, 'Emperor Charles VI: the early years of the reign', *Trans. R. Hist. Soc.* 5th ser. vol. XII (1962), pp. 80–4; cf. above, p. 604. The commercial treaty gave the Austrians freedom of trade throughout the Ottoman empire, besides substantial tariff and consular concessions.

expense of Venice, another loser at Passarowitz. With her finances in ruin, Venice acquiesced in the surrender of the Morea (with Tine and Aegina), although she kept her conquests in Dalmatia, Santa Maura and the Gulf of Arta, and regained Cerigo. This island, with its redoubtable privateering record, remained her forward base, between the Ionian and Aegean seas; but Venice was never again at war with Turkey.

The Peace of Passarowitz proclaimed in effect that the Turks were no longer a military danger to their neighbours. The defeats at Peterwardein and Belgrade had shown how a much smaller but well-controlled army, at least under a commander of Eugene's cool presence of mind, could defeat Turkish forces far inferior in leadership and equipment. But there was more to it than this. The Turks had demonstrated, again and again, their powers of endurance and eagerness to give battle, and also what massive quantities of war material they could raise. They failed on the whole to make the best of these advantages because they were utterly outclassed in the efficient concentration of resources, in reconnaissance, in the adroit handling of cavalry and field-guns, and in the organization of a high command. Tactically, they relied too much on the terror of a mass assault and on hand-to-hand encounters, just as at sea they preferred ramming and boarding to an artillery engagement. Their high reputation as gunners was based on the big brass of sieges. They had not really caught up with the tactical revolution wrought by the mobile field-gun, let alone by the flintlock musket.[1] Their march as well as battle discipline was inferior to the German. No doubt the sheer size of their field armies added to the logistical problems of Balkan campaigning; although they had long experience of this and an elaborate supply organization, they moved with too many impedimenta and camp-followers. Of course there was a practical purpose for the treasure that was found after capture in the grand viziers' tents, but it required many hands to pitch and decorate these multi-chambered silken apartments, together with those of other pashas. Not the least striking fact about the débâcle at Zenta had been that the booty included 9,000 wagons and 60,000 camels.

The Turks now lost all hope of Hungary; they might be fortunate if they held on to their remaining possessions in Rumelia. No Turk, it is true, could reconcile himself to the loss of Belgrade, but the days of great expeditions seemed gone for ever. All classes longed for a durable peace. The newly-installed grand vizier, Ibrahim Pasha, from Nevshehir in Anatolia, to whose influence acceptance of the hard terms of the treaty was mainly due, was to respond fully to that longing and to the preference for rural retirement which the sultans had shown since the days of Hunter Mehmed. Brought up in the Seraglio, Ibrahim had been placed in Ahmed's service while the prince lived in seclusion—the Ottoman method of keep-

[1] See *NCMH*, vol. vi, pp. 746 ff.

ing heirs to the throne out of harm's way—and they were partners at chess. Upon his accession, Ahmed nominated Ibrahim Efendi as his secretary, and he was offered the post of grand vizier after Silahdar Ali's death; he refused it then, but was persuaded to become deputy (*Kahya*) when Halil Pasha proved unfit. An extremely supple courtier, he managed to keep himself afloat in the seas of palace intrigue and to preserve the sultan's confidence. His exceptionally long vizierate (1718–30) is remembered as *Lale Devri*, the 'Age of Tulips', for 'tulipomania' now became the characteristic passion of the court and of wealthy circles in Constantinople; no less than 1,200 varieties,[1] some very costly and objects of keen competition, imported as a rule from Holland or Persia, are said to have been cultivated; sale of a rare bulb outside the capital was even punishable with exile. Under the April moon, the sultan and all the higher dignitaries of the empire, attended by dancers and musicians, would abandon themselves to exquisite and extravagant festivals in the tulip-gardens, hung with lanterns and singing-birds, and with vases of Venetian glass for the finest tulips. In winter, there were helva parties, at which Chinese shadow-plays might be performed and philosophical discussion alternate with the distribution of sweets, jewels, and robes of honour. In summer, elaborate sea-fights and fireworks were staged. The most famous poet of the time, Nedim, glorified the beauties of the 'Palace of Felicity' (*Saadabad*)—the name given to Kagithane[2] on the northern side of the Golden Horn where pleasure-pavilions (kiosks) of the utmost luxury were built, often hinting at Chinese or French designs. For a brief spell faithful Osmanlis were shocked by the advent of the rococo, but it seemed as if their rulers were determined to forget their military humiliation in these fabulous gaieties and to demonstrate how profoundly they had now been converted into devotees of peace.

Besides these organized pleasures, Ibrahim Pasha promoted cultural activities of enduring value. Musicians, singers and poets found ample scope in the new atmosphere, as did the decorative arts. Although the celebrated Ahmed III fountain near Hagia Sophia is a monument to the foreign influence of the time, native Ottoman culture was still far from exhaustion. A vigorous historiographical tradition did not disappear with the death of its greatest representative, Naima, in 1716; not long afterwards, a learned commission was appointed to translate important works, above all of history, from Arabic and Persian. As had happened earlier in Spain, the decline of empire fostered self-criticism, in which contemporary Ottoman historians took the lead. The spread of knowledge

---

[1] B. Miller, *Beyond the Sublime Porte: the Grand Seraglio of Stambul* (Yale, 1931), p. 124. On the powers of Ahmed III's new court officer, the Master of Flowers, see *ibid.* pp. 223–4.

[2] See the map of 'Istanbul and its environs' in A. D. Alderson, *The Structure of the Ottoman Dynasty* (Oxford, 1956), p. 78. It was on the meadows here that the ceremonial processions of the gilds and corporations of Constantinople traditionally took place; the great naval arsenal of Kasim Pasha lay immediately to the east (Mantran, pp. 68, 365).

was encouraged by the opening of five public libraries. In 1721 a Turkish envoy in Paris had instructions to 'make a thorough study of the means of civilization and education, and report on those capable of application' in Turkey; his son, Said Chelebi, returned with an enthusiasm for the art of printing.[1] The most striking innovation of this period, indeed, was the foundation in 1727 of the first Muslim printing press in Turkey by Ibrahim Müteferrika (1674-1745), a Hungarian by birth and a critic of Ottoman backwardness in many fields, who selected, edited and printed some thirty books—the incunabula of Turkish printed books—with the aid of presses and typographers imported from the West.[2] His achievement was only made possible by the support of the grand vizier, against strong opposition from the army of scribes who made their living as copyists, and from the ulema, who were able to prevent the printing of religious works and in 1742 to stop the enterprise altogether.

Ahmed III, whose love of pleasure and the arts fully matched that of his predecessor, was well content with his grand vizier, who became his son-in-law and so addressed as 'Damad'. But Damad Ibrahim had a free hand only at the cost of pandering to his master's avarice and concealing the true state of the empire. In these years the Venetian Residents reported a scarcity of hard money, much unemployment and severe annual epidemics. Pest-ridden Salonica, the largest town in the Balkans, was vacated by two-thirds of its population in 1719.[3] Food prices were exceptionally high; in 1719 the harvest failed in the Black Sea area and the provisioning of Constantinople, always a major concern of the authorities, caused pressure on alternative sources. There is reason to believe that the empire had already entered a new cycle of inflation.[4] At Cairo, which had rioted over the tombs of saints in 1711,[5] there were serious disturbances in 1721.

Even the sultan was slowly awakened to reality by the sensational revolution in Persia, where an Afghan invasion led rapidly to the downfall of the Safavi dynasty. Shah Husein asked for help at the end of 1720, but only his flight in 1722 stirred the Porte to action. It might not have reacted strongly even then had not the tsar moved his troops to Astrakhan in the summer. Peter had waited for no appeal before acting. He at once occupied Darband and proceeded to bar the Turks from approaching the Caspian. In 1723, Shah Tahmasp yielded to him all the provinces bordering that sea to the west and south. But Daghestan, Shirvan, and part of

[1] Lewis, *Modern Turkey*, pp. 45-6.
[2] Jewish, Greek and Armenian presses had long flourished in Salonica, Constantinople and other cities (*ibid.* pp. 47, 50-1).
[3] M. L. Shay, *The Ottoman Empire from 1720 to 1734 as revealed in the Dispatches of the Venetian Baili* (Urbana, Ill., 1944), pp. 20-4; cf. Svoronos, pp. 135-6.
[4] *Ibid.* pp. 86-7; Mantran, p. 279. On the elaborate organization for feeding the capital, see *ibid.* pp. 185 ff.
[5] All foreign visitors were impressed by the manifold cults and ceremonies of Egyptian piety: for a good later description see E. W. Lane, *An Account of the Manners and Customs of the Modern Egyptians* (3rd edn. 1842).

Azerbaijan had been under Ottoman rule before 1612: the Russian advance beyond the Caucasus therefore played into the hands of Turkish irredentists, still smarting from the humiliation of Passarowitz. So in 1723, when the Russians occupied Baku, the Turks seized Tiflis. From this year onwards, for a decade, Turkish policy abroad was dominated by the revolutions in Persia and the threat of a Russian Caspian.

The Porte had never ceased to be worried by the growth of Russian power. More than once it had had to call for the withdrawal of Russian troops from Poland, the maintenance of whose integrity was to remain an axiom of its policy down to the Russo-Turkish war of 1768, itself largely the result of Russian interference in Poland. It was also known that Peter was trying to cast the Georgian and Armenian Christians for the rôle formerly played in European Turkey by the Montenegrins. In 1721 there was news of Russian fort-construction in the Terek valley, of a Russian survey party on the Caspian coast.[1] Distrust of Peter was now, moreover, fostered by the British government, which had worked for a renewal of Russo-Turkish hostilities during the Passarowitz negotiations.[2] Stanyan, with Austrian support, had been authorized to spend 10,000 piastres to accomplish this. His efforts were cleverly countered by the Russian ambassador and his French colleague. These two finally succeeded in bringing the Porte to accept, in June 1724, Peter's novel proposal for a dismemberment of the Persian provinces. While the Porte acknowledged Russian occupation of the Caucasus and the south coast of the Caspian, the Russians recognized Turkish occupation of Georgia, Shirvan, Ardabil, Tabriz, Hamadan, and Kirmanshah. This was the first and last occasion on which the Russian and Ottoman empires agreed upon the partition of a neighbouring state—a Muslim state, though the only one which professed the Shi'a devotion. The partition proved of no lasting value to either beneficiary. With the appearance of Nadir Shah all their conquests were soon to be annihilated.[3] Quite early, in the summer of 1730, he forced the Turks out of Hamadan, Kirmanshah and Tabriz.

These reverses, crowned by rumours that peace talks were in progress after troops and taxes had been raised for war,[4] at a time when pro-

---

[1] L. Lockhart, *The Fall of the Safavi Dynasty and the Afghan Invasion of Persia* (Cambridge, 1958), p. 217. For the mapping activities of Soimonov and Van Verden, cf. *ibid.* pp. 239 ff.

[2] Michael, vol. I, p. 364. Britain was chiefly anxious to divert Peter from northern Europe, but she also feared Russian domination of the Persian trade: I. Jacob, *Beziehungen Englands zu Russland und zur Türkei in den Jahren 1718–1727* (Basel, 1945), esp. ch. VII.

[3] L. Lockhart, *Nadir Shah* (1938), pp. 24–106. From this time also dates the virtual independence of the great vilayet of Baghdad. Cf. *NCMH*, vol. VI, p. 739.

[4] Shay, p. 27. In 1722 Stanyan had reported that the common people of Turkey hated the Persians for their persecution of Sunni Muslims (Lockhart, *Safavi Dynasty*, p. 215). A contemporary pamphlet, 'composed from Original Memorials drawn up in Constantinople' and first published in French at The Hague, states that the renewal of war with Persia, 'always disagreeable and often fatal to the Turks', was a cause of rebellion, not least

visions were dear, precipitated one of the bloodiest revolutions in Turkish history. It began on 28 September 1730 with a mutiny of a handful of janissaries in the capital, while the court was across the water at Scutari. Patrona Halil, by origin an Albanian seaman and later an attendant of the Common Bath near the Bayazid square, now a janissary and clothes-seller, gave a party for his friends and told how the overthrow of the tyranny of the sultan's ministers had been revealed to him. His movement was secretly sponsored by some of the ulema, but not joined by the chief janissary officers. In face of the inaction of the authorities,[1] and thanks to the obscure mechanics of a janissary rising, sedition soon spread through the soldiery. After two days the rebels were in control of the arsenal and able to cut off supplies of food and water to the Seraglio. The sultan tried appeasement by ordering the strangulation of his lifelong friend and son-in-law, whose body, with those of the deputy grand vizier and the Kaptan Pasha, was given to the crowd. Angry that these ministers had not been sent to them alive, the rebels called on the sultan to abdicate. On the night of 1 October, Ahmed III resigned the throne to his nephew Mahmud I, a prisoner of the Seraglio since his father's own abdication in 1703. The Chief Mufti went into exile; the *Reis Efendi* concealed himself.

Unassuaged by the new sultan's promised gratifications, the rioters put to the flames the summer-kiosks on the Golden Horn and pillaged the houses of proscripts in Constantinople itself. There are signs that the leaders tried to stop indiscriminate violence.[2] Some Jewish houses and Greek churches were plundered in Galata while it was without a district governor, but the rebels claimed also to be champions of the religious minorities against oppression. Nevertheless, the mutilated body of Damad Ibrahim Pasha, after a wholly exceptional vizierate of twelve years during which he had unlimited powers and immense fortunes in his hands,[3] was a terrible reminder of the licentiousness always present in the capital, for all its elaborate policing. Its narrow streets were full of unemployed immigrants. Yet Patrona's rebellion also sprang from deep forces in Turkish nature, hatred of the infidel and a habit of satirizing men in power. It was at once an outburst of xenophobia and a protest against the luxury and avarice of the higher Ottoman dignitaries. The insurgents

because the janissaries had shut up shop and incurred expenses for a march which was halted at Scutari, the rebel leader having himself laid out his savings in purchasing arms and clothes for resale during the campaign: *A Particular Account of the Two Rebellions, which happened at Constantinople in the Years MDCCXXX and MDCCXXXI...*(London, 1737), pp. 2–5.
[1] Most of the responsible pashas were out of the city when the revolt broke out, or quickly fled from it, like the Aga of the Janissaries, whose own guard refused to act against the rebels. On the return of the court to the Seraglio there were divided counsels and bitter recriminations.
[2] *Ibid.* pp. 8, 15, 30, 38–41.
[3] The rebels are said to have found the hoards of the grand vizier and his deputy, amounting in cash alone to the equivalent of £1,350,000 and £1,875,000 respectively (*ibid.* pp. 26–7).

called not only for war on Russia but for domestic reforms, such as the abolition of leases for life. It seems prophetic that they adopted red turbans. They claimed to stand for the good and honour of the State, and it is unlikely that terrorism alone brought them their large if uncertain following.

For nearly two months Patrona Halil, still wearing his torn clothes, and his mate, an eloquent young fruit-vendor and fellow-janissary named Muslubeshe, held in their hands practically the supreme power in the State, living in the houses of deposed ministers and visiting the palace when they pleased. They vetoed high appointments and proscribed many judges. They tried to increase their janissary following from 40,000 to 70,000 men, and to get their own nominees elected as officers, with a lavish use of the money they had taken. As early as 13 October, however, when the new sultan ordered the reopening of the shops, some of the janissaries were becoming detached from the movement, partly under the influence of the ulema; and on 5 November Patrona admitted that he relied in the last resort on his 12,000 Albanians, some of whom had been put in charge of the prisons. Even his own companions complained of his greed. He demanded a palace for his concubine, the great office of Kaptan Pasha for himself, the rule of Moldavia for a Greek butcher who had supplied the rebels. Perhaps this swagger was not without a macabre sense of humour, for Patrona seems to have foreseen that his luck would not last.[1] The resistance of the court was stiffened by the return of Janum Hoja as Kaptan Pasha, and by Kaplan-Girei, the new khan of the Crimea, who astutely advised concessions likely to provoke the janissaries. The end came when Patrona and his chief associates were summoned to the palace on pretext of a meeting with the Divan, ostensibly to debate their demand for war. There they were murdered in the sultan's presence on 25 November. It is reported that 7,000 of their accomplices were killed within three days, and that for weeks 'the Bosphorus was continually covered with Cadavars, agitated at the Pleasure of Winds and Waves'.[2]

For more than a year this counter-terror went on, costing many innocent lives and helping to precipitate in March 1731 a small janissary revolt, which the widow of Damad Ibrahim Pasha was suspected of having encouraged. Another plot was uncovered six months later. Cards were found in mosques denouncing the sultan's dependence on favourites. Repeatedly the public baths, taverns and coffee-shops were closed by the police.[3] Within a few years Constantinople is said to have been depleted, by death and banishment, of 50,000 people. The Bath near the Bayazid Square is still connected with the name of Patrona Halil and the restless days of his rule.

[1] *Ibid.* p. 53.
[2] *Ibid.* p. 79. The Venetian *bailo* stated that 10,000 janissaries lost their lives in 1730 (Shay, p. 32).   [3] Shay, pp. 36–7.

BIOGRAPHICAL NOTE

The bibliography of Ottoman history is dominated on the one hand by works in Turkish (Ottoman primary sources and modern studies based on them), and on the other by older European works (primary sources and secondary studies, the latter by now rather badly dated). Some of this literature, the second category in particular, is indicated in the footnotes to the preceding chapters. But for the purposes of the western student coming to grips with Ottoman history for the first time, this literature is for the most part either inaccessible or unhelpful. The primary purpose of this note is therefore to indicate a small number of recent works in English or French from which the beginner is likely to benefit.

I. SURVEYS

The following are helpful surveys of wide areas of Ottoman history:

C. Cahen, *Pre-Ottoman Turkey*, London, 1968 (for the historical background)

P. Wittek, *The Rise of the Ottoman Empire*, London, 1938 (short and incisive)

H. Inalcik, *The Ottoman Empire: The Classical Age, 1300–1600*, London, 1973 (basic)

P. M. Holt, *Egypt and the Fertile Crescent, 1516–1922*, London, 1966 (for the Arabic-speaking provinces)

There is no comparable survey for the later period. A brief account is given in the relevant chapters of

The Cambridge History of Islam, 2 vols., Cambridge, 1970, vol. i, part III

A somewhat indigestible survey of the state of the empire is provided by

H. A. R. Gibb and H. Bowen, *Islamic Society and the West I: Islamic Society in the Eighteenth Century*, 2 parts, London, 1950–7

A certain perspective on the period may also be gained from the early chapters of two works on the later evolution of Ottoman history:

N. Berkes, *The Development of Secularism in Turkey*, Montreal, 1964

B. Lewis, *The Emergence of Modern Turkey*, 2nd edn, London, 1968

For economic and social history the most interesting approach is provided by the relevant sections of

F. Braudel, *The Mediterranean and the Mediterranean World in the Age of Philip II*, 2 vols., London, 1972–3

2. MONOGRAPHS

The student who is prepared to tackle the more specialized monograph literature may learn something from such works as:

U. Heyd, *Ottoman Documents on Palestine, 1552–1615*, Oxford, 1960

R. Mantran, *İstanbul dans la seconde moitié du XVIIᵉ siècle*, Paris, 1962

N. H. Biegman, *The Turco-Ragusan Relationship according to the Firmāns of Murād III, 1575–1595*, The Hague and Paris, 1967

M. A. Cook, *Population Pressure in Rural Anatolia, 1450–1600*, London, 1972

C. M. Kortepeter, *Ottoman Imperialism during the Reformation: Europe and the Caucasus*, New York, 1972

A. Cohen, *Palestine in the 18th Century: Patterns of Government and Administration*, Jerusalem, 1973

U. Heyd, *Studies in Old Ottoman Criminal Law*, ed. V. L. Ménage, Oxford, 1973

3. ARTICLES

There is increasingly a literature of conference papers and articles in periodicals which are worth the student's attention. With regard to conference papers, the following volumes contain some useful studies in the Ottoman field:

B. Lewis and P. M. Holt (eds.), *Historians of the Middle East*, London, 1962

P. M. Holt (ed.), *Political and Social Change in Modern Egypt*, London, 1968

M. A. Cook (ed.), *Studies in the Economic History of the Middle East*, London, 1970

N. R. Keddie (ed.), *Scholars, Saints, and Sufis*, Berkeley, 1972

With regard to articles in periodicals, the following is a brief selection:

H. İnalcik, 'Ottoman methods of conquest', in *Studia Islamica*, 1954

N. Itzkowitz, 'Eighteenth century Ottoman realities', in *Studia Islamica*, 1962

B. Lewis, 'Ottoman Observers of Ottoman Decline', in *Islamic Studies*, 1962

V. L. Ménage, 'Some notes on the *devs̲h̲irme*', in *Bulletin of the School of Oriental and African Studies*, 1966

H. İnalcik, 'Capital Formation in the Ottoman Empire', in *The Journal of Economic History*, 1969

In addition, there is now again a periodical devoted to Ottoman studies: *Archivum Ottomanicum*, The Hague 1969–

4. PRIMARY SOURCES

To get an impression of Ottoman writing from the later period, try:

    L. V. Thomas, *A Study of Naima*, ed. N. Itzkowitz, New York, 1972

    A. Pallis, *In the days of the Janissaries*, London, 1951 (Evliya Chelebi)

    Kâtib Chelebi, *The Balance of Truth*, tr. G. L. Lewis, London, 1957

    W. L. Wright, *Ottoman Statecraft: The Book of Counsel for Vezirs and Governors of Sari Mehmed Pasha*, Princeton, 1935

To sample European writing, try:

    E. S. Forster (tr.), *The Turkish Letters of Ogier Ghiselin de Busbecq*, reprint, Oxford, 1968

    J. C. Davis, *Pursuit of Power: Venetian Ambassadors' Reports on Spain, Turkey, and France in the Age of Philip II, 1560–1600*, New York, 1970

To go further, use the helpful bibliography given in İnalcik's *The Ottoman Empire*, cited above.

INDEX

Note: the sign ~ between dates denotes intermittent periods of activity

Abaza Hasan Pasha of Aleppo, 143, 155, 164–5
Abaza Mehmed Pasha, beglerbeg of Erzerum, 7, 142–3
'Abbās I, shah of Persia (1587–1629), 116, 120, 130–1, 143, 144
'Abbasids, 9
'Abd al-Halīm, see Kara Yaziji
Abdi Pasha, commander of Buda, 189
abode of war, see dār al-ḥarb
Abū Su'ūd, Abu'l-Su-'ūd, grand mufti, 101, 108
Abyssinia, 4 n.1, 89, 99, 160, 179 n.2
Acciaiuoli family, rulers of Athens, 54
'Adalet-name (Book of Justice) of Murād IV, 148
Adana, 51, 59, 60, 211
Adbina, battle of (1493), 58
Aden, 89, 90, 157
'adet-i 'othmaniyye (Ottoman customs), 133
Adharbayjan, see Azerbaijan
'Adiljevaz, 94
administration: organization of the marches, 14th c., 15th c., 32–7 passim; centralized government, 6–9, 28, 34–5, 45–53 passim; idea of empire, 1–9 passim, 41, 42; see also devshirme, economy, fratricide, grand viziers, ghulām, intrigue, janissaries, reforms, sipāhīs
Adrammytion, see Edremid
Adrianople (Edirne), 21, 22, 27, 28, 30, 33, 34, 68, 157, 158, 168, 191; the 'Affair' (1703 revolt), 201; peace of (1713), 208–9
Adriatic Sea, see Venetian–Ottoman wars passim
Aegean Islands and Sea, 18–19, 37, 42, 51, 178, 185; see also Venetian–Ottoman wars passim
Aegina, 199, 210
Afghanistan, 216–17
Afiun Karahisar, Afyonkarahisar, Karahiṣār-i Devle, 10, 11, 12, 73; battle (1511), 65
Afrasiyab, house of, 143
Africa, East, 99, 100, 122
Africa, North (Barbary States): Spanish–Ottoman conflict, 16th c., 37, 86, 87, 88, 89, 100–1, 109, 110; Ottoman suzerainty, 17th c., 157, 161, 178
Afyonkarahisar, see Afiun Karahisar
Age of Tulips, 215–18
agha (commander), 46, 191
agriculture, 19–20, 50, 157–8, 183; see also levendāt, peasants

Ahmad Grañ, 4 n.1
Ahmed I, sultan (1603–17), 131, 134, 136, 142, 143, 149
Ahmed II, sultan (1691–5), 135, 192
Ahmed III, sultan (1703–30), 201, 202, 214–16, 218
Ahmed, son of Bāyezīd II, 65–70
Ahmed Ghāzī, medrese of, 20
Ahmed Pasha, beglerbeg of Anatolia, 59
Ahmed Pasha, beglerbeg of Rumeli, 79
Ahmed Pasha, beglerbeg of Rumeli (1543), grand vizier, 93, 95, 98
Ahmed Pasha of Egypt, 80
Aḥmedi, author, 20
al-Ahsa desert, 143
Aidin, see Aydın
'Aintab, 74
'ajemioghlanlar ('foreign youths'), 104, 122, 204 and n.1
'Ajlun, 145
akçe, akche, asper (coin), 105 and n.1, 126, 127, 181 and n.2, 191, 194
Akhaltzikhé (Altun Kal'e), 93, 114
akhī, akhiler (members of associations of young men), 17
Akhlat, 94
akınjıs, 23, 31–4, 79 and n.2, 161
Akkerman, 58, 91
Ak-Koyunlu dynasty, 43, 44, 55, 64, 65
akritai (Byzantine warriors), 17
Aksaray, 51
Akshehir, 11, 13, 44, 70, 73
al-: names beginning thus are indexed under the capital letter immediately following the prefix
'Alā ad-Daula, prince of Albistan, 59, 60, 65, 70, 71, 72
'Alā ad-Dīn, son of Prince Ahmed, 69
'Alā'iyya, 10, 51
Alans, 15
Alashehir (Philadelphia), 13
alay begi (chief sipāhī officer), 105, 106
Alazan see Kanak
Albania, Albanians: Skanderbeg (Iskender Pasha) and Hunyadi (1448), 30; Skanderbeg's rebellion (from 1443), 43; in Venetian–Ottoman war (1463–79), 42, 44; under Ottoman control (1478–9), 54; in Venetian–Ottoman war (1499–1502), 61, 62; in Venetian–Ottoman war (1570–3), 109; mercenaries serve Venetians, 16th c., 17th c., 61, 151, 192; and Habsburg plan of local resistance, 17th c., 150; and Patrona Halil's rebellion (1730), 219; and dev-

224

INDEX

Chaldiran, *see* Tchaldiran
Chamber (Council) of Petitions, 46–7
Chanak, 162
Chandarlı Khalīl Pasha, grand vizier, 30–1, 40–1, 46
charitable trusts, *see* waqf
Charlemagne, emperor, 4
Charles II, king of Spain, 198
Charles III, king of Spain, *see* Charles VI
Charles V, emperor (1519–58), Charles I, king of Spain, 82, 84, 86–9, 100–1
Charles V, duke of Lorraine, 173, 174, 175, 189
Charles VI, emperor (1711–40), Charles III, king of Spain, 210–14 *passim*
Charles VIII, king of France, 57
Charles XII, king of Sweden, 202–3, 206–7, 208–9
Chaul, battle of (1508), 89
Chiarenza, battle of (1499), 62
chift resmi (plough dues), 35
Chihirin, 174
China, ancient, 2 n.4
Chingiz Khān, 27
Chingizids, 2, 5
Chios (Scio), 152, 154, 193
Chirmen, battle of (1371), 22
Chocim, *see* Chotin
Chorlu, *see* Tchorlu
Chorlulu Ali Pasha, grand vizier, 202, 209
Chotin (Chocim, Khotin), 180; battle (1621), 149; battle (1673), 171, 189
Christian League in Aegean (1332), 18–19; *see also* Holy Leagues
Christianity: and ancient invasions, 1, 3; contrast with Islam, 3
Christians in the Ottoman Empire, *see* akınjıs, Armenian, Balkan, Catholics, Caucasians, *devshirme*, djizye, Greek Orthodox, Levant trade, Maronites, Protestants
Chukurova, *see* Cilicia
Çighāla-zāde Sinān Pasha, beglerbeg of Baghdad, grand vizier, 116, 129, 131
Çildir, lake, battle of (1578), 114
Cilicia (Chukurova), 10; Mamluk–Ottoman war (1485–90), 58–60 *passim*; Turcoman revolt (1526–8), 82; and *jelālī* rebellions (1596–1610), 130
Circassians (Çerkes), 113, 115, 157, 179, 180
civil wars, Ottoman: the interregnum (1402–13), 27; Jem and Bāyezīd (1481–2), 48, 55–7, 134; Selīm, Korkūd and Ahmed (1511–12), 48, 65–70, 134; Selīm, Mustafā and Bāyezīd (1558–61), 48, 96–9, 134, 140; *see also* fratricide, succession
coinage, *see* currency
Colijer, Jacobus, Dutch resident in Istanbul, 192 and n.3, 207 n.1, 208, 213
'Commander of the Faithful', 4 n.1
commerce, *see* trade

Congregatio de Propagada Fide (1622), 151
Constantine the Great, 204
Constantine XI Palaeologus, 40
Constantinople (*after 1453 see* Istanbul): Ottoman threat (1354), 22; Ottoman blockade (1394), 25–7; Ottoman siege and encroachment (1422–44), 29–31; Ottoman capture (1453), 3, 39, 40–1, 46, 48, 51
Contarini, Alvise, Venetian envoy, 147–8
Córdoba, Gonzalo de, Venetian commander, 62
Corfu, 88, 210, 211
Corinth, 43, 62, 210
Coron, Koron, 43, 61, 62, 63, 65, 87, 210
Corpus Christianum, ideal of, 117
corsairs, Christian, 61, 88, 108; *see also* St John, St Stephen
corsairs, Muslim: aid to Ottoman navy, 16th c., 61, 63, 87, 88, 101; conflict with Spain, 16th c., 89, 109, 110; conflict with Venice (1638–9), 151–2; and Venetian–Ottoman war (1645–69), 152, aid to Ottoman navy, 17th c., 18th c., 178, 185, 193, 210
corvées, 34–5
Cosimo II, grand duke of Tuscany, 145, 146
Cossacks: raids on Polish–Ottoman border, 17th c., 149, 161; raids in Black Sea, 17th c., 149 and n.1, 180; and Polish–Ottoman conflict (1616), 149; and peace of Buzsa (1617), 149; conquest of Azov (1637–42), 149 n.1, 180; and independence of Ukraine, 171, 203, 208, 209; and Polish–Ottoman war (1672), 171; rebellion (1706–8), 200 n.1; and Charles XII of Sweden, 202, 203, 209; in battle of Pruth (1711), 206
Council of State, Ottoman, *see* Dīvān
Counter-Reformation, the 150–1
craft gilds, *see* gilds
Cresswell, Joseph, Catholic propagandist, 125
Crete: and the *Shariʿa*, 6; Venetian–Ottoman war of Candia (1645–69), 151–5, 162, 163, 165; Ottoman conquest (1669), 155, 169, 178
Crimea: Ottoman occupation of Genoese ports (1475), 42, 54–5; Ottoman vassal state from 1475, 7, 45, 55, 161, 180; rebellion in Persian–Ottoman war (1578–90), 115; and Ottoman slave trade, 161, 180; Russian tribute remitted (1699), 199, 202; Girei dynasty, 58, 67, 69, 173, 190 and n.2, 202 and n.2, 219; Russian province (1783), 199; *see also* Tatars
Croatia: Ottoman raids, 15th c., 57, 58; border conflict, 16th c., 90–1; in Habsburg–Ottoman war (1526 ~ 66), 81, 93; and Habsburg marches, 17th c., 117; and Ottoman extent (1672), 178;

228

INDEX

Hungary
and idea of nationhood, 7 and n.1
and Balkan crusade (1366), 22
and Wallachia (1373), 23, 24; conflict with Ottomans for Wallachia and Serbia, 14th c., 25, 29
Hunyadi's defence (1441 ~ 8), 30; battle of Izladi (1443), 30 and siege of Constantinople (1453), 40; conflict with Mehmed II (1454–63), 42–3; alliance with Venice (1463), 44
Ottoman raids (1490–5), 57–8; struggle for power in Moldavia, 60
and Venetian–Ottoman war (1499–1502), 62–3; truce with Ottomans (1503 ~ 20), 77
border conflict, 77
campaigns of Sulaimān I (1521–62), 79–101 passim; Ottoman capture of Belgrade (1521), 79; Ottoman capture of Buda (1526), 81; battle of Mohács (1526), 81–2; Habsburg-Ottoman–Zápolyai conflict for Hungary and Transylvania (1526 ~ 66), 82, 91–2, 95, 101, 118; political strategy of Sulaimān I, 82–3; Ottoman campaigns (1529, 1532), 83–5; border razzia, 90–1; Ottoman campaigns (1541–7), 92–3; Ottoman campaigns (1552–62), 95–6; border fortifications, 96; tripartite (1562), 96
border fortifications, 116–17
and the Corpus Christianum, 117
Ottoman campaigns (1593–1606), 117–21, 139; English involvement, 125–6; peace of Zsitva-Torok (1606), 120–1, 150
Kleinkrieg, 17th c., 149–50
and Habsburg–Ottoman war (1663–4) 169–70
as Ottoman client state (c. 1672), 178, 180, 183 and n.1
Thököly's rebellion against Habsburgs (1678–86), 172, 189 and n.2
and siege of Vienna (1683), 172–6 passim, 188–9
Habsburg occupation (1683), 176
Serbian exodus to (1690), 188
and Habsburg–Ottoman war (1683–99), 188–93 passim, 198; in Habsburg possession after peace of Carlowitz (1699), 199, 213
Francis Rákóczi as Ottoman vassal king (1716), 211; Habsburg-Ottoman war (1716–18), 211–14 passim; remains in Habsburg possession after peace of Passarowitz (1718), 213
Hunyadi, John, Hungarian leader, 30
Ḥusām al-Dīn Choban, Seljuk emīr, 13
Husein, shah of Persia (1694–1722), 216
Hüseyn Efendi, 155

Hüseyn Hezarfenn, 2 n.3
Hüseyn Pasha, commander in Crete, grand vizier (1656), 153–4
Hüseyn Pasha, governor of Adana, 211
Hüseyn Pasha, grand vizier (1697–1702), see Köprülü

Iaşi, see Jassy
Ibn Baṭṭūṭa, historian, 19–20
Ibn Hanush, Arab chieftain, 76
Ibn Iyās, historian, 73 and n.1
Ibrahim, sultan (1640–8), 135, 155, 161–2
Ibrahim Beg, ruler of Karaman, 55
Ibrahim Müteferrika, printer, 216
Ibrahim Pasha, commander of Buda (1683), 173
Ibrahim Pasha, grand vizier (1523–36), 80–3 passim, 85, 88, 90, 101
Ibrahim Pasha, grand vizier (1718–30), 214, 215–16, 218
Ibrahim Pasha, military commander, 189
Ibshir, Ibşir Mustafa Pasha, grand vizier, 143, 155, 163
ich-oghlans (slaves educated at sultan's court), 28
Idrīs, historian, 71, 72
Il-Khāns, īl-khāns (Mongol rulers), 13, 16, 20, 28
imam (caliph), 5 n.1
Imbros, 54
Imereti principality, 114, 115
India: trade, 15th c., 50, 51; Portuguese conquest of Goa (1509), 89; in Portuguese–Ottoman war for spice trade, 16th c., 88–90, 99–100, 122–3; and foreign currency, 17th c., 181
Indian Ocean, 88–90, 99–100, 122–3, 153
inflation, Ottoman, 126–8, 139–40, 162, 181, 200, 216
Innocent VIII, pope, 57
Innocent XI, pope, 173, 189
'inside boys', 204 n.1
Interregnum, the (1402–13), 27
intrigue and Ottoman decline, 107, 135–7, 147, 155, 159, 161–2, 179, 186, 215
Iraq: Ottoman conquest in Persian-Ottoman war (1534–5), 85–6, 90, 111; and peace of Amasia (1555), 94, 111; and Ottoman ship-building, 16th c., 100; and Persian–Ottoman war (1578–90), 116; and Persian–Ottoman war (1623–39), 143–5, 146–7; and peace of Zuhab (1639), 147, 148; and desert Arabs, 17th c., 178–9
'Īsā, son of Bāyezīd I, 27
Isabella, consort of John Zápolyai, king of Hungary, 92–3, 95
Isaqça, 149
Ishāk, ruler of Karaman, 58
Iskender Bey (George Castriotes, Scanderbeg, Skanderbeg), 30, 43, 54
Iskender Pasha, beglerbeg of Erzerum, 94
Iskender Pasha, kapdan, 66, 68

INDEX

Kösem, *Walide Sultan*, 137, 155, 161, 162, 177
Kosova, Kosovo Polje, battle of (1389), 24, 38; battle (1448), 30
Kotor, *see* Cattaro
Kozmin, battle of (1497), 61
Krems, 175
Krim Tatars, *see* Tatars
Kroja, *see* Croia
Kuban river, 112, 115, 199, 202 n.2
Küçük Ahmed Pasha, beglerbeg of Damascus, 145, 146
Kula, 13
kullar, see ghulām
Kulpa river, 116, 117
Kumkale, 165
Kunfidha, 180
Kura river, 115
Kurdistān, Kurds, 55, 65, 71–4 *passim*, 85, 94, 143, 146, 157, 180 and n.1
Kutahia, Kütahya, 10–11, 12, 65, 73, 99
Kuyuju Murād Pasha, grand vizier, 130, 131, 142
Kythera, *see* Cerigo
Kyzyl Elma ('Red Apple', symbol for conquest of Vienna), 170, 172

La Goletta, 87, 110
Laibach, 62
Lale Devri, the Age of Tulips (1718–30), 215–18
Languschi, Giacomo de', Italian observer, 41
law, civil, *see qānūn, 'urf*
law, religious, *see Sharī'a*
Lebanon: indirect Ottoman rule, 17th c., 145, 179; power of Fakhr al-Dīn II, 145–6; traders in Ottoman Empire, 181; Christians and Ottoman tolerance, 76, 179 and n.1
Lefort, François, Russian naval commander, 195
legend and myth, Ottoman, 14, 17–18, 32
Leghorn, 181
Lemburg, 50
Lemnos, 45, 54, 154, 161, 164, 165
Leopold I, emperor (1658–1705), 169–70, 173, 174, 189, 204
Lepanto, 61, 62, 63, 178; battle (1571), 101, 109–10
Lesbos, 54, 63
Leszczyński, *see* Stanislas Leszczyński
Leukas, *see* Santa Maura
Levant Company, English, 123, 213 n.2
Levant trade and Europeans, 18, 19, 42, 50–1, 89, 90, 100, 108, 122, 123, 124, 152, 153, 181, 213
levendāt, levends, leventi (rootless men): and brigandage, 98, 128; and *jelālī* revolts (1596–1610), 129–30, 141–2; recruitment to Ottoman army, 140–2, 159, 185 and n.2; *see also gönüllü, mustahfiz, sarıja, sekban*

Lewis I, king of Hungary, 22
Lewis II, king of Bohemia and Hungary, 81, 82
Lewis, margrave of Baden, 191
Limberg, Andreas, mayor of Vienna, 174
Linz, 174, 189
Lippa, 95
Lisbon, 90, 100
Lonska, 93
Lori, 115
Louis XII, king of France, 62
Louis XIV, king of France, 170, 173, 189, 192, 205, 210
Lukaris, patriarch of Constantinople, 151
Luristān, 116, 143
Lutfī Pasha, grand vizier, 4 n.2, 5 and n.1, 128
Luther, Martin, 17
Lwów, 171

Macchiavelli, Niccolo, 69 and n.1
Macedonia, 22
Magedon, 12
Magnesia, *see* Manisa
Mah-Firuze, mother of Osmān II, 136
Mahmūd I, sultan (1730–54), 218
Mahmūd II, sultan (1808–39), 194 n.2
Mahmūd Beg, Ramazan-oghlu prince, 74
Mahmūd Gāwān, Bahmanid *wazīr*, 99
Mahmūd Pasha, beglerbeg of Rumeli, grand vizier, 44, 46–7
Maina, Mainotes, 150, 154
Makran, 99
Makri, gulf of, 10
Malabar, 90
Malatia, Malatya, 25, 73
Malindi, 100, 122
Malkoch, Malkoch-oghlu dynasty, 32 67
Malkoch-oghlu Bali Beg, governor of Silistria, 61
Malplaquet, battle of (1709), 210
Malta, Maltese, 86, 101, 152, 181–2, 189, 212
Maltepe, 56
Malvasia, 190
Mamluks of Egypt: comparison with Teutonic Knights, 7 n.2; and Timurtash Noyon (1328), 16; and Bāyezīd I, 25, 27; and Ottoman conquests in Anatolia (1466–70), 44, 45; and Florentine trade, 15th c., 51; Mamluk–Ottoman war in Cilicia (1485–90), 55, 58–60; naval war with Portuguese (1508–16), 89–90; and Korkūd, son of Bāyezīd II, 66; Mamluk–Ottoman war (1515–17) and Ottoman conquest of Syria and Egypt, 72–7; obsolete military technique, 72, 79; revolt (1523–4), 80; and Ottoman reforms (1524–5), 80–1, 90
Ma'n, house of, 145–6
Manchus, 2 n.4
Manisa, Manissa (Magnesia), 16, 20, 66, 99

236

INDEX

Paphlagonia, 14
Párkány, 188
Parkins, Christopher, English envoy, 125
Parthenios II, patriarch, 164
Parthenon, destruction of (1687), 190
Passarowitz, peace of (1718), 213–14, 217
Passau, 174
Patras, 153
patriarchs, 42, 151, 164, 204
Patrona Halil, rebel, 218–19
Paul III, pope, 88
Pavia, battle of (1525), 86
payment of troops: and unrest and revolts,
127–9 passim, 136, 139–41 passim, 194,
201; and reforms, 148, 155, 163; see also
timar, zi'âmet
peasants: in Balkans, preference for Ottoman rule, 31, under Byzantine rule, 34,
and Ottoman administration, 34–6; in
the Ottoman Empire, flight from the land,
128, 129, 181, 183, 200, see also levendât
Pechin, 20
Pécs, 93
Perekop, isthmus of, 195
Persia: Mongol internal conflict, 13th c.,
13; Uzun Hasan's wars with Ottomans
(1463–73), 43–4, 55; growth of Safawiyya (q.v.), 63–5; Persian–Ottoman
war (1511), 65; and Ottoman civil war
(1511–13), 65–70; battle of Tchaldiran
(1514), 70–1, 85; Persian–Ottoman war
(1514–16), 70–2, 85; involvement in
Mamluk–Ottoman war (1515–17), 72–6
passim; border warfare, 16th c., 85;
Persian–Ottoman war and Ottoman
conquest of Iraq (1534–5), 85–6, 93;
Persian–Ottoman war (1548–55), 93–5,
97; peace of Amasia (1555), 94, 111;
and Ottoman civil war (1558–61),
99; Safawid–Sunnī conflict, tribal and
internal tensions, 16th c., 111–14; relations with Christian states, 111; Persian–Ottoman war (1578–90), 114–16,
121, 139, 140, 143; Persian–Ottoman
war (1603–18), 130–1; loss of Ottoman
possessions, 17th c., 131, 141, 143;
Persian–Ottoman war in Iraq (1623–
39), 143–5, 146–7; peace of Zuhab
(1639), 147, 178; and Arab capture of
Basra (1694), 179; Afghan invasion
and Safawid downfall (1722), 216; revolutions, 18th c., 217; Russo-Turkish
partition of provinces (1724), 216–17;
conquered by Nadir Shah (1729), 217;
and rebellion in Istanbul (1730), 217
and n.4; literature translated into
Turkish, 20; silk trade, 15th c., 50;
and Ottoman trade, 17th c., 181; and
tulipomania, 18th c., 215
Persian Gulf, 89, 90, 99–100
Pertev Pasha, vizier, 101
Pervâne, see Mu'īn al-Dīn Süleyman
Pest, 81, 120

Peter I (the Great), tsar of Russia (1682–
1725): and the navy, 195 and n.3, 200
and n.1, 207; and religious problems,
195, 204–5, 207; for his campaigns from
1696, see Russia
Peterwardein, 82, 191, 193, 198; battle
(1716), 211–12, 214
Petrovich, Daniel, Serbian bishop, 205
Phanar, the, 207, 208 n.1
Philadelphia, see Alashehir
Philip II, king of Spain, 3 n.2, 4, 5, 101, 109
Philip III, king of Spain, 145
Philippopolis, 180
Phocea, 51
piastre, 163 n.1, 181 and n.2, 194
pilgrimages, 39, 108, 111, 157, 199
pious foundations, Ottoman, see waqf
pirates, see corsairs, St John, Uskoks
Pīrī Pasha, grand vizier, 79
Pīrī Re'īs, naval commander, 99
Pius II, pope, 42–3
Pius V, pope, 109
Piyāle Pasha, kapdan, 101, 108
plough dues, see chift resmi
Podolia, 171, 178, 189, 199
Poland: conflict with Ottomans, 15th c.,
16th c., 58, 60–1, 77; and John Zápolyai
of Hungary (1527), 82; and Hungarian–
Ottoman war (1593–1606), 118–19;
Polish–Ottoman war (1616–17), 149;
peace of Buzsa (1617), 149; Polish–
Ottoman war (1620–1), 136, 149;
Polish–Ottoman war (1672), 171; Otto-
man power in Podolia (1672–99), 171,
178, 189, 199; Sobieski and siege of
Vienna (1683), 175–6, 189; and peace of
Carlowitz (1699), 199; and Russo-
Turkish war (1711), 206, 208–9; and
Charles XII of Sweden, 203, 208–9; and
Cossacks and Tatars, 58, 149, 171, 203;
and Moldavia, 58, 60, 61, 118–19,
149, 189, 190; and Russia, 17th c., 171,
203, 206, 208–9, 217; aristocracy and
the state, 8
poll tax, see djizye
Poltava, battle of (1709), 202
Pomerania, Swedish, 203
Poniatowski, Count Stanislas, adherent of
Charles XII, 203, 209
popes, see papacy
population: Turkish movement into Europe under early Ottomans, 35–6;
Istanbul, repopulation after 1453, 51–2,
population, 17th c., 182 n.2; in the
Ottoman Empire, increase and unrest,
16th c., 17th c., 126, 139, 140, population, 17th c., 157; rural depopulation,
16th c., 17th c., 128, 129, 183 and n.1;
in the Morea, increase, 17th c., 209 n.2
Porte, Sublime, 186 and n.2, 188, 193, 195,
208
Portugal, Portuguese: conquests to gain
spice trade, 16th c., 89, 153; war with

240